CLASS STRUGGLE AND RESISTANCE IN AFRICA

CLASS STRUGGLE AND RESISTANCE IN AFRICA

EDITED BY
LEO ZEILIG

Haymarket Books
Chicago, Illinois

First published in 2002 by New Clarion Press, Cheltenham, UK

This edition published in 2009 by Haymarket Books
P.O. Box 180165
Chicago, IL 60618.
info@haymarketbooks.org
773-583-7884
www.haymarketbooks.org

Trade distribution:
In the U.S. through Consortium Book Sales and Distribution, www.cbsd.com
In the UK, Turnaround Publisher Services, www.turnaround-psl.com
In Canada, Publishers Group Canada, www.pgcbooks.ca
All other countries, Ingram Publisher Services International, ips_intlsales@ingramcontent.com

Special discounts are available for bulk purchases by organizations and institutions. Please contact Haymarket Books for more information at 773-583-7884 or info@haymarketbooks.org.

ISBN: 978-1-931859-68-4

Library of Congress Cataloging-in-Publication Data is available.

Entered into digital printing May 2018.

CONTENTS

CONTRIBUTORS

All the contributors are political activists, involved in a variety of organizations in Africa and Europe.

Leo Zeilig is an activist and socialist based in South Africa. He is a research fellow at the Centre for Sociological Research in Johannesburg and teaches sociology at the University of the Witwatersrand. He is a member of the organization Keep Left. Email: leo.zeilig@hotmail.co.uk

Anne Alexander is a writer and researcher specializing in modern Middle Eastern history and politics. She is the author of a biography of Gamal Abd-al-Nasser, entitled *Nasser: His Life and Times* (Haus and American University in Cairo Press, 2005). She is a member of the Socialist Workers Party. Email: r_annealex@hotmail.com

Azwell Banda was forced into exile from Zambia, where he was a leading socialist. He is currently working as a researcher for the Eastern Cape Social Economic Consultative Council in South Africa. Email: azwell@ecsecc.org

Peter Dwyer worked as a campaign organizer for a South African NGO. He has extensive research and campaign experience, developed whilst working with social movements in South Africa. He is currently a lecturer in economics at Ruskin College, Oxford. He is a member of the Socialist Workers Party. Email: pdwyer@ruskin.ac.uk

Munyaradzi Gwisai is a leading member of the International Socialist Organization of Zimbabwe. He is a lecturer at the University of Zimbabwe. Email: munyag@hotmail.com

Miles Larmer is currently a lecturer in International History at the University of Sheffield. He has written widely on Zambian political and labor history and on social movements in Southern Africa. Email: M.Larmer@sheffield.ac.uk

David Renton is a barrister working in employment law at Islington Law Centre. He has been a lecturer at Rhodes and Johannesburg Universities in South Africa and at Nottingham Trent University in England. He is an activist in tenant, union, and housing campaigns and a member of the Socialist Workers Party. Email: davidkrenton@googlemail.com

David Seddon is widely recognized as an authority on popular movements in Africa and the Middle East. Email: J.D.Seddon@uea.ac.uk

Jussi Viinikka has worked with Nigerian labor activists in England. He is currently teaching in London. Email: jussi@totalise.co.uk

Interviewed contributors

Femi Aborisade is a leading Nigerian socialist and lecturer at Ibadan polytechnic. He has written widely on Nigerian labour history and politics. Email: aborisadefemi@yahoo.com

Tafadzwa Choto is a leading member of the International Socialist Organization of Zimbabwe. Email: tonytaffy2000@yahoo.co.uk

Ahmed Hussain is a human rights activist in Egypt.

Austin Muneku is the director of research for the Zambia Congress of Trade Unions. Email: amuneku@yahoo.co.uk

Trevor Ngwane is a leading socialist and anti-capitalist campaigner in South Africa. Email: trevorngwanesoweto@yahoo.com

FOREWORD

Azwell Banda

The real world for the vast majority of the Earth's working peoples is one of globalized anger, frustration, and despair. After September 11, 2001, fear and insecurity became globalized, in a world driven and managed by private greed and the urge to dominate and conquer. No one will ever again live under the illusion of post–Cold War safety and security. The response of the American government to September 11 guarantees this outcome. For more than five hundred years, for us African workers, every day has been a September 11. Becoming workers has been a violent, dehumanizing process and this violence continues unabated today.

Many books have been written about colonialism, apartheid, imperialism, the globalization process, and the forces that have shaped the history of Africa. Some accounts of African history are purely romantic and fanciful, others racist and Eurocentric. The concrete reality of the situation is domination and resistance, which has been the true nexus linking Africa to America and Western Europe. Plunder, domination, and the conversion of able-bodied men and women into desperate laborers have characterized Africa's contact with Western and American civilization. Africa's physical resources and its human beings have been prized raw materials for American and Western European industries and world markets.

The story, however, that remains to be fully told is how Africa has resisted this domination. During each phase in the history of Africa and its relationship with American and European domination—slavery, colonialism, apartheid, neo-colonialism—leading elements of the African liberation movements have used different ideologies to appeal to the only class capable of carrying the day: the African working class. This has been the case whether the movement was to end exploitation in the first factories set up by European capital or ultimately to break the political back of colonialism.

The story of the central and pivotal role of the African working class in the struggles against oppression has not been well told. This book attempts to start the process of reclaiming, for African workers and their organizations, their role in the struggles of the global working class against capitalist exploitation. It is an ambitious project, since it is framed in the only viable prism through which African workers can view history—a Marxist perspective.

This book is published at a time when many political thinkers of all ideological hues are celebrating the illusion of the end of classical Marxism and the end of the Marxist interpretation of social reality and history. Some of these thinkers, drunk with the successes of the imperialist conquest of the world, have gone insane, denying the very existence of the class struggle. We are told that history has come to an end with the triumph of imperialist globalization. The possibility of socialist revolution is denied, as if its very denial can erase popular social change. But how else can the situation of the majority of the Earth's peoples, who live in conditions of crushing domination and exploitation, be turned to their advantage?

Disdain for any analysis that locates workers and their organizations at the center of historical change permeates political and social analysis. As for the African working class, at best a philanthropic curiosity may be given to it, and at worst it is simply ignored. After all, Europe and America can now survive and thrive without Africa and its numerous problems. Africa and its peoples are now reduced to objects of imperialist charity or blamed for spreading diseases and harboring terrorists. Why, then, should anybody in their right mind write about Africa and its working class?

The decay and decomposition of the postcolonial African state, the disintegration of former liberation movements and the universal penetration of American and European imperialism have led to the joyous celebration of the end of the class struggle. The role of workers and their organizations is confined to the dustbin of history. Western governments and local ruling classes continue to siphon vast sums of money and natural resources out of Africa and into the old colonial metropolises at the expense of Africa's working class and other poor people.

Desperate for clean water, medicine, food, clothing, shelter, education, and a life in which the fruits of their toils will go to enriching their lives, the majority of African workers have been reduced, particularly in the last twenty years, to a life without proper work and an early grave. Here in Africa, the brutal reality of imperialist exploitation and oppression confronts the African worker every day.

The inevitable decay and collapse of the colonial state that was bequeathed to the African political class at the point of independence has ushered in an age of primitive militarization. The African ruling class, desirous of outperforming the departing colonial and imperialist masters, wasted no time in deteriorating further the already deplorable condition of the African working class and the poor. I live with working mothers and fathers who cannot feed their sick, unclothed children.

A huge volume of books and papers has been written about how postcolonial Africa has failed to create conditions conducive to sustaining the modern state. Racist rubbish has often been spoken about the apparently inherent inability of Africans to govern themselves. In the latest addition to the chain of independent African states, black South Africans continue to be warned "not to go the African way" or be like "all the other African countries." Today, as the South African rand continues to fall against other currencies and the prices of basic goods and services soar, a white caller to a popular morning radio talk show can tell black South Africans that under a black government prices continue to rise, while under the former white government prices were low. This is happening barely seven years after South Africa attained its nominal political freedom from racist oppression.

There are many African workers living as refugees in the numerous diasporas across the world. Many more continue to live destitute lives on the continent away from their own home countries, as economic and political refugees. I am one of these African workers. I fled from Chiluba's regime in Zambia soon after the attempted military takeover at the end of 1997. I was then the secretary-general of the Zambia Democratic Congress (ZDC) and a serving member of the secretariat of the Alliance of Opposition Parties.

In 1981 the IMF and the World Bank ordered Kaunda (then president of Zambia), as part of the structural adjustment program (SAP), to cut the government's social spending. Kaunda moved quickly and removed direct state funding to students in tertiary education institutions including the University of Zambia. As president of the Federal University of Zambia Students Union, I led the first student rebellion against the SAP. We mobilized students from all higher education institutions in the country and eventually forced Kaunda to reintroduce state funding for students. This did not endear me to the Kaunda regime and the then-minister of education, Raja Kunda, bluntly told me that I would not finish my education at the University of Zambia. I was latter expelled from the university.

In April 1984, students went on a nine-day stoppage against the Kaunda regime, the university administration, and the general deteriorating standards of life in the country largely resulting from the SAP. I was detained and interrogated, but not tried, for my participation in the student demonstrations.

The Kaunda regime was then a one-party state, and with more than 80 percent of the economy in Kaunda's hands, when Kaunda blacklisted you, you were cut out of normal life. I could not get a formal job or continue my studies in any of the other state institutions. I lived from 1984 to 1991 hand to mouth, teaching in private schools and doing anything to survive. During this time I made a number of attempts to form an underground working-class organization. But as political organizations were banned under the one-party state, it was very difficult and dangerous to mobilize outside the ruling party and the Zambia Congress of Trade Unions (ZCTU).

At the end of the 1980s and the beginning of the 1990s, one-party states were swept away as the Soviet Union and the Eastern European regimes crumbled. We in Zambia grasped the opportunity to win back the right to organize in political parties. I formed the first structures of the Movement for Multi-party Democracy (MMD) in the Eastern province of Zambia and was elected as first provincial chairperson.

The MMD was initially founded as a protest movement against the social and economic decay resulting from more than ten years of Kaunda's half-hearted but fatal relationship with the IMF and the World Bank. The ZCTU, possessing a national organization and carrying with it the aspirations of the majority of the working class in Zambia, quickly came to occupy a central place in the MMD. Chiluba, the chairperson-general of the ZCTU, was initially elected operations secretary.

Our fundamental mistake, on the left in the MMD, was not to unite as a solid group and to rally labor to our side. This was largely due to more than seventeen years of one-party rule, when all forms of organization, even those only remotely connected to politics, were banned. There was also the problem of the demagogic hold that Chiluba had on the ZCTU in particular, and on the ordinary workers and the poor in general.

In April 1990 I spent days with Chiluba at his home trying to persuade him to participate in creating a workers' organization capable of taking over from Kaunda, but he had other ideas. When Chiluba was elected president of Zambia, I quietly left the MMD and returned to the university to finish my studies in natural sciences. I was elected the first national general secretary of the Zambia Labour Party—a radical, left-wing party. We had running battles with the leadership of the ZCTU, whom we regarded as failing to place the demands of the workers at the center of politics in Zambia, and allowing Chiluba to take power on the back of the workers.

The search for the formation of a credible workers' organization, to drive a clear agenda, continues in Zambia. The current collection of political groupings does not give much hope. And the ZCTU leadership's inability to clearly define a political platform for its membership robbed workers of an opportunity to articulate their political demands during the December elections in 2001.

As an exile, there have been for me the usual uncertainties and insecurities of physical and personal dislocation. It is perhaps a funny twist in my personal history that I should flee to a country whose political refugees, as a political activist in my country, I played a small but militant part in looking after. People here laugh when they learn that I am in exile. They know Zambia as the home of their political leaders, during the days of their liberation struggle.

Since I stepped on to South African soil I have shed many illusions. There are trade unionists, communists, and other ordinary people whose dedication to radical social change I have come to admire. I have also come to learn that the war is not won, either against imperialism or for real liberation. My faith in the working class of Africa is restored when I witness the political militancy of the ordinary working people here. The growth of the anti-capitalist movement has also shown the possibility of linking the movement for a better world, North and South.

Workers and the poor people of Africa must break their chains of oppression. Among the first solid steps toward this must surely be to study and appreciate the central role that the workers' movement has played, and continues to play, in the continent's struggles for social change. Only when we clearly understand this, and the fact that socialism can only be won by the collective action of the working class itself, can the people of Africa finally overthrow their oppressors and will true liberation begin. This book begins that task.

The book retells the story of mass struggle and working-class resistance in Africa. The first chapter considers the experience of Marxism in Africa since independence, looking at the role of the class struggle in shaping political change on the continent and how Marxism has been distorted by Stalinism. In the second chapter, David Seddon then gives a historical overview of the African working class and the development of capitalism on the continent, from one of the continent's first strikes in 1874 in Sierra Leone to the struggles against the first governments of national independence. The third chapter, by Anne Alexander and Dave Renton, examines the role of popular struggle and the working class in Egypt. Jussi Viinikka in the following chapter shows how Nigeria has been continuously convulsed by general strikes and mass protest. The importance of these movements and their potential to transform Nigeria is clearly demonstrated. The Zambian trade union movement created and led the Movement for Multi-party Democracy, which saw the victory of Frederick Chiluba in 1991. But even before these events the labor movement shaped Zambian politics. In the fifth chapter, Miles Larmer looks at the development of the working-class movement in Zambia.

Peter Dwyer in the sixth chapter examines the recent history and legacy of the anti-apartheid struggle in southern Africa and looks at the prospects for the left. Munyaradzi Gwisai considers recent developments in Zimbabwe in the seventh chapter. Munyaradzi is a leading activist and socialist in Zimbabwe. Mass demonstrations and strikes shook the country throughout the 1990s. This led to the creation of the Movement for Democratic Change (MDC), which represents a potential turning point for the region. The chapter explains the nature and background of this struggle, which is the high point of popular resistance in Africa today and shows directly the importance of revolutionary socialists in Africa. Each of the five case studies is followed by an interview with a key activist, trade unionist, or socialist from the country. The final chapter, by Leo Zeilig and Peter Dwyer, examines the anti-capitalist movement and the challenges for revolutionaries in Africa.

I am convinced that a return to mass struggle and resistance in Africa, against globalization and the market, can transform the continent. And if we understand the processes at work, we can build the movements that will finally overturn our world.

Azwell Banda
South Africa
January 2002

ACKNOWLEDGMENTS

The idea for the book came from a whispered conversation with Peter Dwyer during a meeting on Zimbabwe at the annual Marxism conference in London in July 1999. Originally it was conceived as a millennium project, to celebrate and retell the rich history of class struggle and resistance across Africa at the start of a new century. The century that was just finishing deafened us with a cacophony of rubbish about a "hopeless continent" that could only be brought to its senses by the good sense and helping hand of the "international community." Without Peter's judgment, support, and endless enthusiasm the book would have taken until the next millennium to complete.

It is appropriate for a book that celebrates collective struggle and resistance to have come through many hands, but perhaps unfair to implicate them all in the final outcome. However, thanks must be given to Charlie Kimber, Nigel Harris, Peter Alexander, Caroline O'Reilly, Jimi Adesina, John Lea, Gillian Zeilig, Maurice Caplan, Rachel Cohen, and Momar Coumba Diop. In addition, without the ceaseless support, solidarity, and judgement of Andy Wynne and the foresight of Chris Bessant the book would not have emerged.

The book is dedicated to Femi Aborisade—an outstanding and courageous socialist.

The first edition of this book sold out within two years, demonstrating more than anything else a desire by a new audience—particularly those influenced by the emergent anti-capitalist movement—to understand the history of protest and class struggle in Africa. With the second edition Haymarket Books has given the arguments and politics in this collection a chance to reach a new audience, for this the editor and contributors are deeply grateful.

Workers will not achieve anything except through struggle, unity and solidarity. Our objective is to ensure that class and property will be wiped out of our society once and for all... In the final end of the struggle, there should be no property because there will be no capitalism.

—Alhaji Sunmonu, Nigeria
May Day 1980

Introduction to the 2009 edition

RESISTING THE SCRAMBLE FOR AFRICA

Leo Zeilig and David Seddon

I n the six years since this book was first published the continent has been in the grip of what has been called the "new scramble for Africa," or more precisely the scramble for African resources. The new thirst for Africa's mineral and oil wealth was triggered by a number of factors. In the post–9/11 world the United States became particularly concerned with the inadequacy of its post-1945 global oil strategy that rested on the tenuous stability of two regions—the Middle East (principally Saudi Arabia, Iran, Iraq) and South America (notably today Venezuela). Even if the United States was prepared to intervene in Iraq in 1990 and to invade and occupy Iraq in 2003 to secure these supplies, Africa was regarded as an important alternative source. The continent—with Nigeria preeminent—has become a central focus in the global hunt for oil supplies. Oil explorations have proliferated. The Gulf of Guinea in West Africa has become an area of frenzied and contested activity that has seen international corporations competing for oil contracts. The commodity boom—another important element in the recent scramble—has been fueled by additional demand from China, and to a lesser extent India. Africa has again become a disputed site for geopolitical competition, today between the United States, China, and the EU. But still some commentators were ready to pro-

1

nounce this moment as one of great possibility for the continent. The IMF's *World Economic Outlook* stated excitedly in October 2007: "Sub-Saharan Africa is clearly enjoying its best period of sustained growth since independence."[1] The recent scramble for resources in Africa gives us no reasons to be cheerful.

Angola is an example of the current boom, recently promising to become the "African Dubai."[2] Riding high on oil and peace Angola turned its back on assistance from the International Monetary Fund (IMF). Boasting an average economic growth of 13 percent between 2004 and 2007, the country succeeded in paying off two-thirds of its $2.3 billion of debt owed to the Paris Club. Angola has earned records amounts from oil, estimated at 585 million barrels of oil worth over $30 billion (£15 billion) in 2007. Though Angola is the second-largest oil producer on the continent little has changed for the poor. Child mortality rate has stuck at 260/1,000—meaning one child in every four dying before they reach five years old—since 2002. As oil wealth has poured into the state's coffers the country has actually seen its position on the UNDP index fall, to "rest" at 161 out of 177.[3]

Money is being spent on glory projects for the rich. This includes an obscene mall, Belas Shopping, which opened in 2007 in the capital, Luanda. This is a $35 million project that includes exclusive shops and restaurants—the indoor shopping mall is surrounded by slums and poverty. Other projects include an $800 million investment in the bay of Luanda, for land used to build a luxury waterfront zone. But local politicians and businessmen see the development as a sign of the health of the economy, one commenting soon after its completion, "It is a reflection of the new mood of optimism in Angola. As the standard of living rises and disposable income increases, naturally people would like to have nice places in which to spend it." This "civilizing" influence will even prevent the country from returning to chaos and war—final proof of the efficacy of trickle-down economics.[4]

Nigeria, long the reliable ally of foreign companies and western countries, has also become central to the new "boom." In 2007, $55 billion was earned from oil and this was expected to increase in 2008 to $76 billion. The new oil boom has led to almost crazed predictions for Nigeria's future. The London *Financial Times*, in a elaborate supplement on the country in June 2008, could barely contain their jubilation: "the private sector has mostly flourished. Demand for services, such as mobile phone lines and bank accounts, and goods from televisions to cement, has far exceeded expectations." Much of this boom, and excitement, is fueled by increased competition for Nigeria's oil and resources. Yet despite several years of high economic growth—estimated by the IMF to reach 8 percent in 2008—the country fails to provide minimum basic services for most of the population, unable even to provide affordable fuel or electricity, a particular obscenity in an oil-rich country. After some investment by the former government of Olusegun Obasanjo, the national grid still only supplies approximately 5 percent of national demand. An estimated half of the 140 million population lives in severe poverty.[5] This picture follows a pattern. Since oil production began in 1956, the Nigerian government has earned approximately $600 billion in revenue. From this amount the World Bank estimates that as much as $200 billion may have been stolen by successive governments, civilian and military alike. The result, as Michael Watts reports, is "that oil has probably not added to the standard of living of average Nigerians. This is a stunning indictment."[6]

Expanding jobs for a small layer of Nigerian graduates and returned professionals can be found in the banking, telecom, or oil sector. This group has in turn fueled a growth in the retail sector. In 2004, Silverbird Group opened their first shopping mall on Victoria Island in Lagos. Similar to luxury malls around the world, it includes classy boutiques, fast-food outlets, hair salons, and The Galleria, a multiplex cinema screening recent Hollywood releases. Jonathan Murray-Bruce, general manager of Silverbird Cinemas, expressed the aspirations of this new buoyant group: "We wanted it to be a place where kids can hang out."[7]

Both Angola and Nigeria are insulated by huge oil revenue—and the myriad spin-off ventures around this revenue—which largely shields them from hypocritical western opprobrium of African failures regarding "governance" and "democratization." Both countries spend negligible amounts on public welfare, and are surrounded by mass slums and collapsed infrastructure—but these facts are obscured by oil wealth and the importance of these resources in the global economy. Both states can be described as "successful failed states," in providing wealth for a tiny minority and securing the backing of international companies yet offering nothing for the overwhelming majority.[8] In Angola it is the state oil company that provides for this illusory stability, which sees the creation of a shadow economy that seals off local conditions—of poverty, crisis, and collapse—while securing for oil companies a legal framework and logistical competence. The national oil giant Sonangol is almost the only state institution that functions, and has guaranteed the flow of wealth to the rich since the 1970s. Yet this "success" acts out in conditions of "state dereliction, civil conflict and utmost impoverishment. Its tools and professional expertise…are put to service not of broad-based prosperity, but the enrichment of the few."[9] Actual capitalist growth, as it exists in much of Africa, offers no prospect of real broad-based development.

Oil companies operate in "First World" enclaves. Yet the fragility of this insulated world of profit and exploitation is demonstrated in Nigeria by the attacks on oil installations and company-related interests by Niger Delta militants. These attacks have increased rapidly since 1999—and particularly since the emergence of Movement for the Emancipation of the Niger Delta (MEND) in 2006—amounting to what Nigeria expert Michael Watts has described as an "oil insurgency."[10] Watts argues that "the future of oil in Nigeria is now in question in an unprecedented way. As we speak, something like 25 percent of Nigerian oil is locked in or deferred because of the attacks by militants." Federal forces in the country have been unable to subdue this "insurgency," which has become a source of major concern to the United States. Escalation of U.S. military presence in the region can be interpreted as a desire to help quell internal and potential unrest in oil-producing states.[11]

The ex–Portuguese colony of Sao Tomé and Principle, an island state in the Gulf of Guinea, has become a focus of the latest lust for oil. Promised lavish dividends from oil—and the promise to turn this small and underdeveloped state into a wealthy African Kuwait—a contact was signed in 1997 with a U.S.-based company, Environmental Redemption Holding Corporation (ERHC). The deal guaranteed ERHC exclusive exploration and exploitation rights for twenty-five years and half of the profits. In return Sao Tomé received $5 million. The various oil blocks have attracted fierce competition. The best of these, a Joint Development Zone held with Nigeria, went to auction in 2003. The bid, made by a consortium led by Chevron and Exxon-Mobil, won through. Though oil in commercial quantities has so far eluded companies who have begun drilling, the area is a hive of activity and symbolizes continental developments.[12]

If the focus is on oil-rich West Africa, no area of the continent is left untouched. The rising oil prices have recently increased the interest of multinationals, so prospectors can be found sniffing around many parts of the continent. Ghana, Gambia, Somalia, Uganda, and Mozambique are all being targeted, with the promise of a glut of petrodollars if deposits are found.

In some ways South Africa is prophetic of what African capitalism may become. No other country in Africa has embraced with such craven enthusiasm the agenda of privatization and the free market. The country boasted average economic growth rates of 4.5 percent between 2003 and 2007. This has resulted in considerable dividends for the rich and the middle class. Here, the wealthy, like their Angolan counterparts, live behind their security gates—shuttling between home and shopping mall. Nowadays, this privileged section of South African society does everything at the malls—all social and consumer activity takes place there, including trips to the cinemas, restaurants, and bars. This group, though predominately white, has been expanded by a new layer of black professionals. The striking division in wealth induces a state of schizophrenia. South African's move between wealth and misery, from the city and mall where they work to the old, largely unreformed townships. This is what the boom represents—the familiar formula, noted years ago across the Third World, of growth without development.[13]

Despite the so-called "success" of South Africa—often presented as a model for the rest of Africa—official unemployment (16 percent in 1995) rose to 31.2 percent in 2003, but if those who have given up the hunt for work are included the figure rises to 42 percent. Formal employment has collapsed in many "traditional" sectors. During the 1990s, the number of jobs declined 47 percent in mining, 20 percent in manufacturing, and 10 percent in the public sector.[14] The recent xenophobic attack against non–South African immigrants in townships across the country reflects, above all, the response of those who experience firsthand the devastation of unemployment and where it can lead.

But instead of these "booms"—each arriving with more ridiculous hype from economists and journalists—signaling economic growth and development, the opposite has been the case. After decades of structural adjustment, described in detail in this collection, the devastation to basic infrastructure is now in many places almost complete. The new "growth" that has followed the commodity boom has been built on the rubble of a world that for a brief, post-independence moment in the 1970s offered development to the continent's working class and poor. Take Zambia. No country illustrates more the chimera of the boom in commodity prices. Chinese involvement in African mining has seen previously abandoned mines reopened. Though the Chambishi copper mine was the site of the worst mining disaster in Zambian history in 2005, when fifty-two workers were killed, it also represents an area of formal sector expansion. When the mine was purchased by a Chinese state-owned enterprise in 1998, employment was boosted to 2,200 from 100.[15] However, in the new privatized world of contemporary Zambia nothing is the same. Formal jobs have not returned in the same form, and few of the miners who are now employed in the reopened Zambian copper mines have pensionable contracts, a situation that contrasts dramatically with the previous practices. Today mining communities have been ravaged by HIV/AIDS, and little exists in the way of health care. Housing that was provided for miners does not exist on any significant scale, and townships, where most workers now live, are without proper services. The effect of years of privatization has also meant that the partial "recovery" has not benefited the national state. So when copper was $2,280 a ton in 1992 the state-owned mining sector earned the Zambian government $200 million from four hundred thousand tons of production. In 2004 at similar production levels but with copper selling at an increased price of $2,868, only $8 million was contributed by private mines to the state treasury. There is no more powerful example of the devastation wrought by privatization on the continent.[16]

The new scramble for Africa has also seen a growing interest on the part of China in the continent's oil reserves and minerals. This has led to hysterical condemnation, typical of which was London's *Daily Telegraph*, which in August 2007 had an article titled, "Why China is trying to colonise Africa." Western corporations and countries are not sprayed with the same vitriol.[17] Though Chinese investment on the continent has grown by great strides, it still does not come close to matching the involvement of the EU or the United States. The volume of trade has increased from $3 billion in 1995 to $55 billion in 2006, but this figure amounts to only 10 percent of Africa's total trade (compared to 32 percent with the EU and 18 percent with the United States). It is, however, projected to keep growing to $100 billion by 2010.[18] China, in some cases, has managed to offer African countries less onerous loans, which have helped to secure their place at the trough. Between 2005 and 2007, China advanced Angola credit lines estimated to be more than $5 billion, thus funding some of the country's "reconstruction." Angola is China's primary source of imported oil.[19]

The structural adjustment programs—now euphemistically renamed poverty reduction programs—of the IMF have over a period of twenty years devastated the continent, plunging country after country into economic crises that are often played out through the political manipulation of so-called ethnic divisions. Even where there is some recovery of jobs and economic growth, as we have seen, it still rests precariously on the prices of one or two commodities set on international exchanges in Chicago, New York, and London. When jobs return in these areas, the reduction in services and collapse of health systems, education, and welfare ensures the continuation of desperate poverty and hardship.

The European Union is aggressively pushing its own brand of adjustment. In 2008, the EU's trade negotiator, Peter Mandelson, managed to persuade eighteen African countries to sign interim Economic Partnership Agreements. Since 2002, EPAs have attempted to supplant the failed trade talks through the World Trade Organization. Similar bilateral agreements are now common for both the United States and China. These EPAs insist on investment protection, competition policy, and government procurement—each measure is designed to protect corporate profit and foreign access to African markets. Ghanaian activist Gyekye Tanoh argues that through these agreements "Europe is gaining 80 percent of our markets in exchange for what is effectively just 2 percent of theirs."[20] Another requirement of the EPAs is government investment in port infrastructure, a vital requirement for the stable outflows of primary commodities and cash crops—a classic feature of colonialism.

The Democratic Republic of Congo illustrates the collapse of a country into a maelstrom of disaster and war, largely provoked by structural adjustment programs and implemented by a political elite. Much of the boom, described briefly above, is carried out with apparent "legality," but foreign multinationals, mining firms and speculators in the DRC were quite happy—according to a UN report in 2001—to operate regardless of "unlawfulness." Another UN report in 2002 identified eighty-five foreign countries operating in the DRC. The nature of their involvement, however, changed dramatically during the long decade of conflict.[21] In the first war of 1996–97 the mining companies played an important, speculative role in the conflict. In the ensuing chaos and war of 1998 and onward, the companies were an essential element. One example is fairly typical. At the time of the second war, American Mineral Fields purchased diamond concessions in the Cuango Valley along the Congolese-Angolan border from a firm of Belgian speculators. This was a familiar pattern; entrepreneurs—known as "minors"—would acquire concessions and then sell them on at increased prices to bigger players. The deal was celebrated by the company in a press release, "The joint venture asset is a 3,700 square kilometre mining lease in the Cuango Valley, and a 36,000 square kilometre prospecting lease which borders the mining lease in the north." This activity, that sped up as the country moved toward a settlement and elections from 2003, saw the exploitation of minerals and the funding of rebel groups that fed into global networks of international business.[22]

The "peace" in 2003 signaled by the transitional government triggered two important processes. The first saw the return of some multinational companies to regions that they had previously watched from a distance. There were attempts to reintroduce gold mining and to start oil exploration. The peace agreement saw the central government attempt to reclaim control over the country's resources. It signed oil exploration licenses with the Canadian-British Heritage Oil Company which, mindful of the region's political turbulence, made contacts with local chiefs and rebels in one eastern province in 2002. The second process tied to the 2003 peace deal was just as predictable. Rebel commanders responsible for much of the killing and slaughter in the war were encouraged to become incorporated into the Congolese army. This process failed when several former rebel commanders in the east refused, and insisted once again on resisting the central government in the name of regional and local interests, but all too often in order to establish their own fiefdoms. Conflict continues throughout much of the eastern region, as does the exploitation of local resources.

"Popular participation" shorn of any real pretense of empowerment and economic equality provides a "legal" or ideological front to the old exploitation. Much of the new lip service paid to "democratization" and "good governance" on the continent is this: the veneer of respectability in the context of the scramble for riches. The reality is close to the surface, as we have seen recently in Nigeria, Angola, DRC, Kenya, Zimbabwe, South Africa and others.

Meanwhile the western powers, notably Britain, France, and the United States, have maintained their strategic interests on the continent. The United States in particular, under the auspices of its global "war against terror," has escalated military and strategic surveillance across the continent. The frantic attempts by the U.S. Defense Department to set up the new Africa Command (Africom) on the continent have run up against local reluctance to cooperate, but the motivation even to propose such an agency, to direct U.S. strategic interests on the continent, illustrates the renewed importance of African resources, particularly oil, for the United States. As part of this project George Bush was desperate for new allies on the continent to collaborate in the scramble for Africa and the global "war on terror."

Africom could not find a suitable African home. Traditional U.S .allies on the continent can no longer be relied on. Ethiopia is embroiled with the U.S. in the disastrous intervention in Somalia, while Kenya's domestic political crisis ruled out another reliable ally. So the White House was finally forced in February 2008 to base its Africa-watch outfit in the well-known African capital of Stuttgart, in Germany. Even friendly governments were reluctant to house the U.S. imperial project. Liberia was the sole volunteer.

But cooperation between the US and African governments, centred on the global "war on terror," has grown rapidly in recent years. Joint Combined Exchange Training (JCET) exercises conducted by units of the U.S. Army have provided training to African armies. So in August 2007, for example, approximately 350 U.S. troops were in Mali for three weeks of counterterrorism exercises with personnel from Algeria, Chad, Mali, Mauritania, Morocco, Niger, Nigeria, Senegal, and Tunisia. These "maneuvres" were part of Operation Enduring Freedom—

Trans-Saharan Counter-Terrorism Partnership (TSCTP) that links eight African countries to the United States.[23]

The important region around the Gulf of Guinea is now policed by the U.S. Navy. So U.S. naval forces regularly patrol the Gulf of Guinea. U.S.S. *Fort McHenry* an amphibious assault ship undertook a six month tour of duty in the region in the first part of 2008, operating as a "floating schoolhouse" to train local forces in oil-rig and port security and search and rescue mission. These requirements fit precisely to regional needs with the escalation of hostage taking of foreign oil-rig workers by rebel groups operating from Nigeria.[24]

Monolithic subjects?

If the continent is being plundered in a new wave of exploitation and imperialism, what are the prospects for resistance? Recently many have come to see the possibility of the African and Third World working class generating emancipatory change, or even limited social reform, as slight or having been entirely extinguished by the forces described above and by the ruling elites who benefit from the new scramble for Africa only if their own populations are effectively repressed and broken. Mike Davis has developed the most sophisticated recent critique of the political project for progressive change of what he sees as a fragmented and broken Third World proletariat. Though Davis's principal arguments in his book *Planet of Slums* concern the extraordinary growth of "mega-cities," he also raises questions about the role of class in a world transformed by "market reforms" since the 1970s.[25] He argues that the "supernova growth of a few cities like Lagos (from 300,000 in 1950 to 13.5 million today) has been matched by the transformation of several small towns and oases like Ouagadougou, Nouakchott, Douala, Kampala…and Bamako into sprawling cities larger than San Francisco or Manchester."[26] This growth, he suggests, has confused the distinction between rural and urban, as cities stretch out to include small towns and previously rural villages. As a consequence we are confronted with "the emergence of polycentric urban systems without clear rural/urban boundaries."[27] This explosion of cities both confirms and confounds the dynamic of global urbanization predicted in the nineteenth century.

But the growth of urbanization on the continent, which continues unabated, does not, in his view, signal the growth of an industrial working class or even in many cases the growth of formal wage labor. As Davis writes, "Since the mid-1980s, the great industrial cities of the South…have all suffered massive plant closures and tendential deindustrialization…. Urbanization has been more radically decoupled from industrialization, even from development *per se* and, in sub-Saharan Africa, from that supposed *sine qua non* of urbanization, rising agricultural productivity."[28] Historically, Davis argues, the movement to urban centers was accompanied by the growth of industrial manufacturing and the concomitant increase of formal wage labor, Marx's industrial proletariat. This development was also often associated with a growth in agricultural productivity to feed swelling cities, through the application of modern farming techniques. But in many parts of Africa at least, the opposite has occurred; "urbanization without industrialization is an expression of an inexorable trend: the inherent tendency of silicon capitalism to delink the growth of production from that of employment."[29] The culprit, Davis argues, is the twin evil of the 1970s debt crisis and the IMF and World Bank restructuring of Third World economies. So today urbanization becomes synonymous with falling wages, factory closure, and massive unemployment.

Davis is clear what this means: "From Karl Marx to Max Weber, classical social theory believed that the great cities of the future would follow in the industrializing footsteps of Manchester, Berlin and Chicago."[30] But he suggests something different has taken place. Today urbanization in Africa and Asia signals simply poverty, not industrialization. Slums, in Davis's account, symbolize the total reconstitution of class structures in the Third World. Unemployed slum dwellers are not the urban proletariat, spearheading and powering political, economic and social transformation. At the end of *Planet of Slums* we are left with a question: "To what extent does an informal proletariat possess that most potent of Marxist talismans: "historical agency'?"[31] To what extent, one might also ask, given the picture drawn by Davis, are they even a "proletariat" at all? In the world of neoliberal slums, Davis suggests there is "no monolithic subject…[but] myriad acts of resistance," that emerge from a chaotic plurality of "charismatic churches and prophetic cults to ethnic militias, street gangs, neo-liberal NGOs and revolutionary social movements [*sic*]."[32] It is tempting, however, to ask when, even at great moments of working-class action, there has ever been a "monolithic subject"?[33] The answer: "rarely, if ever"—suggests that Davis's thesis may be misleading and misguided.

Davis is, we would argue, right about the culprits of the recent devastation of the potential for genuine development on the continent, but wrong about the working class and the significance of popular protest. Actual class reconfiguration, and how it has manifested itself in the "myriad acts of resistance" in the South, does not, we believe, suggest a working class entirely dislodged from its "historical agency." There has, of course, been a long—and often skeptical—academic debate about the nature, and even existence, of an African working class. David Seddon, in this collection, deals impressively with these arguments. Writers doubted whether bonds of solidarity and consciousness were strong enough for a "real" working class to bring about social transformation, and suggested that the so-called working class was in any case excluded from other groups in society as an "aristocracy of labor." It is undoubtedly true that that the formation of the working class has been characterized by a complex and often heterogeneous process of "proletarianization" in most parts of Africa in the nineteenth and twentieth century—from migrant labor in the mines in southern Africa from the 1900s to labor in oil extraction and processing in the Niger Delta from the 1970s. Davis's vision of "desperate millenarianism" can be situated within the considerable body of literature questioning the capacity of a Third World or African working class to play its "historical role." For Davis, if this class existed, it did so in the past, but now, under the impact of neoliberalism, it has again been recast into a hybrid slum dweller, a lumpen proletariat, unable to lead new progressive social movements on the continent. We disagree.

The case of Soweto

Let's deal with the question of the slum, township, and urban expansion.[34] The sheer breadth of Davis's account is itself problematic, insofar as he includes in his account of the African situation numerous and extensive global slum and shantytown areas of extraordinary diversity and complexity. Africa is not, uniquely or universally, a space of undifferentiated "de-industrialisation" where the working class has been uprooted from formal employment. Take one example. Davis writes about Soweto—referring to its "backyards" and how "residents have illegally constructed shacks that are rented to younger families or single adults."[35] Soweto is South Africa's largest township, home to an estimated two million residents, twice the number of those recorded in a survey nine years ago.[36] It is a place of phenomenal diversity, including wealthy suburbs serviced by modern shopping malls and a golf course, as well as "respectable" working-class communities in modest apartheid-era housing. These areas, however, sit cheek-by-jowl with the squatter camps and informal settlements that are taken by Davis (as they have been by other commentators before him) to typify the slums and shantytowns of Africa—and indeed the South—as a whole.

Sowetan diversity expresses, with far more nuance than Davis's accounts allows, the nature of class diversity and change and the relationship between "slums," "shantytowns," and social classes. Recent research suggests a reality quite different from the fashionable view that unemployment in South Africa has "polarised the labour market by increasing the resources to some of the 6.6 million in the core who are formal, permanent workers while at the same time reducing the resources" to the rest.[37] The research suggests far more fluidity between the 6.6 million and the rest. In a Soweto-wide survey, conducted by the Centre for Sociological Research in Johannesburg, more than three thousand people in 2006 were asked to describe their lives. Not far short of a quarter of the total (23 percent) respondents were in "employment"; a slightly larger proportion (24 percent) were "unemployed," and overall, around half (50.12 percent) of respondents were "not in formal employment." This requires some explanation. Some of these were "partial workers," who explained that they did not work but occasionally did piecework, others were "fill-ins," who were engaged in small businesses, similar to the petite bourgeoisie, but who would accept paid work if it were offered. These "businesses"—in the much celebrated entrepreneurial world of the new South Africa—might be hawking sunglasses or bootleg videos by the side of the road, or perhaps more often in Soweto selling a few fruits and vegetables on the pavement. None of these people, however—a full 26 percent—are counted in the official unemployment statistics. These figures could be used to issue a devastating verdict on the neoliberal laissez-faire policies of the both Mandela's and Mbeki's governments.

There seem at this point to be no surprises. The statistics do not challenge the argument that the effects of mass unemployment—typical of deindustrialized urban life in the South—have created a new class of the wageless poor, excluded from the world of work. The working class seems now, by implication, a tiny and privileged group, many of whom live outside the township slum and have interests separate from the majority of the urban poor. However, a closer look at the statistics reveals something quite different. If we examine the household, we can see extraordinary mixing of the different and seemingly divided groups of the poor. For example, in only 14.3 percent of households were there no employed or self-employed. This means that less than a sixth of households were *entirely* unemployed or self-employed. We can go even further: 78.3 percent of households contained a mix of adults who were employed, self-employed, and unemployed. There is no "wall of China" between work and unemployment, as those in different economic statuses (or "class positions") from the "poor" to the "middle class" live side by side, and often in the same household.

What does this mean in terms of people's lives—and the potential for action and change? Claire Ceruti gives several examples, "Mr. Khumalo…was a teacher and now works as a driver. He lives with his wife who is a nurse, and his three children. One child is at university. He supports his brother and his sister. His brother has been unemployed for two years after the factory closed." Mr. Khumalo describes himself as "working class…trying to push to be middle class." Ceruti concludes from her case studies that "the employed and the unemployed are integrated at the level of the household. These stories show that the polarization of the labour market, far from making the stable employed into a privileged layer, may have the reverse effect of increasing the responsibilities on their wages."[38] The wages earned by the "workers" contribute significantly to their households, which may also include the "self-employed," the "unemployed," and the part-employed.

This brings us to another argument. In Soweto, an extraordinarily mixed urban space, the majority of people do not live in "shacks," as Davis pictures them. The spread of housing types across Soweto shows that 76 percent live in a range of formal housing, from council housing to recently built government housing. This is not to suggest that there is not a housing crisis in Soweto. On the contrary, a shocking 24 percent of people live in "informal" shacks, hostels, or "backrooms" (often corrugated iron extensions tacked onto the side of brick houses). In addition, new housing has simply not been built since 1994 in anything like the numbers required (or promised). According to the statistics, RDP houses, as this housing stock is popularly labeled (after the Reconstruction and Development Program introduced briefly after 1994), account for only 4.2 percent of the total housing types in Soweto.

What do these figures tell us? Put simply, and of course limited to Soweto, the jobless and formally employed are not hermetically sealed from each other, neither in terms of the household nor neighborhood.

They are not clustered in the so-called "informal" slum settlements of Soweto. This does not imply that the effects of unemployment have not had a dramatic and devastating effect on the poor. In fact the picture derived from the survey is that most families have been shaken by the hurricane of job losses. But this has important consequences for the character and pattern of social unrest. If there is no clear divide in the world of unemployment and formal employment, then the potential for a similar crossover exists as regards popular protest and social dissidence. A literal explosion of "service delivery" uprisings in South Africa over the last four years has been documented, in which whole communities have erupted in riots, protesting against the lack of basic services. Though the number of protests seems to have dropped off from the high of the early 2000s, the levels remain impressive. These protests are not small-scale, localized events. The public sector general strike in June 2007, for example, was the largest since the end of apartheid, pulling many people into trade union action for the first time. The potential cross-fertilization of these struggles—of community and workplace—does not live only in the minds of activists, but, as the survey suggests, expresses the real household—and wider community—urban-political economy of contemporary South Africa.

Soweto seems to point to what might best be termed "a complex coherence." The township might be viewed as a meeting point—indeed a "hotbed"—for trade unionists, university students, graduates, the unemployed, and informal traders. The specter of unemployment infects all layers of society. But these groups are not distinct or permanently cut off from each other, and may be found in the same community and even in the same household supporting and encouraging and influencing each other. Though we cannot simply generalize from the experience of Soweto, there seems a reasonable chance that the mix of the formally and informally employed at the level of household, and their intermingling fates, in diverse urban spaces could also be found in Davis's quintessential mega-slum—Kenya's Kibera—and indeed elsewhere also. It is perhaps worth reminding readers that this picture of the "complex coherence" of the shantytown (*bidonville*) resembles and recalls that evoked by early writers, such as Frantz Fanon, who saw in the 1950s and 1960s such emerging "areas" as precisely the likely sources of radical social action.

Fighting back

Like every other proletariat in the world, and in history, the African working class is characterized by and brings together heterogeneous groups. It has never been a "monolithic subject." But these debates can only be fully understood in the context of popular struggles and the actual moments of protest and resistance. This sees class as a relationship brought to life by the real course of events. As E. P. Thompson wrote, "like any other relationship, it is a fluency which evades analysis if we attempt to stop it dead at any given moment and anatomize its structure…the relationship must always be embodied in real people and in a real context."[39] This collection seeks to look at this relationship in concrete struggles that have taken place on the continent. Now we need to briefly consider the recent class struggle as manifested in protest—in strikes, marches, demonstrations, and riots—since this book was first published.

Two examples from 2007 substantially dismantle the myths of a poor multitude dislodging the working class. The wave of strikes in South Africa, including the June public-sector strike in 2008, has seen the increase of strike days from 500,000 in 2003, to 2.9 million in 2006. The public-sector strike was arguably the largest in South Africa's history, with 11 million strike days in June. But workers' struggles have been matched by the struggles among other groups of the poor. Service-delivery demonstrations and riots have skyrocketed to over twenty thousand in 2005–2007 from fewer than six thousand in 2004. In this sense there has been a real convergence of protests that have included traditional working class and the wider poor.[40] The strike in June 2007 was characterized by mass meetings, demonstrations, and strike solidarity committees. It also blew a hole into the traditional loyalty binding the ruling ANC to trade unionists. Claire Ceruti describes a meeting of strikers during the June strike:

> When a speaker on the platform shouted, "Viva ANC!" I listened as usual for the loudness of the reply to judge the popularity of the ANC. I heard something I had never heard before—dead silence, followed by a sprinkling of insulting phrases. Soweto activist Trevor Ngwane commented, "You could hear the audience thinking in that silence, 'Do we still support the ANC'?" Throughout the strike one striker after another repeated the refrain, "We put them where they are and look how they treat us." The implication, still only half grasped, is that power lies below—a lesson that has been disguised by years of policy battles.

It is not only in South Africa that we can find evidence of rising working-class action and popular protest. In the words of President Umaru Yar'Adua, a four-day general strike in Nigeria also in June 2007 "wreaked havoc on the economy and our people." The strike succeeded in closing down government departments, petrol stations, and stores. Export of the country's largest commodity—oil— was paralyzed in all but one terminal. Demands included the reversal of the N10 (Naira) increase in petrol prices, a 15 percent pay raise for public-sector workers and a review of the privatization of oil refineries and state power plants. But still the strike was called off four days after its start, without the full demands being met. However, Femi Aborisade, who is interviewed in this collection, is right to argue that "Regardless of the weaknesses of the strike, the working class has shown that based on a united force of organisations of the poor, it is a force to reckon with."[41]

Huge riots and protests, often simplistically (but not entirely misleadingly) called "bread riots," have punctuated the first decade of the new century in the Third World. In April 2008, recent price rises were labeled "mass murder" by Jean Ziegler, UN special rapporteur on the right to food.[42] Linked to oil price increases and speculation in the aftermath of the sub-prime crisis, price rises of basic foods have been astronomical—the UN Food and Agriculture Organization has shown that the food import bill for poorest countries is probably going to increase to $169 billion in 2008, with prices unlikely to return to previous levels.[43] By early April 2008 the effects were clear; protests had broken out across Africa including in the Ivory Coast, Guinea, Senegal, Mauritania, Morocco, Mozambique and Burkina Faso. In Burkina Faso, a three-day general strike took place in April against the rise in food prices with trade unions demanding a 25 percent wage increase for all public-sector workers. Ziegler explained that one day the starving poor could stand up against their oppressors: "It's just as possible as the French Revolution was."[44] He is right except for one crucial point: they are already are—every day and in most cities, towns, and villages across the continent.

But to see these instances of protest as simply spontaneous explosions of a slum-dwelling multitude is nonsense. More often they are organized or semi-organized expressions of political dissidence—movements based on a combination of anger and outrage at government failures and pressures of globalization—that carry demands for social and economic transformation. From protesting food price increases and demanding affordable bread, some of these movements have insisted on an across-the-board increase in the national minimum wage. Old political masters lose their credibility as economic questions become suffused with political actions and slogans. This criss-crossing of political and economic demands constantly folding over one another is a common feature of mass strikes.[45]

Nowhere has this process been clearer than in the extraordinary wave of protest and strikes that has swept Egypt in the last two years. Mentioned in the chapter on Egypt in this book, which refers mainly to popular protest between 1977 and the 1990s, Egypt has been the setting since 2000 for major demonstrations, one of the most significant of which has been that of the democracy movement that pulled in a range of opposition groups under the slogan "Kefaya" ("Enough"). In May 2006 pro-reform judges challenged the state's authority, and the previous year (in the November elections) the Muslim Brotherhood, despite violence and intimidation, won a large share of the parliamentary vote. But more significant still has been the wave of strikes that have broken out from December 2006, involving something like two hundred thousand workers and justify comparison to the strike wave in Egypt after the Second World War and during the protests of 1977–78. The recent strikes of the textile city of Mahalla al-Kubra have been central to Egyptian working-class action. Anne Alexander, who writes on Egypt in this book, has described this more recent upsurge in popular protest and working-class action:

> During the two strikes of December 2006 and September 2007 the area was transformed into a tented city where workers ate and slept. Workers' representatives reported back to mass meetings of thousands of strikers on the progress of negotiations. Lively protests with chants, drums, placards and palm branches communicated the strikers' determination to the authorities and kept their spirits high.[46]

These strikes have also exposed another fallacy that sees the informalization of work, temporary contracts, and unemployment as a barrier to real working-class action on the continent. The first strikes at the Mahalla textile factories were launched by women, few of them with formal contracts and most suffering terrible conditions in the factories. These workers, often on temporary contacts for three months, then fired and then again rehired, were among the most radical. They moved between sites and pulled out male workers. Sameh Naguib, an Egyptian socialist, emphasized, "Most of the women are fully veiled, but they are extremely militant, spending the night in the occupation alongside the men. If you lose the image of the veil you'd think they were militant socialists, and they are often leading men in the struggle."[47]

Zimbabwe tells us another related story. The chapter on Zimbabwe in this collection still provides excellent background to the current situation. Between 1996 and 1998, Zimbabwe had its *biennio rosso* of rising working-class militancy. Old shibboleths were overturned and the regime, once a symbol of the armed and victorious resistance to white settler rule on the continent, became synonymous with the cankerous rot of a corrupt postcolonial elite. Knighted by the British monarch in 1994, President Robert Mugabe was congratulated at the time for bucking the continental trend of tyranny and dictatorship. His ruling party, ZANU-PF, was the willing midwife to repeated programs of structural adjustment. But out of these reforms emerged a movement of impressive force, which by 1999 had decided to organize itself into a political party. On September 11 that year the Movement for Democratic Change (MDC) was formed, principally by the nation's trade union federation, the Zimbabwe Congress of Trade Unions Congress (ZCTU), but with a complex configuration of class forces supporting it.

Such opposition parties, in which the working class played a significant but not necessarily decisive role through the trade unions, were important to many of the developments that had taken place earlier in the decade on the continent. The nature and development of mass parties—often formed by the protest and opposition movements in the 1990s—were contested, however, by those socialists who were active in the opposition movements. In Zambia, for example, trade unions were central to the growth of resistance to President Kenneth Kaunda's ruling party, the UNIP. Frederick Chiluba was the leader of the Zambia Congress of Trade Unions and took a leading role in the formation of the opposition coalition. But trade unionism alone is insufficient to determine the progressive and revolutionary orientation of opposition politics. Azwell Banda was a socialist who tried to influence the processes at work. He explains, in the foreword to this book: "In April 1990 I spent days with Chiluba at his home trying to persuade him to participate in creating a workers' organization capable of taking over from Kaunda, but he had other ideas." Eventually the Movement for Multi-Party Democracy (MMD) was formed and went on to win elections held in

1991. The party, a coalition of business interests and trade unions, continued with the politics of adjustment and neoliberalism—all that the party came to represent was the vacuous notion of "change."

The failure of those socialist forces to assert themselves on the new and frequently trade union–based parties had a crippling effect. In the face of the weaknesses of the political left—that could and did argue for a "workers' organization capable of taking over"—these social movement parties were prey to domination by a new or more usually recycled elite, often led by ex–trade union leaders, who argued for a continuation of structural adjustment, liberalization, and a new form of comprador capitalism. For those countries that overturned regimes in the 1990s—during what was called the "democratic transitions"—all too often, new parties and coalitions resumed neoliberal reforms once in power. These new governments delivered a quick death to the African renaissance that was momentarily promised to the continent in the mid-1990s.

Activists and trade unionists who have fought in the recent riots, strikes and protests against price rises are, however, a new generation that needs to be won to the idea of socialist politics and organization. These are not novel needs or demands. After the general strike of 1964 in Nigeria—which involved over five hundred thousand workers—one strike leader argued that "although the cause of the strike was based on economic demands, yet in its development it has raised possible political action which, with a developed Marxist-Leninist party, could have led to a proletarian revolution."[48] The failure to build these alternative voices, proposing, arguing, and organizing a break with "the Washington consensus" and allied "reactionary consensus in Africa" has been a disaster for ordinary African people. In Zimbabwe, those forces created in the ferment of political protest and uprisings were unable to challenge effectively a regime that has cynically and brutally attacked the Left, and indeed wide swaths of the opposition movement. At the same time the opposition has itself leaned on an accommodation with the Washington consensus and neoliberalism and not relied on its original foundations as a movement of trade unions and students. However, there is an alternative—to which this book is dedicated—that looks to the power of the national and regional working class.[49]

On April 16 news spread around the world of the arrival of a Chinese cargo ship, the *An Yue Jiang*, owned by China's state shipping company, in the major container port in Durban, South Africa. The ship included three million rounds of ammunition and 1,500 rockets bound for Zimbabwe, two days drive from the port. The South African government explained to the world that there was nothing they could do: this was a legal transfer of cargo that had already been paid for by a neighboring sovereign state. The problem was that the sovereign state of Zimbabwe was busy stealing an election and crushing the opposition. The South Africa Transport and Allied Workers Union (Satawu) refused to be browbeaten by claims of legality. The union refused to unload the ship, while Satawu truckers said that they would not transport the cargo by road. The ship was paralyzed in "outer anchorage" in "off-port limits." Within a few days, trade unions with members in ports near Zimbabwe followed suit: Mozambique and Namibia also refused to unload the weapons. The ship was forced to sail to Angola, where dock workers "maintained a watch" to ensure that the seventy-seven tons of weapons were not unloaded.[50] This was a signal and heroic action.

However, while we can celebrate the extraordinary and complex vitality of class struggle and resistance in Africa, we also need to build and organize political alternatives. In each country socialist politics, based on the strengthening of popular resistance and working-class struggle, can, we believe, bring an end to adjustment, poverty, and underdevelopment. It was in order to harden and strengthen this project that this book was originally conceived. Now, republished several years later, it can continue to assert not only the relevance but also the centrality of a combination of popular protest, working-class action, and socialist organization for the real development and future of Africa.

MARXISM, CLASS, AND RESISTANCE IN AFRICA

Leo Zeilig and David Seddon

For almost forty years the ideas of Marxism were seemingly omnipotent in Africa. They dominated every serious intellectual debate about the continent and occupied the minds of those who sought independence. It was assumed that the poverty and underdevelopment of the continent could only be reversed by the application of socialism, or more specifically the Soviet model of economic development, state capitalism. The speed with which the leaders of national liberation movements proclaimed their faith in scientific socialism, or extolled the virtues of African socialism, or saw the future of Marxism in the new governments of China and Cuba, was enough to confuse the most level-headed. The proliferation of Marxism(s) would surely have led Marx to proclaim again "all I know is that I am not a Marxist."[1] In more recent times, however, the careful application of Marxist analysis to African realities has become rare, as have claims by popular movements to be Marxist or even to be inspired by that tradition of theory and practice.

This book reasserts the relevance of Marxism to modern Africa. We argue that the Russian model of socialism from above (state capitalism) and free market capitalism, whose virtues are extolled by the World Bank and most governments, have been equally disastrous for the mass of the populations of African countries. In contrast, we argue for a return to the classical Marxism of socialism from below, where socialism is seen as the self-emancipation of the working class.

In a book that seeks to use the classical Marxist method to analyze African political economy, it is essential to examine both the origins and the demise of "Marxism" and to consider to what extent current realities are still amenable to a Marxist analysis.[2] Why was "Marxism" so influential in Africa and what were the international factors underpinning the predominance of these ideas? Why has "Marxism" become less influential and what precisely explains heightened working-class struggles and popular resistance?

The chapter will follow the key turning points on the continent in the last fifty years. Roughly three periods can be discerned. Firstly, between 1945 and 1970 came the first wave of independence in Africa and the consolidation of state-led development, often by avowedly socialist regimes. Secondly, the years 1970–85 saw a second wave of liberation struggles by radical movements that were critical of independence and at the same time a decline in the state-capitalist model of development. And lastly, the period from 1985, associated with the rapid demise of the Soviet Union (the principal source of African Marxism) and the ascendancy of neoliberalism and globalization, brought structural adjustment and the privatization of the state in Africa. Each of these periods, from state-led socialist development to the neoliberalism of the International Monetary Fund (IMF) and World Bank have failed to bring economic development for the overwhelming majority of Africans. This failure and the role of Stalinism will be the subject of the earlier sections of this chapter. Later in the chapter we address the issue of contemporary working-class and popular struggles and their revolutionary potential.

The rise and fall of the Russian revolution

If Russian revolutionaries saw 1917 as the first part of a permanent, world revolution for socialism, how did the notion of "socialism in one country," the idea of independent (national) socialist development, become transformed into the raison d'être of the Third World communist movement? Had the Russian revolution collapsed under the pressure of foreign intervention and civil war, or did the rise of Stalin symbolize the victory of the revolution over these forces? Although many Marxists argued that the Bolshevik revolution had been strangled by the failure of successive attempts to spread the revolution, for others the isolation of Russia became the unique strength of the revolution and the international socialist movement. For many in the colonial world the isolation of the Soviet Union, its ability to "delink" from the capitalist system, was seen as the key to its industrial development. But it was precisely this delinking, forced on the initially successful Russian socialist revolution, that led to its reversal and, with the rise of Stalin, state capitalism.[3]

Prior to 1917 most Marxists believed that the struggle for socialism would be led by the advanced capitalist countries. But the first revolution of the twentieth century took place in what was seen as a cultural and social backwater, tsarist Russia: a country with a small working class concentrated in a few industrial centers but in which the overwhelming majority of the population were peasants. The conservatism and traditions of the tsarist empire were transformed into the militancy and urgency of a socialist revolution. Yet the only way that revolution could survive was through an international struggle for socialism. Russia then would be the signal, the detonator for world revolution. As Marx had pointed out, in 1848 the bourgeoisie, as the historical authors of capitalist development, proved that they were indecisive, cowardly, and weak.[4] If they had failed to organize or lead the European revolutions in 1848, what chance would they have in the twentieth century? This convinced Marx and Engels of the necessity of the "permanent revolution"—a small and relatively inexperienced proletariat, who were always the radical and most determined element in revolutionary struggle, must lead the fight for socialist transformation until it was victorious across the globe. This would be all the more so in the colonial world, where a national bourgeoisie was hardly able to raise its head as an independent power under the weight of the European metropolis. Russian revolutionaries regarded national seclusion and independence as problematic in the modern world.[5] The evolution of international capitalism predetermined and insisted on international revolution. As Lenin repeated endlessly, "We began our work counting exclusively upon world revolution."[6]

Leon Trotsky, a leading member of the Bolshevik government, was responsible for developing the theory of "permanent revolution." He understood that revolutionary change might start not in the developed economies but in regions peripheral to the centers of capitalist production, including the colonial world. But its victory could be assured only if the revolutions became "permanent" and spread to the developed economies. Tony Cliff highlighted the six principal aspects of the theory:

1. A bourgeoisie that arrives late on the scene is fundamentally different from its ancestors of a century or two earlier. It is incapable of providing a consistent democratic, revolutionary solution to the problem posed by feudalism and imperialist oppression. It is incapable of carrying out the thoroughgoing destruction of feudalism, the achievement of real national independence, and political democracy. It has ceased to be revolutionary.... It is an absolutely conservative force.

2. The decisive revolutionary role falls to the proletariat, even though it may be very young and small in number.

3. Incapable of independent action, the peasantry will follow the towns, and in view of the first five points, must follow the leadership of the industrial proletariat.

4. A consistent solution of the agrarian question, of the national question, a breakup of the social and imperial fetters preventing speedy economic advance, will necessitate moving beyond the

bounds of bourgeois private property. "The democratic revolution grows over immediately into the socialist, and thereby becomes a permanent revolution."

5. The completion of the socialist revolution "within national limits is unthinkable.... Thus, the socialist revolution becomes a permanent revolution in a newer and broader sense of the word; it attains completion only in the final victory of the new society on our entire planet." It is a reactionary, narrow dream to try to achieve "socialism in one country."

6. As a result, revolution in...[economically less developed] countries would lead to convulsions in the advanced countries.[7]

In 1917 this was not an obscure political theory but the self-evident reality (and an indispensable political strategy) in a globalized capitalist economy. At the time most Russian revolutionaries were clear on two things: firstly, socialism could not exist in a single country, even an industrially advanced one; and secondly, imperialism and the socialist revolution could not live side by side—one had to triumph.

Following 1917, every effort was made to strangle the Russian revolution: more than a dozen foreign armies invaded the country while a crippling blockade helped starve the revolution. Nevertheless the Bolsheviks held on, waiting and hoping for revolutionary victory in either the east or the west, a victory that would finally break their isolation. But the revolutions that broke out after the First World War went down to defeat. Stalin's rise to power was the symbol not of the glorious victory of the Russian revolution but of its crushing defeat and isolation. The ideas that grew up around this defeat—socialism in one country, the two-stage theory of revolution and the people's front—were exported from the Soviet Union in the name of "Marxism-Leninism."

When Mao Zedong's Communist Party proclaimed the People's Republic of China in 1949 it seemed to provide further evidence, if more was needed, that national liberation and socialism could be achieved only by disengaging from western imperialism.[8] Mao also gave a breath of life to a generation who had grown critical of Stalinism, and seemed to offer an answer to the question of the peasantry bedeviling the Third World. The Chinese revolution promised the equality of the town and countryside and avoided "the forced extraction of surplus" that had led to the forced collectivization of the peasantry in the Soviet Union.[9] It also seemed to guarantee a worker and peasant alliance, even if workers were effectively written out of the revolution and towns became regarded not as the hub of the revolutionary movement but as the center of a pro-imperialist petty bourgeoisie.

In the Soviet Union, China, Eastern Europe, and Cuba, self-proclaimed communist parties had come to power in countries that were largely peripheral to capitalism and not part of the project of colonial expansion in Africa. They were corners of the world that were regarded as sharing certain African realities: large peasant economies with often coastal-based industries and a small, relatively inexperienced working class. The argument of many at the time was that the organizing center for the revolution would, as China had illustrated, be the countryside and the guerrilla movement. By the 1960s the writing was on the wall: the responsibility for Marxist transformation had shifted from the European working class, who had abdicated their role at the forefront of international socialism—often because they were regarded as having been implicated in the "pillage of the Third World"—to popular, nationalist movements in the Third World.[10]

In practice, the working class was often regarded by these governments as at best a passive element and at worst a reactionary fifth column. This did not prevent Maoists from using the language of proletarian internationalism even when there was not a member of the working class in sight. Che Guevara explained how he greeted comrades in the foothills of the eastern Congo in a spirit of "proletarian internationalism" and set about building the "International Proletarian Army."[11] Like in "The Emperor's New Clothes," very few were heard shouting from behind the crowd, "He's naked, there is not a member of the working class in sight!" The anxieties about whether an African working class exists, a question that has turned many academics gray, often arose simply because they were not "visible" in the new "revolutionary" paradigm.

Even so the working class did play a leading role in the struggle for independence in many African countries (see Chapter 2). In 1945 the first general strike in Nigerian history paralyzed the colonial machine for six weeks and led to a period of "labor nationalism" (see Chapter 4) throughout the late 1940s. This mass struggle also encouraged the founders of the left-wing Zikist Movement, who called for strikes and boycotts and attacked Nigerians who collaborated with the colonial state. In Senegal, the extraordinary railway strike of 1947 was a major factor in the birth of the nationalist movement.[12] Similarly, the uneasy alliance between the Zambian trade unions and the nationalist Northern Rhodesian Congress illustrates how the trade union movement in Africa often predated the nationalist struggle and refused to be subsumed by it. The problem was not the existence or activity of an African working class, but arguably, as Femi Aborisade claims, the "lack of a visionary and strategic labour leadership" (see pp. 150–56).

But essentially, the lesson of October 1917 was lost: the idea that a small, industrial working class could lead the revolution in a movement *linked to* the international struggle for socialism. Even in countries where the peasantry was numerically dominant, it was only the working class who had the organization and consciousness necessary for a successful socialist revolution. The essence of classical Marxism, the self-emancipation of the working class and the oppressed, was rejected in the Stalinized "Marxism-Leninism." Internationalism, the lifeblood of Bolshevism, became merely a slogan used in international diplomacy. The democratic, national revolution that had been subsumed by the struggle for socialism in 1917 became the prerequisite first step or "stage" towards socialism in the Third World. Socialism, the world was assured, would follow the national struggle. National liberation *and* socialism, it was claimed, were too much for one movement and the people were told that, like U.S. President Gerald Ford, they could not walk and chew gum at the same time.

Students and intellectuals: deflecting the revolution

What happened to Trotsky's theory of the permanent revolution in Africa? Despite the central role of working-class resistance in the years immediately before decolonization, the African working class failed to lead those movements to "permanent revolution." By the early 1960s, contrary to the theory, the role assigned to the working class seemed to have been taken by a radical intelligentsia. This was not accidental. In the absence of revolutionary politics on the continent—paralyzed by Stalinized communist parties—and with the relative inexperience of the working class, a group of students and intellectuals was able to lead the movements for national independence, a process that Tony Cliff described as "deflected permanent revolution." The revolutionary role of the working class is not an absolute rule, without the vital intervention of revolutionary organizations.

The coherence of these intellectuals was in direct proportion to the lack of organization and cohesion of the working class in colonial Africa. In this vacuum they saw themselves as the liberators of Africa, representing the emergent nation. As Cliff wrote about the intelligentsia: "They are great believers in efficiency.... They hope for reform from above and would dearly love to hand the new world over to a grateful people, rather than see the liberating struggle of a self-conscious and freely associated people result in a new world themselves."[13] These factors helped to make the Soviet state-capitalist model of economic development an enticing objective for African socialists.

The economic success of state capitalism was very attractive. In 1913 the old tsarist regime had contributed only 6 percent to the planet's "national incomes" and 3.6 percent of the world's industrial production. Within a few decades this picture was transformed. By the 1950s, the Soviet Union was one of a handful of "superpowers," and even after two decades of decline, in 1986 the Soviet Union still produced 14.6 percent of the world's industrial output.[14] The success of the Soviet economy seemed to prove that national industrial development would follow independence. For Kwame Nkrumah, who became Ghana's first president, the Sputnik, the Soviet rocket launched in 1957, seemed to symbolize the potential to overcome the debilitating and, for the group that saw themselves as Africa's future, humiliating underdevelopment.

In addition to this, capitalism had failed to spread the industrial revolution across the globe, and remarkably little industrial development took place in Africa during the period of colonization. The hub of industrial capitalism was still located in Western Europe and North America. This fact, lamented by delegates at the Pan-African Conference in 1945, reinforced the attraction of state-led development, with the Soviet Union as an oasis of industrial development in a capitalist world.[15] The model appeared to indicate that independence and development could be achieved by "delinking" from the capitalist world.

So the Soviet Union influenced not simply African geopolitics after independence, but also the ideological formation of a group of Africans in the 1940s and 1950s. Future leaders developed their politics in student groups like the West African Student Union in London and the Black African Student Federation in Paris. Nkrumah even boasted about reading the newspaper of the British Communist Party on the London underground. These groups achieved a certain intellectual and organizational hegemony that was unparalleled in colonial Africa.[16]

The African working class, without its own revolutionary organization and leadership, was unable to push the national and democratic struggle forward to socialist revolution, but within months of the national flag replacing the colonial one they resumed the struggle against their "own" ruling class. And Nkrumah showed as much hostility to striking workers as his colonial predecessors.

1945–70: imperialism, socialism, and the Cold War

After the Second World War, the command economies of "socialist countries" were seen as the only way for radical Third World states to advance. As Keynesianism had become the economic orthodoxy in the West, so state capitalism became the doctrine of African states. This coincided with a period of rapid and largely state-directed economic growth in the West after the war. The protectionism and state capitalism of the interwar period gave way to a widespread belief in an active, interventionist state that would continue to provide the conditions for rapid economic growth. The "long boom" that followed the war was largely fueled by intense military competition between the Soviet Union and the United States, but it was built on the ideological premise of economic interference in national economies.[17] The ideas of the economist John Maynard Keynes came to symbolize the economic success of the period. Most would have concurred with Nkrumah when he wrote, "Government interference in all matters affecting economic growth in less developed countries is today a universally accepted principle."[18]

In the first ten years of independence, even states that were not explicitly "Marxist" expressed an allegiance to socialism and an admiration for the Soviet Union. The list includes many of the most famous leaders of independent Africa: Nasser, Nkrumah, Sekou Toure, Julius Nyerere, and Ben Bella. Several African leaders were also in the process of adapting the ideas of Marxism in an attempt to make them more applicable to what were regarded as African realities. So Tom Mboya of Kenya maintained that socialism was an idea intrinsic to traditional African culture. "African socialism has an entirely different history from European socialism," which, he argued, arose from the

division of society between a capitalist class and an industrial proletariat. However, "There is no such division into classes in Africa...so
there is no need in Africa to argue over ideology or define your actions
in terms of doctrinaire theories."[19]

In Algeria, independence was the subject of long and brutal struggle. After eight years of war—a war that had left over one million dead
and which had been conducted with brutality by the French government[20]—Algeria finally became independent in 1962. Colonial Kenya
was typical of the situation in white settler states in fighting a war
against the courageous Mau-Mau movement.[21] However, Ghana's
largely peaceful transition to independence provides an example of a
process of "handover" that was experienced more widely. Although
Nkrumah had created the Convention People's Party (CPP), a popular
mass party that had been agitating for political change throughout the
1950s, he quickly abandoned the movement when independence had
been achieved. Expressing the sentiments of many new leaders, Léon
M'ba, the first president of Gabon, assured the French government
that "Gabon is independent, but between Gabon and France nothing
has changed; everything goes on as before."[22] Ruth First, the brilliant
activist and writer on Africa, observed several years after independence
that decolonization had been nothing more than a "bargaining process
with cooperative African elites.... The former colonial government
guarded its options and...the careerist heirs to independence preoccupied themselves with an 'Africanization' of the administration."[23]

But what were the experiences of these regimes for ordinary
Africans? The result was that so-called socialist states and capitalist
countries on the continent were for most Africans indistinguishable.
It was believed that the state, capitalist or socialist, must lead the drive
to industrialization in the interests of the nation. The reality was that
capitalist and socialist regimes used the same heavy-handed state apparatus, whether in Nkrumah's Ghana or M'ba's Gabon.

To a growing, radical generation of Africans, independence was
gradually being seen as a charade barely disguising the imperialism of

former colonial powers. No country illustrated the hollow claims of independence better then the ex-Belgian Congo. As soon as independence had been won, the left-wing prime minister, Patrice Lumumba, was faced with a mutiny, the secession of the country's mineral-rich province, Katanga, led by Moise Tshombe, and (within months of their departure) the return of Belgian troops. The United Nations, invited by Lumumba, arrived in an attempt to defend the country's borders the same year. In 1961, after Lumumba requested Soviet support, he was overthrown by the country's president and then assassinated by Tshombe, who followed plans laid by the Central Intelligence Agency (CIA). By the end of the year, the United States had helped to prevent the defection of a mineral-rich country and the battle lines of the Cold War in Africa had been drawn.[24]

Later, in 1964, the Congo was convulsed by a series of rebellions under a left-wing Lumumbist alliance. One of these rebellions was being led by Laurent Kabila and supported by Che Guevara, who hoped the struggle would draw in and weaken "Yankee imperialism." American anxiety was heightened by the left-wing movement in Zanzibar that led to the unity of Tanganyika and Zanzibar the same year, and to make matters worse the Afro-Shirazi Party in Zanzibar were strong supporters of the recent Cuban revolution. The fear in Washington was that Africa was about to turn "Cuban," so the CIA funded, supported, and armed the Congolese government in its fight against the rebellion. Cuban exiles, recently routed from Cuba, were recruited to fly missions against the rebels and the Americans suggested the use of white mercenaries from southern Africa, who were eventually organized by a veteran of the Second World War, Colonel Mike Hoare. In one of the first operations in 1964, Belgian paratroopers were flown into Africa using U.S. Air Force planes, from a British and later a Congolese base. The air support was provided by B-26s flown by Cuban exile pilots who had been trained and were controlled by the CIA. The mercenaries were also a thoroughly international force, which included British, French, Belgians, Germans, Italians, South Africans, and Rhodesians. The Congo had become an imperialist battlefield awash with racist armies and military advisers.[25]

In the next few years a number of other first-generation, self-styled African socialist leaders were also toppled or assassinated. For example, Ben Bella in Algeria was overthrown in a coup by his defense minister; Nkrumah, who had become increasingly unpopular at home, was removed while abroad; and the Moroccan oppositionist Ben Barka was kidnapped and assassinated in Paris. But what had been their legacy? The experience of Ghana, illustrative of the period, had revealed two things: the difficulty of industrial development in a world dominated by western imperialism, and the façade of African socialism.

The centerpiece of Ghana's attempts to industrialize was the Akosombo Dam on the Volta river. It was hoped that the dam would provide energy to allow the local supplies of bauxite to be turned into alumina. Instead the American company Kaiser, which ran the aluminium works, imported semi-processed bauxite from Jamaica. It claimed that it did not make economic sense to use local sources of bauxite one hundred miles away when they could import it from an island 2,500 miles away! As Robert Biel has put it, "the four big companies which dominated the world aluminum industry were brought together through the personal intervention of U.S. leaders Nixon and Kennedy, to ensure that Ghana did not establish a basis for independence."[26]

The second lesson of the Ghanaian experience was the very socialism that the state claimed it was based on. Ghana had experienced a period of mass mobilization between 1949 and 1951 that led to limited self-government. But from independence the movement that had been built and mobilized was forgotten, and increasingly what counted "was the exercise of power rather then the mobilization of the masses."[27] Nkrumah was isolated in the political administration and centralized state that he inherited from colonialism. Support had disappeared and opposition had grown by the time of the coup that toppled him in 1966. For regimes like Ghana, Mali, Mauritania, and Guinea, which were regarded at the time as radical, social change was instigated by a state machine that bore a close resemblance to the colonial state that they claimed to have broken with.

1970–85: the new "Marxist-Leninists" and the state

The period between 1970 and 1985 held many contradictions for African radicals. There was a combination of new struggles in Africa and a deepening economic crisis that brought to an end the myth of rapid economic development directed by the state. It also marked the end of the long boom that had stretched precariously and unevenly around the world since 1945. By the early 1970s industrial production had slumped in the advanced economies by 10 percent in one year, while international trade had fallen by 13 percent.[28] The resulting recession had a devastating effect on Africa. Still locked into economic dependency, most African economies relied on the export of one or two primary products. By the mid-1970s, for example, two-thirds of exports from Ghana and Chad were coffee and cotton respectively, while the fall in copper prices meant that by 1977 Zambia, which depended on copper for half of its GDP, received no income from its most important resource.[29] Regions already marginal to international capitalism were further marginalized and even the protective edifice of state capitalism that was still being constructed in Africa was impotent to resist the violence of these slumps.

The struggle for independence from Portugal represented, for some, a renaissance of socialism in Africa.[30] Since the crisis in the Congo, guerrilla movements had multiplied in Africa, the most effective fighting under the leadership of Amilcar Cabral in the small West African state of Guinea-Bissau. Amilcar Cabral, intellectual and activist, was a symbol of the new generation of African socialists, and he managed to demoralize and humiliate the Portuguese army. The Portuguese army was also involved in Angola and Mozambique in an increasingly desperate bid to hold on to Portugal's African empire.

The armed struggle was launched in Guinea-Bissau after the famous dockworkers' strike in 1959. On August 3 the police attacked strikers on the Pidjiguiti waterfront in the capital, Bissau. Fifty strikers were killed and more than a hundred were wounded. The massacre convinced Cabral that the struggle for liberation must be rooted in the rural areas. Following the massacre, Cabral left Guinea-Bissau for neighboring Guinea, where he started to organize a struggle that would, from now on, take place in the countryside.[31]

Although the new leaders of liberation movements were often committed to "Marxism-Leninism," they remained critical of the experience of decolonization. The MPLA in Angola and FRELIMO in Mozambique both faced external invasions from South Africa and internal destabilization by movements funded by the United States. But these movements still highlighted the upsurge of radicalism on the continent. The Portuguese revolution that followed a military coup in 1975 was both precipitated and inspired by the struggle for national liberation in Africa.

Elsewhere in Africa, the early and mid-1970s also seemed to mark a period of political transformation. The strikes, protests, mutinies, and demonstrations that gripped Ethiopia in 1974 turned Addis Ababa into "a permanent seminar. Everything was discussed, everything examined closely.... Drunk with their freshly acquired liberty...Addis Ababa took to the streets again."[32] The unrest spread from the capital to provincial cities, where the demand grew for the dismissal of government officials and even the senile emperor, Haile Selassie.

The emperor was deposed in September and the Derg (council) proclaimed itself the Provisional Military Administrative Council. Although there was no opposition to the removal of Haile Selassie, the military government was immediately condemned by the trade unions and a wider protest movement. There were calls for a "people's government," demonstrations, and threats of a general strike. But the leaders of the Confederation of Ethiopian Trade Unions were arrested and the Derg, under the authority of Mengistu Haile Mariam, moved quickly to consolidate its power, killing sixty members of the imperial army and suppressing the civilian opposition.

In the absence of sustained political opposition, a small but tightly organized group within the army took the streets back from the students, the trade unions, and the urban poor. "Marxism-Leninism," conspicuously absent from the Derg's previous pronouncements, was taken up as the state ideology and by 1975 Soviet military assistance began to arrive. The Soviet Union had first supported the Eritrean People's Liberation Front, then abandoned them and backed Ethiopia's war for "national sovereignty" against the Eritreans, not the "behavior they expected of the 'father of socialism.'"[33]

Economic reform, austerity, and popular protest in the 1970s and 1980s

If the "second wave" of political transformation increasingly appeared compromised during the second half of the 1970s and into the 1980s, all paths of autonomous national development adopted by existing African regimes were increasingly undermined as the global economic crisis deepened. Although the economic crisis of the late 1970s and early 1980s was a global capitalist crisis, much of the pain of adjustment was borne by the developing countries, and particularly by those that relied heavily on oil imports and on borrowing from the West.

Loans turned into debts as the process of global adjustment and restructuring required for the resolution of the international capitalist crisis proceeded. More and more African states found their options constrained and their macroeconomic policies increasingly shaped by the conditions imposed by the International Monetary Fund (IMF), the World Bank, western governments, and the private banks.[34] By the time the free market governments of Thatcher and Reagan had been elected, development policy had shifted to focus on the market and the private sector. The IMF and World Bank became the central players in this policy. As the World Bank reported at the time, "Africa needs not just less government—[but] government that concentrates its efforts less on direct intervention and more on enabling others to be productive."[35]

For most African economies, "structural adjustment" preceded more far-reaching economic and institutional reform, leading to varying degrees of economic liberalization. The costs of economic liberalization and the austerity policies that accompanied it, however, fell unevenly on different social classes. The poor and working class, particularly in urban areas, felt the pain of adjustment most acutely. But they did not just suffer passively, as victims of the crisis; they struggled in various ways, resisted, and protested.[36] In general, for the poorest and most vulnerable, survival strategies of various kinds were deployed on an individual and household basis. Social networks have always been a crucial part of the real economy in Africa, and these were increasingly mobilized to provide security. But, contrary to the view of many on the left, the reaction of the working class and poor was not only defensive and geared toward survival; it was also offensive—aimed at resisting, protesting against, and changing the policies, and at challenging those interests that so evidently oppressed and exploited them. The targets of popular protest included the international financial agencies (particularly the IMF), the governments that adopted the austerity policies and the representatives of the big corporations (foreign and national) that benefited from liberalization.

Across the continent through the late 1970s and the 1980s, popular struggles against the austerity policies of their governments brought people out on to the streets in demonstrations, marches, strikes, and other forms of protest action. These helped to build their resistance and their anger against the governments that had introduced and implemented wage restraint and budgetary cutbacks. The wave of popular protest that swept across the African continent—as it did across the developing world as a whole[37]—during the late 1970s and the 1980s drew its strength and effectiveness from being based on broad coalitions, in which the working class was as often supporting as leading. These popular struggles were strengthened by their association with the trade union movement, labor movements, and working-class actions, but were also often broader in their social class composition, including the lumpen proletariat of the shantytowns and elements of the new petty bourgeoisie.

We reject the suggestion that these popular struggles can be written off as "defensive, ephemeral, even destructive," or as "irredeemably populist," "unsustainable" and "utopian."[38] We argue that, while they were indeed to a large extent spontaneous and directed predominantly toward current economic reforms and austerity measures, they also contained the potential to become more orchestrated and systematic political opposition movements. In some cases, within a matter of days or weeks, they took on the character of political opposition, challenging policies and in a few cases leading directly to the overthrow of the government. In most cases they redefined the terrain of class struggle and provided the basis for the emergence at a later stage of political movements aimed at changing governments rather than just policies.

In North Africa, with the exception of Libya, every state experienced major outbreaks of popular protest against the economic reform and liberalization policies of their governments during the decade 1977–87. They started in Egypt in 1977, when the government's decision to raise food and gas prices as part of a program of financial stringency and economic reform designed under the auspices of the IMF, provoked long and fierce rioting in major cities across the country. The wave of popular protest also involved four out of the five countries of the Arab Maghreb Union—Morocco, Mauretania, Algeria and Tunisia—and also Sudan. In all of these countries popular protest had a political impact; in virtually all cases, it produced a rapid reversal of cuts in subsidies, and a far greater awareness of the political limits to rapid structural adjustment and economic liberalization; in some cases it resulted in political changes and a greater degree of political openness; in Sudan it resulted in the rapid development of a movement of opposition to President Numeiry, which ended in the overthrow of the regime. In sub-Saharan Africa also, during the 1980s, as economic reforms continued, so too did the popular protests, although by now they were becoming less "spontaneous," more organized, and more overtly political (see pp. 15–19).

The military and the new economics in the 1980s

Many countries followed the trajectory of Ghana after the fall of Nkrumah in 1966: successive military coups, each promising a fresh start and national reconstruction. In the fifteen years after the coup that removed Nkrumah, Ghana experienced no fewer than eight "transitory" governments. As each regime came and went, the economic situation for ordinary Ghanaians deteriorated. In 1981, after a strike wave paralyzed the country, the government declared that in the event of further action all strikers would be arrested. The strike movement helped precipitate the collapse of the Limann administration, but it was the military that profited from the instability, and Flight-Lieutenant Jerry Rawlings led a coup on December 31, 1981. Rawlings became the latest in a line of military "saviors," committing his first government, the Provisional National Defense Council, to sweeping and "revolutionary" change. He immediately appealed to the Trades Union Congress in Ghana to withdraw their wage claims.

Rawlings's first government was a contradiction. While he made populist appeals to the nation and called for the poor to defend the "revolution," the regime adapted to the exigencies of international agencies. After several years, left-wing opponents were imprisoned and attempts were made to silence the trade unions.[39] At the same time, the regime became a test case for structural adjustment. Rawlings oversaw the introduction of the Economic Recovery Program and called for "austerity and sacrifice." Phase two was initiated in 1987 and in acknowledgement of the government's achievements international organizations pledged $575 million for further programs. Rawlings the revolutionary became the darling of the IMF and the World Bank.[40]

The reaction of urban workers in Ghana to the economic reform program implemented from the early 1980s by Jerry Rawlings's quasi-military regime was initially limited but gradually became more militant. In 1984–85, twenty-five thousand redundancies were announced, and they were followed by a further thirty-two thousand during the next year. By the start of 1986, there was widespread dissatisfaction among the well-organized Ghanaian trade union movement. But when workers gathered in Accra to protest against the arrest of several trade union leaders who had voiced their opposition to the job losses, they were met with an estimated ten thousand police who, with armored cars, sought to control the protest. Even after the working class had been ravaged by privatization and structural adjustment, the TUC boasted a membership of five hundred thousand in seventeen affiliated unions in the early 1990s.[41]

Rawlings recognized that the consensus that had supported the idea of state-led development had shifted. As Chris Harman wrote, the "pendulum swung from one extreme to another…African state direction could not break the vicious circle of underdevelopment, impoverishment, political corruption and dictatorship."[42] Around this time the phenomenon of the "Asian Tigers" developed. South Korea, Taiwan, Hong Kong, and Singapore saw their growth rates soar. This was seen as confirmation that free market capitalism could bring economic development to the Third World. It was believed that, while the economies of those countries that espoused socialism or advocated state intervention declined, other Third World countries that expressed economic allegiance to the capitalist system were experiencing rapid growth.

Some writers have maintained that the Asian experience is proof of the continuing ability of capitalism to bring development.[43] But in reality the expansion of manufacturing and investment has been increasingly concentrated in the heartlands of western capitalism and a limited number of newly industrialized countries (NICs). World manufacturing exports for the 102 poorest countries fell from 7.9 percent to 1.4 percent in the 1980s, not the picture of a dynamic, expanding capitalism. However, the myth of rapid industrial development is central to the idea of the NICs—if they did not exist, it would be necessary to invent them. As Robert Biel has put it, even "large areas of the South which…central capital will never view other than as a passive reservoir of cash crops or raw materials, might be reconciled with the system if it seemingly opens up an avenue for advancement."[44] The African ruling class has searched high and low for "African Tigers": President Mubarak of Egypt talks about building a "Tiger on the Nile," while Senegal's President Abdoulaye Wade dreams of mass industrialization and high-tech growth in Africa. Both continue to call for prudence and austerity, an obscenity in the face of mass poverty and the conspicuous displays of wealth by the ruling class.

On the left, revolutionary politics had been paralyzed by the Cold War, by an absurd and Stalinized view of socialism and the ubiquitous and nonsensical notion that there was not a "real economic working class" in Africa. Where socialists were forced to admit that there was a working class on the continent it was dismissed as "Africanized" and unable "to achieve the solidarity and coherence that could have moved them toward empowering socialist political movements."[45] But from the late 1980s Africa underwent a political revolution hardly noticed in the West, but as far-reaching as the changes that brought down the state-capitalist regimes of Eastern Europe. In the words of the long-standing (and no doubt fearful) president of Gabon, Omar Bongo, "the winds from the East are shaking the coconut trees."[46]

The winds from the South: mass protest and political transformation in the 1990s

Throughout the 1970s and 1980s the Soviet Union and its client Eastern European states were increasingly exposed to the effects of the international recession. The effects of military competition with the West and the fall in commodity prices had helped to paralyze the East. By 1987 vodka and oil were the principal source of the economy's national income. However, East and West continued to be bound up with the Cold War, played out to horrifying effect in Africa.[47]

Even Angola's President dos Santos had begun by 1985 to move away from the failure of state-led development based on the Soviet model. He was not alone. Soon leaders who had previously adhered to state-led development and socialism rushed forward to welcome neoliberalism and the free market. The transition was easy: African leaders who had repeated the mantra of "proletarian internationalism" for thirty years now called for privatization of the state and "international competition."

The idea that African states were in some way a barrier to the free market and globalization was a self-evident absurdity, but this was lost on most commentators. They rushed to proclaim a new faith in the market after the collapse of the state-capitalist regimes in Eastern Europe. Andre Gunder Frank was typical in arguing at the time that these policies resulted in "enormous strides in the...economic and political direction" of the Third World.[48] Even by the mid-1980s, regimes that had kept the banner of "Marxism-Leninism" flying introduced programs mirroring IMF-led structural adjustment. Structural adjustment programs were the conditions attached to IMF and World Bank loans. The terms of the loans required states to "adjust" their economies, privatize national industries, remove tariff barriers, and "open up to the outside world," exposing their economies to international competition and the free market.[49]

But the protests that marked the start of the 1990s were eloquent testimony to the devastation that structural adjustment and the free market had already brought to the continent. A second wave of popular protest, now more explicitly political and with more far-reaching aims and objectives, spread across the continent like a political hurricane. From 1989, political protests rose massively across sub-Saharan Africa. There had been approximately twenty annually recorded incidents of political unrest in the 1980s; in 1991 alone eighty-six major protest movements had taken place across thirty countries. By 1992, many African governments had been forced to introduce reforms, and in 1993, fourteen countries held democratic elections. In a four-year period from the start of the protests in 1990, a total of thirty-five regimes had been swept away by protest movements and strikes, and in elections that were often held for the first time in a generation. The speed with which these changes took place left commentators breathless: "Compared with the recent experiences of Poland and Brazil...African regime transitions seemed frantically hurried."[50] The effects of the IMF and neoliberalism in the region at the end of this period had only one benefit: they brought together on an unprecedented scale workers, peasants and the poor, who fought with extraordinary militancy and courage against food and fuel rises and political oppression, and often for wholesale political transformation.

In 1989, the movement started in the West African state of Bénin. Students demonstrated against the government in January, demanding overdue grants and a guarantee of public sector employment after graduation. The government, crippled by financial scandals, capital flight, and falling tax revenue, thought it could respond as it had always done, by suppressing the protest. But the movement grew during the year to incorporate trade unions and the urban poor. In an attempt to preempt the movement, the president, Mathieu Kérékou, declared that his party, the People's Revolutionary Party of Bénin (PRPB), had jettisoned "Marxism-Leninism" and agreed that multiparty elections could be held in the future. In a pattern followed by other countries he set up a commission that would eventually create a national reconciliation conference that included the opposition movement, trade unions, students, and religious associations.

Emboldened by events, trade unionists, led by postal workers and teachers, left the government-controlled National Federation of Workers' Unions of Benin (UNSTB). By the end of the year the capital, Cotonou, was convulsed by mass demonstrations. When Kérékou attempted to befriend demonstrators during one of these protests he was jeered and threatened, forcing him to flee. In February 1990 the National Conference of Active Forces declared itself sovereign and dissolved Kérékou's national assembly. Obstinately he still insisted, "I will not resign, I will have to be removed." After being defeated in the presidential elections held the following year, he asked humbly for forgiveness and asserted his "deep, sincere and irreversible desire to change."[51]

In Ivory Coast, severely affected by the drop in the international price of cocoa and coffee, violent unrest between March and May 1990 threatened the government's austerity program and shook the regime. The austerity program was designed to fill a £236 million gap in the budget, and had been agreed the previous July with the World Bank and the IMF. Three weeks of protests and strikes by workers in all sectors delayed the imposition of measures to cut public sector salaries and increase taxes, while student protests added fuel to the flames. The army was brought in by Félix Houphouët-Boigny (the first president of Ivory Coast, who held the office from 1960 to 1993) to control the protests, and the president rejected growing demands for a multi-party state. Cuts and the taxes were imposed, together with price cuts aimed at softening the blow of the salary reductions.

But protests continued, and businesses resisted the proposed reductions in prices. On March 23, soldiers used tear gas to disperse more than one thousand people protesting in the center of Abidjan in support of a group of women who had staged a sit-down protest on Abidjan's main street, bringing traffic to a halt. Doctors voted for an indefinite strike and withdrew emergency cover in protest at mass arrests of demonstrators. A ban on demonstrations, imposed on March 26, proved ineffective and in April the austerity measures were suspended after public protest and political pressure (from France as well as from within) forced a review of government policy. In May, lower ranks in the army started a series of demonstrations, culminating in their taking temporary control of the main airport, in support of their demands for better pay and conditions.

Ethiopia's Mengistu, who had appeared unassailable in 1987, moved as quickly away from the Soviet Union as he had moved toward it in 1975. His army of half a million, the largest anywhere on the continent, disintegrated in the face of an alliance between the Eritrean People's Liberation Front (EPLF) and the Tigray People's Liberation Front

(TPLF), whose leader Meles Zenawi became the new president of Ethiopia. Meles Zenawi, following the trend, abandoned his adherence to (Albanian) socialism, which he had held for years, and embraced liberal democracy and the "new world order." The United States organized the transition in 1991 and at a peace conference in London, Assistant Secretary of State for African Affairs Herman Cohen advised the TPLF to occupy the capital, Addis Ababa.

If the early part of the 1990s saw a number of efforts by former dictators (both civilian and military) to maintain themselves in power by masquerading as democrats, the second part of the decade saw an undoubted deepening and widening of democracy, although not necessarily within the formal arenas of party politics and more often in the public spaces of the major cities. Saul and Leys were still asking, in 1999, "to what extent might this climate of democratization also open up space for popular initiatives that could prove more transformative?"[52] But the evidence of the last few years is there for all to see.

Mass demonstrations and general strikes forced the pace of democratic change on the continent. Unions together with a variety of popular forces fought regimes hanging on to power in Burkina Faso, Burundi, Cameroon, the Central African Republic, Chad, Comoros, Congo, Côte d'Ivoire, Gabon, Ghana, Guinea, Kenya, Lesotho, Madagascar, Mali, Mauritania, Nigeria, Swaziland, and Zaire. Even if elections were not held and heads of state clung to power, the pattern was the same: trade unions "sought not simply to protect the work place interests of their members but have endeavoured to bring about a restructuring of the political system."[53] The trade union movement demonstrated greater independence and militancy than at any time in its history.

We have to be clear that this wave of political movements in Africa during the 1990s took diverse forms and attracted diverse social elements, often giving rise to serious misgivings about the extent of their progressiveness among leftist commentators, particularly in areas where the populists used the religious ideology of Islam or Christianity to mobilize support. While some of these political movements remained closely linked to working-class struggles, others, particularly those rooted in the rural areas, took on the dimensions of ethnic, tribal, and religious struggles.

The great turn toward militant Islam in the 1990s constituted a major development in northern Africa as the poor discovered an authentic voice in which to express their profound disillusionment with capitalist "development" and with the corrupt and authoritarian regimes that presided over it. The possibility that these Islamist movements were also themselves liable to a distinctive form of populist authoritarianism greatly preoccupied leftist analysts and those remaining on the secular left in those countries where Islamist movements gained greatest ground (as in Egypt and Algeria).

Aid or imperialist plunder?

The "African renaissance" launched by Nelson Mandela was going to transform the continent in the mid-1990s. There was good reason to suppose that a rebirth had taken place. Mass movements had cast aside hated and despised regimes and black South Africa had finally defeated apartheid. But it was another false dawn. If the generation of African leaders who had spent years advocating "Marxism-Leninism" were not overthrown, like Benin's Mathieu Kérékou, then they converted rapidly to the Washington consensus: "it soon became apparent that many newly elected governments lacked the...willingness to tackle criticism...without resorting to the authoritarian measures of the past."[54]

There is no better example of this than South Africa since the end of apartheid. Leaders of "liberation movements" who used the language of socialism to mobilize resistance to apartheid have become evangelical advocates of "open" markets and foreign investment. Beating the Stalinist path, the South African Communist Party argued that socialist transformation could only follow national liberation, the two-stage theory. But today the Central Committee of the Party are members of a class who have enriched themselves while arguing, "in the name of the nation," for "patience and privatization." South Africa, like the rest of the continent, was paralyzed by the Stalinist notion that the national, democratic stage of liberation was distinct from the struggle for international socialism. Socialism, true to the pattern, was forgotten after "independence."

But there is no excuse for the South African "experience." For years it had been clear that the movements of national liberation disintegrated into state oppression and corruption once the nation had been "won." Where mass movements had existed they were crushed, as in Ethiopia after 1974, or in Angola, where the independent mass movement, the strikes against foreign companies and the "people's power" movement of 1975–76, were savagely suppressed in the "national interest" and for "national production." This suppression was often carried out with the aid of Cuban "socialists," who insisted with the Russians to be allowed to "aid" Angolan economic recovery. The same political families in Angola used their positions to benefit from liberalization policies in the 1990s. Before 1989 these countries remained neo-colonies tied to a network of "bipolar" imperialist control, and since then they have been subject to a similar process of subjugation that is now called "globalization."

Economic devastation in the 1990s left Africans consuming 25 percent less than they had in the 1960s and spending less on education and social services than at any time since independence. At the same time, economic disparities grew at a rate that defies belief. The United States had an annual income of $10,000 billion, yet contributed an astonishing one-hundredth of 1 percent to assist development in sub-Saharan Africa.[55] The IMF and the World Bank have been advocates of the neoliberal charade. While promising "debt sustainability" and "open markets" for Africa, they have overseen policies that have led to the deaths of millions who have had no access to basic health care and nutrition.

It is estimated that Africa will have 71 million fewer people by 2010 as a result of AIDS because the ability to fight the disease has been destroyed by policies designed by international "donors."[56] While per capita health spending in Africa is $7 per year, what the continent pays in interest on foreign debts alone is four times the complete budget for health and education. At the same time, the most powerful G8 countries in the world contribute on average 0.19 percent of their national wealth to the Third World—less even then the derisory 0.7 percent that they promised at the UN thirty years ago. Africa, in short, has continued to be a net contributor to the "development" of Western capitalists.[57]

The result of the widespread decimation of health services, mass unemployment, and deprivation has been catastrophic. Communities are often held together by only the informal economy and remittances from abroad. Certain states that were already marginal to the international economy have ceased to function or where they continue they have become "criminalized." The wars in the West African states of Sierra Leone and Liberia are seen to be characteristic of this disintegration in Africa.[58] As Jean-François Bayart has stated, "the process of criminalization...has become the dominant trait of a subcontinent in which the state has literally imploded under the combined effects of economic crisis, neoliberal programs of structural adjustment and the loss of legitimacy of political institutions."[59] Since Siad Barre was overthrown in 1990, Somalia has also lapsed into stateless criminality. "International" forces, as in these examples, intervened in an attempt to restore national authority and reorganize the chaotic and anarchic criminality of the collapsed state.[60]

But theorists of the "criminalized state" tend to underestimate the extent to which international capitalism is involved in and has profited from the criminality of the African state. The involvement of international business in the Congo has helped to sustain both the war and regional governments active in the conflict. According to a UN report, foreign companies "were ready to do business regardless of elements of unlawfulness.... Companies trading minerals which the Panel considered to be 'the engine of the conflict in the Congo' have prepared the field for illegal mining activities in the country." De Beers and American Mineral Fields signed contracts with rebel leader Laurent Kabila that were estimated to be worth $3 billion a year when Mobutu was still the legally recognized president of the Congo.

While the World Bank funded and praised Uganda and Rwanda for being good examples of economic stability and transparency on the continent (awarding them debt relief through the HIPC initiative), their economic success was being built on the exploitation of Congolese minerals. They started to export large quantities of coltan (used to make mobile phones and Playstations), cobalt, and gold. Despite deafening and sanctimonious calls for openness, anti-corruption, and transparency in economic "governance," Western donors never questioned the export of minerals that had clearly originated from the Congo. Rwanda's balance of payments increased from $26.1 million in 1997 to $51.5 million in 1999, exactly during the period of its intervention in the war.[61]

Angola has been undergoing a similar process. International firms have been given stakes or "water blocks" in offshore oil exploration in exchange for arms deals.[62] The global web of illegal deals in a region recently labelled the "Kuwait of Africa" has involved international businesses and politicians.[63] Nigeria is another famous example; the country is the thirteenth-largest crude oil producer in the world and the sixth-largest supplier to the United States. Western-owned firms with the Nigerian National Petroleum Company (NNPC) have been able to act with impunity in the oil-producing South. Despite $275 billion earned from oil since the mid-1970s, life expectancy in Nigeria has fallen to fifty-one years, while 34 percent of the population in the oil-rich Niger Delta lives in absolute poverty. Some have argued that Chevron, the American oil giant, has been implicated in the murder of dozens of protesters. Using the Nigerian military like a private army is regarded as an unavoidable and, in the case of recent revelations, a "regrettable consequence" of doing business in Nigeria. As one Nigerian academic has observed, to state "that some oil producing communities are threatened with extinction due to oil pollution and poverty [does] not seem to be overstatement."[64]

Oil is also at the center of the shameless involvement of France in Africa since independence. Elf, set up in 1965 by Charles de Gaulle, was used as an arm of the French state in dealing with newly independent African states. "Sweeteners," sometimes in the region of $15 million, were frequently paid to African leaders to ensure Elf was awarded oil contracts. Elf often acts like a sovereign power within African states, while French governments have shown shocking but honest disregard for the distinctions between diplomacy, politics, and business.[65] While three-quarters of Gabon's foreign investment comes from France, Gabon was often responsible for more than two-thirds of Elf's profit. In return for sacrificing "independence," Gabon's leading political family had access to enormous amounts of wealth, while France could use the state to organize "Francafrique."[66]

Frequently the West disguises contemporary "intervention" in Africa under the terms of "ethical foreign policy" and "humanitarian assistance." The catastrophe in Somalia is symbolic of the tragic farce of 'humanitarian intervention." Operation Restore Hope was going to be practical evidence of George H. W. Bush's humane New World Order: when U.S. forces left in 1993, a small UN force remained under American leadership. When it was forced to flee in 1995 Somalia was in tatters: the warlord General Aideed's popularity had risen by resisting foreign intervention; an unknown number of Somalis had been killed (perhaps several thousand) and the country was further plunged into warring chaos that would last for years. But the failure was a clear indictment of the hypocrisy and incompetence of the UN. It had constructed a fortified "city" for its staff that included a High Street shopping mall, leisure center, and high-tech sewage system, built for $160 million from the Somalia aid budget. In a country where life expectancy is forty-six years, the only truly astonishing fact about the débâcle is how few UN personnel were murdered.[67]

The tragedy in Rwanda also shows how western intervention and "structural adjustment" have been responsible for what writers have termed the "new barbarism." The destructive spiral of events in Rwanda was triggered by the collapse of the International Coffee Agreement in 1989, instigated by Washington, which acted in the interests of U.S. coffee importers who were anxious for lower prices. This plunged the Rwandan economy, of which coffee is the chief export, into an economic crisis. In a situation of absolute deprivation it was not difficult for the regime to mobilize the tried-and-tested politics of ethnic hatred. Then between 1990 and 1994 the Rwandan president Juvenal Habyarimana, using funds made available through structural adjustment program, purchased $83 million worth of arms—transactions assisted by the future UN secretary-general Boutros Boutros-Ghali. As early as 1992 western powers knew of the plan to eliminate Tutsi and moderate Hutus opposed to the government of Habyarimana. While the international community armed and funded the genocidal government in Rwanda, Washington and the "market" ensured that a fall in coffee prices set the genocide in motion.[68]

Conclusion

If much superficial commentary on African political economy in the 1990s has consistently drawn attention to the undoubted setbacks experienced in many regions, there are also many instances, as we have shown, where popular protest and working-class struggles have evolved into more organized and effective political opposition, with significant political consequences. Whatever one's skepticism regarding the real meaning of the dramatic move toward multi-partyism in Africa, or the result of the undoubted upsurge of democratic struggle in the 1990s, the greater political openness in much of Africa is to be welcomed. It creates more space within which popular, working-class movements can take shape and exert greater influence on the direction of government policies, and it moves the terrain of class struggle to a higher plane.

Africa has a rich history of independent working-class action, as we have indicated in this chapter, and as the rest of the book describes in greater detail. But what is also needed are working-class parties that are able to guide and coordinate this spontaneous revolt. Such parties should help to make trade union action more successful and, at the same time, lead to a growth in confidence in working-class self-activity. This should, in turn, lead to greater support for parties that articulate and encourage such independent action.

In a number of African countries, such parties are in the process of being built. They shun both the experiences of the Soviet state-capitalist model and the free market capitalism of the World Bank and western countries. Both have failed Africa catastrophically in the last fifty years. In contrast, we propose the classical view of Marxism as a radical critique of capitalism and a view of socialism as the self-emancipation of the working class.

Franz Fanon, the activist and writer, saw better than any of his contemporaries the nature of political power on the continent; he understood how the class of nationalist leaders becomes "a sort of little caste, avid and voracious...only too glad to accept the dividends that the former colonial power hands out to it."[69] He was also clear about the answer: only in the field of revolutionary action—in alliance with European workers, once they had stopped playing their game of "Sleeping Beauty"—could the worldwide struggle for freedom finally be won. As Marx wrote of the working class during the "national democratic" revolution in Germany in 1848: "Their battle cry must be: The Permanent Revolution."[70]

POPULAR PROTEST AND CLASS STRUGGLE IN AFRICA: AN HISTORICAL OVERVIEW

David Seddon

Imperialism and class struggle

Under imperialism, capitalism expands and develops on a world scale, subordinating pre-capitalist modes of production and associated social formations to its demands, ensuring both their transformation and the establishment of a global capitalist political economy.[1] This process is historically combined and uneven, and "there are crucial distinctions to be made between the 'classic' form of capitalism that developed in Western Europe, and the forms of capitalism which imperialism imposed on the underdeveloped periphery of the world economy."[2] In Africa, the forms of capitalism that exist today are the outcome of a long and distinctive historical process that requires careful consideration and analysis. Eurocentric preconceptions as to what "should be" the path of capitalist development and therefore what "should be" the progressive forms of class struggle in Africa—with which the literature is bedeviled—must be set aside to enable us to consider the actual history of capitalist development and class formation in Africa, both of which have been the result of popular struggle as well of changes in the material conditions within which these struggles took place.

This chapter, therefore, has a historical focus. It demonstrates—
through a condensed overview—that popular protest and working-
class struggle shaped the various paths of capitalist development in
Africa from the earliest times to the immediate post-independence
period.[3] It emphasizes the complexity and contradictions of capitalist
development in Africa, and underlines the fact that, for better or
worse, the African people have made their own history, although certainly not under conditions of their own choosing.

Early capitalist intervention

Slavery and the slave trade

In the classic model of capitalism, the central contradiction or class
conflict is between the bourgeoisie—the private owners of the means of
production, who employ wage labor for profit—and the proletariat, a
class of workers "free" to negotiate the sale of their labor as a commodity
in the market. Yet, historically, labor under capitalism has never been
entirely "free"; it has always been coerced or constrained in some way. In
Africa, slavery coexisted with capitalism for three and a half centuries.

Slavery existed in Africa from early times and the medieval trans-
Saharan trade involved slaves as well as other goods. Until the European
scramble for Africa, however, slavery was a part of a world of distinctive
pre-capitalist social formations; the majority of those traded became
domestic slaves for the rulers and urban elites of the Ottoman Empire.
Although in some cases, such as Egypt, they were also employed as laborers in agriculture and other sectors, it was not until the nineteenth
century that the trans-Saharan trade was directly linked, through the
employment of slaves on the cotton-producing estates of Egypt and
Sudan, to the demands of European industrial capitalism. From the sev-
enteenth century onwards, however, long before labor was ever employed for profit in Africa itself, it was shipped to the "New World" and
set to work under conditions of slavery to produce the raw materials for
emerging capitalist industries in Europe and North America.

It can be argued that "the Third World's first 'proletariat' was nurtured in the plantation economies of Brazil, the Caribbean islands, and the American South."[4] But it was born from the reserve army of labor created in Africa. At the height of the slave trade, in the 1840s, more than one hundred thousand slaves were exported from Africa each year; over the centuries, some twenty million men and women were forced to "migrate." The impact of this trade extended far into the interior, where the European demand for slave labor was filled by local rulers, who waged war on each other to secure slaves for sale. As Marx observed, "the turning of Africa into a warren for the commercial hunting of Black skins, signalled the rosy dawn of the era of capitalist accumulation."[5] Slavery has endured for some three hundred years as part of the history of capitalist development in Africa; for, although it was formally outlawed in both British and French colonies in the second half of the nineteenth century and was increasingly replaced by other forms of labor coercion and control during the first half of the twentieth century (see below), slavery continued to exist as an integral feature of rural class structures until well after independence in many parts of Africa.[6] That slavery is entirely compatible with capitalism can be seen from the fact that it can be found today, particularly in West Africa—the UN estimates that two hundred thousand children are traded and work as slave labor in West Africa, mainly on plantations in Ivory Coast and Gabon, producing cash crops for export—and in Sudan.

While we know something of the forms of resistance, "hidden" and overt, individual and collective, practiced by the slaves of the "New World," we still know relatively little of those adopted initially by the peoples of West Africa and the Sahel in response either to indigenous slavery or to the European (or Arab) slave trade, apart from hiding or running away. For later periods, when slavery had become more deeply integrated within the colonial regime, we know more: that there were periodic slave revolts is certain, but generally the forms of struggle tended to be muted, either by the extreme forms of

repression and violence used by the slave-owning classes on plantations and other relatively large-scale enterprises, or by the highly per-
sonalized relationships involved in the indigenous forms of slavery.[7]

Coercion and resistance

Colonialism in Africa always involved violence.[8] From the very earliest European interventions, there was widespread and often protracted resistance. If the interests of capital, and of empire, were to be
satisfied, then this resistance had to be quelled—and it was, usually
brutally. Some of the earliest collective resistance was in West Africa,[9]
where the Atlantic slave trade first provided the "mode of articulation"[10] of capitalism with indigenous pre-capitalist social formations.
But resistance was encountered subsequently all across the continent,
as Africa was subjected to the uneven advances of European imperialism and colonialism.

Usually, this resistance was orchestrated by local chiefs and tribal
leaders (where they existed) or by prophets and demagogues (where
these emerged), even if it was ordinary Africans who fought and died
in countless skirmishes, battles, and wars against Portuguese, Spanish, French, Belgian, Dutch, British, German, and Italian intervention. In more marginal areas, local warlords and "primitive rebels"[11]
operated on a semi-permanent basis; and there were periodic attacks
on the merchants, missionaries, military outposts and settler communities that constituted both the forefront and the outposts, of European imperialism. Even after the initial "pacification" of African
states and societies, there continued to be uprisings or rebellions
against European rule. That broader popular protest at growing European intervention could develop, however, is shown by the 'Urabi
movement of 1880–82 in Egypt.[12] Resistance to European colonialism continued in some parts of Africa (for example, in the Sahara)
until the 1930s.[13] But, increasingly, as colonial rule was established
and entrenched, many local leaders adapted to and collaborated in
the subordination of their people, becoming a part of the colonial

administrative apparatus and a subaltern fraction of the new colonial ruling class.

Forced labor

In Africa, early European rule was widely accompanied by violence and coercion, often by the state, and by the oppression and exploitation of "unfree" labor. In some parts of Africa, such as South Africa and Uganda, indentured labor from the British Empire in Asia (India, Malaya, etc.) was imported to work on plantations and in other sectors (some forty thousand indentured laborers were brought into East Africa from India between 1895 and 1922).[14] But the coercion of indigenous labor was far more widespread. The lack of comprehensive labor legislation or effective implementation of international labor conventions allowed for the systematic use of forced labor throughout sub-Saharan Africa right up until the Second World War, and afterward.[15]

In the Belgian Congo, forced labor, introduced in the 1890s, became an integral part of the colonial system. In 1923, the Permanent Commission for the Protection (*sic*) of the Natives accepted as "necessary" a maximum of sixty days' forced labor for every male adult, although it mentioned cases where Africans "had to work for 90 or even 104 days."[16] It was not until 1954 that forced labor was officially abolished.[17] The term *chibalo* (or *chibaro*) was used commonly in central and southern Africa from the late nineteenth century onward to describe a variety of oppressive forms of labor introduced by the Europeans. The Portuguese in Mozambique stipulated that all adult males had to perform *chibalo* for six months a year. Commonly used for compulsory labor service on large colonial plantations in Mozambique, *chibalo* was also applied to the forced cultivation of particular crops by small producers on their own land. Conditions on plantations in Mozambique were so bad that many preferred to migrate to South Africa to work as contract labor in the gold mines. Forced labor was still widespread in Portugal's African colonies in the early 1960s.[18]

In French Africa between 1927 and 1936, thousands were conscripted to work on the Dakar–Niger railway and to improve the navigation of the Niger river; this involved three years' service, hard work, and low pay. In 1935 alone, 3.3 million people were subjected to twenty-eight million days of compulsory labor, with only seven million days redeemed by cash payments; another form of forced labor, in lieu of military service, provided 12.5 million workers a year. Although in 1936 the Popular Front government in France tried to end forced labor, the planters and timbermen refused to comply; in the Ivory Coast the lieutenant governor was actually dismissed for attempting to enforce these new measures. The legal basis for compulsory labor was not removed until 1946.

In British East and Central Africa, various forms of compulsion were used; there, private employers set the pace and the colonial administration followed suit. In Nigeria, the administration itself introduced forced labor: Sir Frederick Lugard encouraged it, arguing that "among primitive tribes, a measure of compulsion through their tribal chiefs, in order to obtain labor for railway construction and other important works, is justifiable."[19] Colonial Office pressure ended legally compulsory labor in Southern Rhodesia in 1900.[20] Despite earlier efforts to outlaw forced labor in Natal and British East Africa,[21] extensive use of compulsion was not in fact discontinued until the 1933 Forced Labour Ordinance, and even then exceptions permitted under the International Forced Labor Convention (and originally inserted because of pressure from the colonial powers) were extensive throughout British Africa. Forced labor for public works, porterage, and agriculture was being used as late as 1958 in Nigeria, Gambia, Kenya, Uganda, Tanganyika, and Bechuanaland.[22]

There is little information available regarding resistance to forced labor, although undoubtedly many attempted to avoid being recruited in the first place, and some ran away.[23] The extreme violence of the Belgian colonial authorities toward the indigenous population was certainly linked to their concern to prevent laborers from "deserting." Falling short of slavery, this was nevertheless a form of coercive labor that afforded few opportunities for orchestrated struggle. All of the "hidden forms" of resistance[24] documented for later periods were undoubtedly employed. For example, after 1903 the state in Nyasaland attempted in vain to seal the borders and curtail the emigration of thousands of workers to Katanga, northern Rhodesia, or Mozambique to ensure the availability of cheap labor to domestic plantations. The plantations were, nevertheless, able to expand as a result of the immigration of vast numbers (fifteen thousand–thirty thousand between 1900 and 1903 into one district alone), escaping from the coercion and brutality of the Campanhia do Niassa in Mozambique.[25]

Class formation and class struggle under colonial rule
An overview

The development of capitalist class relations in Africa was specifically constrained by the interests of metropolitan and/or settler colonialism and the actions of the colonial state. As Mbeki has pointed out, with respect to South Africa, "we must bear in mind that the capitalist class does not view itself solely as the appropriator of wealth in contra-distinction to our being the producers. The capitalist class is also heavily burdened with matters of state administration. It has taken on itself the task of ruling our country."[26] European capital, hand in hand with the European colonial state apparatus, ruled supreme. In most of Africa, the colonial state (serving the interests of metropolitan capital and, where settlers became more strongly rooted, of local settler capital) was at pains to inhibit the development of an indigenous African capitalist, or, for that matter, working class.

In some colonial states, particularly in North Africa, the indigenous landowning classes and urban bourgeoisie were able to survive as a subaltern fraction of the ruling class, transforming themselves in the case of the former into commercial farmers and in the case of the latter into mercantile and predominantly artisan-scale capitalists, and then gradually turning to various more developed forms of manufacturing and to "comprador" activities. This was, however, relatively uncommon elsewhere, except perhaps among traders in parts of West Africa. For the most part, despite the efforts of the colonial authorities to constrain the emergence of either an African capitalist class or a proletariat, the increasing demands of the colonial state for revenues to support infrastructural and other capital investment meant that the local population was subject to a variety of taxes and levies. These, in turn, obliged rural producers either to increase sales of farm produce for the market, or to seek wage employment. The result was the gradual emergence of a class of rural petty commodity producers (often referred to even by left analysts as "peasants") and of a smaller, but increasingly significant class of migrant workers, working on plantations, estates (for example, in Egypt, Sudan, Mozambique, and Tanganyika) or, in progressively greater numbers, in town.

In many colonial states, despite efforts to root the masses on the land, there developed an increasing rural exodus and an associated system of internal labor migration, from which there emerged a distinctive African working class, initially strongly rooted in the countryside and reproduced there, but increasingly developing a different identity from those classes still based in the rural areas. This "new" or emerging working class was usually highly heterogeneous, both "vertically" (for example, ethnic and tribal origins) and "horizontally" (such as working conditions and pay). For some on the left, the heterogeneity and internal differentiation of the African working class (into labor aristocracy, lumpen proletariat, etc.) in the colonial period, and even in the early years of the postcolonial period, was a critical constraint on the development of "progressive" class struggle, when this is in fact a characteristic feature of any emerging working class.[27] In any case, as we shall see, this failed to prevent its involvement in widespread and protracted class struggle throughout the colonial period and thereafter.

Also, to degrees that differed significantly from case to case, there began to develop in Africa during the colonial regime what Poulantzas[28] called a "new" petty bourgeoisie of small functionaries and public sector employees—clerks, teachers, nurses and health auxiliaries, soldiers, petty bureaucrats, and so on. Although some of these were recruited to maintain control in the colonial territories (police, soldiers, etc.), it was very often in young radicals and intellectuals from such social origins that the nationalist movements that played such a critical role in the early formation of the postcolonial states of Africa found their inspiration and leadership. Those who would see the history of class struggle in Africa in terms of a narrow definition of the working class must recognize the crucial (but often problematic) role played by the radical elements of the "new" petty bourgeoisie in popular class struggles, during the colonial period and immediately after independence.

Class struggle during the colonial phase of capitalist development in Africa was often couched in ideological terms that prioritized the division between the indigenous populations and the Europeans, despite the undoubted process of class formation within indigenous colonial society. The subsumption of class to national identity is understandable, given the hegemony of European capitalism and the control Europeans exerted, directly (as in settler states) or indirectly (as in the majority of colonial territories) through the colonial state apparatus. But class struggle, particularly on the part of African workers, was from the outset a subjective as well as an objective reality; those who deny this reality have not studied the history of early workers' struggles.

Early workers' struggles

In the early colonial period, the major employer of African labor was the state; and the earliest experience of organized class struggle in sub-Saharan Africa, whether in the form of popular protest or workers' action, was among public sector workers (notably dockers and railway men). One of the earliest strikes in Africa took place in Sierra Leone, in 1874, in Freetown harbor.[29] This was only two years after the Congress of the International Workingmen's Association in The Hague, the culminating point in the development of the First International, which considered "economic struggles" to be a prerequisite (the "lever") for the struggle of the working class against the political power of its exploiters.[30] In Egypt, the first strike movement took place in April 1882—after more than a decade of subjection to European capital and in the aftermath of the nationalist 'Urabi revolt (1880–82)—among coal heavers at Port Said and Suez on the canal. This was followed in June by a massive urban uprising in Alexandria, which began when European troops fired at a crowd, and which left more than 250 Egyptians and fifty Europeans dead after the rioting that followed. The fact that Alexandria was now "in the power of a mob" helped justify the occupation of Cairo by the British later the same year.[31]

Another early strike was that in Lagos in 1897. In April, the governor of Lagos decided to cut the wage rate of public sector workers and to increase productivity by altering the structure of the working day. He foresaw trouble, but was confident.[32] The governor deliberately set out to provoke a strike, smash it, and then dictate new terms and conditions of employment. In July, there was unrest in response to a preliminary tightening up on working practices and when, in August, the restructuring of the working day was initiated, virtually all those employed by the Public Works Department went on strike. After three days, the governor was forced to come to terms. As Hopkins remarks, "the outcome must be counted a victory for the strikers, who returned to work on Thursday 'quite contented', and conveyed to the governor their satisfaction with the new arrangements."[33] This incident can be interpreted without exaggeration as marking the beginning of "the emergence of a Nigerian working class."[34]

The early development of the Rhodesian mining industry was halted by the revolt of 1896–97—a widespread early protest movement—but wage labor was employed from the 1890s onward. Working conditions were appalling: even as late as 1910–11, the Native Affairs Committee noted that families would sell grain or livestock to pay their taxes in preference to working in the mines. In the early days, worker resistance was strongly conditioned by prevailing cultural forms as much as by the actual relations of production. Thus, in the case of the Bonsor, one of the first of the large mines to come into production (in 1898), labor troubles began in June 1899, when word spread that the mine was "bewitched."[35] For a period of two months not a single African applied for work. This forced the management to turn to foreign labor. In October 1900, an attempt was made to recruit five hundred workers from the Transkei, in South Africa, where demand for labor had fallen during the Boer War. Only three hundred were recruited and, as they demanded higher wages than the locals, these rural migrants were considered unsatisfactory; they were passed on to another mine, where they apparently caused disaffection among local workers. The Bonsor was eventually saved from closure by the recruitment of migrant laborers from Portuguese East Africa, who also could not sell their labor in South Africa.

Gradually, across Africa, more developed forms of resistance to exploitation and oppression were adopted as the numbers and self-consciousness of the working class grew. This process was probably most rapid in the mining areas of Central and Southern Africa, although it was of significance also in parts of West Africa (such as Nigeria) and North Africa (Egypt). By the turn of the century, South Africa was a significant emerging capitalist economy. One consequence of this was a substantial and growing demand for labor, which was met from an early stage by migrant workers, often from other territories in southern Africa, establishing a characteristic structure of class relations across the region. In other regions, such as the "Copper Belt" in present-day Zambia, Francophone West Africa, and the Maghreb, long-distance labor migration across borders developed during the colonial period, and even more so after independence, as a distinctive feature of African capitalism. The class consciousness of migrant workers, although frequently belittled by leftist analysts, was appreciable from the earliest days.

The avant-garde in southern Africa

The black labor force in Southern Rhodesia had already grown by 1906 to over seventeen thousand, and by 1920 it numbered over thirty-six thousand. Van Onselen[36] has documented the early development of black worker consciousness and the growth of the black working class in the mining sub-sector of Southern Rhodesia in the first two decades of the twentieth century. In South Africa, where the recruitment of mine workers (both black and white) began in the nineteenth century, the concentration of "free labor" in the Transvaal at the start of the twentieth century was remarkable and gave rise to growing workers' organization. The establishment of the Transvaal Mineworkers' Union in 1902 triggered the first in a series of bitter campaigns against the mining companies. A major strike of Witwatersrand miners in 1907 was followed by the Transvaal Industrial Disputes Prevention Act of 1909, which tried to outlaw strikes. In 1913, one of the most serious disputes in South African history (over trade union recognition) gave rise to strikes all over the Reef (the gold-mining areas around Johannesburg). This led to a judicial commission, which recommended recognition of the South African Miners' National Union by both the Chamber of Mines and the government. But further disputes resulted in the calling of a general strike in 1914. Parliament responded with the Act of Indemnity and a Riotous Assemblies Act designed to prohibit strikes in the public services and make peaceful picketing illegal. The Chamber of Mines, however, as well as several private companies and municipal authorities, accepted the "closed shop" principle and wages rose significantly. Between 1915 and 1918 the unions in South Africa increased their (mainly white) membership from 10,538 to 77,819.[37]

The end of the First World War saw further unrest, this time involving black African workers. In 1919, Clemens Kadalie, a migrant worker from Nyasaland, formed the Industrial and Commercial Workers' Union (ICWU) of Africa, which became the center of African industrial and political struggle for the next decade. The ICWU attracted African workers not only in manual but also in clerical and white-collar jobs, and even professionals. Clemens Kadalie was fêted by the British TUC as the representative of over one hundred thousand workers, and the ICWU applied for affiliation to the (white) South African TUC. In 1919–20, a series of strikes brought the docks and railways to a halt; and in February 1920, forty thousand African miners came out on strike. In early 1922, the Chamber of Mines announced that it would employ larger numbers of African workers and reduce the wages of white miners.[38]

Within nine days a general strike had broken out; it lasted for eight weeks and towards the end became an armed revolt—the Rand Rebellion. Led by white Afrikaner nationalists, dissidents expelled from the Mineworkers' Union and a few members of the Communist Party, the strikers sang "The Red Flag" and marched under a banner that read: "Workers of the World Unite and Fight for a White South Africa." The minority of trade unionists and left-wing political activists who wanted the strike to be a struggle of *all* workers against the Chamber of Mines were overwhelmed by the majority of white miners, and there were serious clashes between the strikers and African and Indian workers. At a mass rally in February 1922, the white strikers called for a Nationalist–Labour coup and the proclamation of a South African Republic. The Nationalist leadership rejected the proposal and in mid-March, Smuts called out aircraft and artillery to smash the strike, killing 230 workers and injuring hundreds more. In 1923, however, the Nationalists did form a pact with the Labour Party and at the 1924 election a Nationalist–Labour coalition swept into power, pledged "to oppose capitalist and monopolistic domination" and to introduce "a civilized labour policy"—which protected white workers. A year later, the Mines and Works (Colour Bar) Act was passed, making the right to skilled work dependent on race and color.[39]

Wage-fixing legislation followed and despite unprecedented economic growth, the mid- to late 1920s saw thousands of African workers unemployed or forced to accept substantially lower wages. Kadalie was urged to review the strategy of the ICWU. The left—backed by the communists—wanted more positive action; the right wanted a 'respectable' organization and the expulsion of the communists. In December 1926, communists were banned. The Communist Party started a new campaign to organize African (and other, non-white) workers, and in 1928 a

Non-European Trade Union Federation was established. In early 1928, the large Natal section disaffiliated from the central ICWU, and this was followed by a series of further splits and secessions; by 1930 the ICWU was in fragments. It foundered in large part because it was unable to make a decisive commitment to either a militant or a moderate line.

It was not until the end of the decade that the South African TUC urged the government to recognize non-white trade unions on the same basis as other workers' organizations. In 1942, it opened the first annual conference of the Council of Non-European Trade Unions, at which twenty-five unions and thirty-five thousand workers were represented. The government's offer of limited "administrative recognition" was strongly rejected by "black" workers. In any case, in 1948 the Nationalist Party came to power and began to establish the racially determined framework within which all class issues would be caught for the next half-century.

Workers' struggles across Africa in the interwar period

Elsewhere in Africa, during the interwar period, workers in both the public and private sectors were widely involved in industrial action and, in some instances, wider political struggles. In Egypt, for example, where workers had long been organized, they were heavily involved in the nationalist movement during the First World War and participated in the so-called revolution of 1919. The first federation of trade unions was established in 1920, two years before Egypt became a formally independent state. Over the next twenty years the Egyptian working class was to develop a relatively high degree of self-consciousness; its relationship, however, to the Wafd nationalist movement, led very much by the Egyptian bourgeoisie and landowning classes, remained ambivalent through this period.[40]

In sub-Saharan Africa, the first recorded strike by railway workers in the Gold Coast took place in June 1918, following the exclusion of skilled and unskilled workers from a war bonus granted to European and "permanent" African staff in the civil service. African railway workers were also involved in strikes in Sierra Leone (1919 and 1926), in Nigeria (1921), and among the Thies-Niger workers in French West Africa (1925). The railway experienced the largest single number of recorded disputes in Nigeria in the interwar period, and was the birth-place of manual worker unionism. In 1930 serious disturbances occurred among the mineworkers in the Gold Coast and among dockers at Bathurst, in the Gambia.

From the outset, industrial action by African workers was regarded as tantamount to rebellion or revolt. The response was often violent and almost always extremely repressive. The 1926 railway strike in Sierra Leone, for example, was described by the governor as "a revolt against the Government by its own servants." Troops were called in, strikers and demonstrators shot, strike leaders imprisoned, exiled or at least sacked, and any tribal association connected with the disturbances banned or dissolved. In Kenya, a general strike organized by the Young Kikuyu Association led to the massacre of some 150 people by the King's African Rifles. In Northern Rhodesia, major strikes by African workers took place on the Copper Belt in 1935 and 1940. The first of these was provoked by an increase in the poll tax and organized through the Watchtower sect and Bema dance societies; the second involved a demand for equal pay with white workers and mobilized some three thousand strikers. The 1940 strike was put down by troops, with sixty injured and seventeen killed.[41]

Working-class struggle was evidently a political as well as an "economic" threat in many countries across Africa in this period. Not surprisingly, the greatest resistance to the organization of African workers was generally experienced in the white settler states, where a significant class of European capitalists had an immediate vested interest in both their exploitation (for profit) and their oppression (for political reasons), and where the white working class had its own concerns about the growing strength of black workers' organizations. As Davies notes, "in the short run—in Algeria, Tunisia, Morocco, the Ivory Coast, Kenya, Tanganyika, Northern and Southern Rhodesia—

the settler elite was able to sabotage all efforts at permitting the growth of African trade unions."[42] In these colonial states, the forms of repression characteristic of the early colonial period elsewhere in Africa continued in force, often until the 1930s and even later. In South Africa, they were to continue, in effect, until the 1990s.

The development of trade unions

Virtually all of these actions were organized and supported by groups of nonunionized workers, in some cases by tribal associations but more usually by an ethnic cross-section of workers. According to Jeffries, the Sekondi–Takoradi railway and harbor workers were the only Gold Coast wage-workers to establish a durable union organization prior to the Second World War.[43] An organization of railway workers may have existed in Tanzania as early as 1929,[44] but generally, outside Egypt and South Africa, the establishment of the trade union movement took place only from the 1930s onward.

The gradual development of labor legislation and the emergence of trade unions in the 1930s and 1940s across most of the continent marked a significant stage in the history of class struggle in Africa. In the British territories, it was only just before the Second World War, following outbreaks of labor unrest in various parts of the empire (including northern Rhodesia), that effective labor legislation was introduced.[45] The need to recruit labor (and soldiers) in support of the war effort further stimulated progress. The Colonial Development and Welfare Act was passed in 1940, stipulating that "no territory might receive aid under its provision unless it had in force legislation protecting the rights of trade unions, and unless the works for which the aid was to be used were carried out under a contract that embodied a fair wages clause, and which forbade the employment of children under the age of 14."[46]

The commitment in the colonies to the implementation of measures conceived in the UK remained strictly limited. In Uganda, one colonial official was dismissed because he "acted in conflict with official policy" by advising unions on negotiation tactics, and the Kenya union adviser, James Patrick, was told that "the time had not yet arrived" for the establishment of trade unionism in Kenya; he should come back in twenty years or so.[47] Indeed in Kenya, although a Labour Trade Union of East Africa was registered as early as 1937 and an African Workers' Federation in 1947, both were later banned because they helped to organize a strike in Mombasa. Meanwhile, the Railway African Staff Union, formed in 1940, built up branches all over the country during the war and played an important intermediary role during a threatened strike in Mombasa in 1945.[48] By 1945, the Railway African Association was the most powerful workers' organization in the territory, with a majority of the seventeen thousand or so railwaymen as members. Railway workers in Tanganyika played a critical role in the general strike of 1947 and in the articulation of broad political demands during that strike.[49] An East African TUC, founded in 1949, was refused registration and various measures were introduced to give the government stronger powers against unions and workers. One of the measures introduced was the Deportation Ordinance aimed specifically at militant Indian workers; the government was worried that the East African TUC was led by "a prominent Communist agitator" who was also an Indian.

Trade unions in most British territories throughout Africa were registered and closely supervised by the colonial labor departments; accounts were scrutinized, political affiliation was discouraged, and the right to strike was circumscribed by the "emergency" actions of governors or by the inclusive definition of "essential services" in which strikes were illegal. During the 1950s, fifteen such essential services were listed in Tanganyika, thirteen in Kenya, and ten in Nyasaland. In 1950, the leaders of the African Workers' Federation of Kenya and the East African TUC were arrested, and a general strike in Nairobi was crushed by armed police, the army, and the Royal Air Force. Three hundred workers were arrested and some union leaders sentenced to "banishment" or jail for declaring illegal strikes. The history of the Kenya unions and the East African TUC, together with the experience of Morocco and Algeria and the Rhodesians, shows the commitment of white settler colonial regimes to repress the workers and block the evolution of labor unions. But by inhibiting these forms of class conflict, they ensured that resistance and protest eventually took more violent forms and contributed to the bitterness of the struggles for national independence in those states.

At the other end of the spectrum was the experience of Sierra Leone. Most of the early unions there were connected with the public sector railways, docks, mines, and schools; most of them involved relatively privileged Creoles from Freetown. Here, Edgar Parry, a British trade unionist who became labor commissioner, helped establish a union structure, presided over by the non-political coordinating body of the Sierra Leone Council of Labour, which operated quietly and effectively from 1946—a model of official colonial union policy in practice. Here, collaboration and co-option were the government strategy, rather than confrontation and conflict. But even so, following a major strike in Freetown in 1955, two of the most prominent union leaders formed political parties with trade union support in 1957 and 1961.[50] By 1958, some 60 percent of the wage labor force were members of unions.

The Nigerian Railways Corporation comprised the single largest concentration of manual wage workers in the region (with some twenty-seven thousand employees in 1953) and the Railway Workers' Union of Nigeria was the first registered union in the country; its leader, Imoudu, was involved in the 1942 and 1945 wage movements, the militant or left-wing trade union centers from the 1940s to the 1960s, and most of the attempts to create worker-based parties or union-party alliances during the postwar period.[51] Differing from the repressive white settler states of eastern and southern Africa, and also from the "collaborative" Sierra Leone case, the development of working-class consciousness was probably greater in Nigeria than almost anywhere in Africa during the later colonial period.[52]

In French West Africa, where the right to form trade unions was granted by the French Popular Front government in 1937, some nineteen thousand Africans were employed in the railways and on the docks. In 1947–48 the longest strike in African union history involved workers of all four railway networks in the French West African territories. Their major demand was for a non-racist labor hierarchy. The Ivorien network returned to work after three months, but the rest remained on strike for 160 days (of the nineteen thousand workers involved, only 858 had returned to work after eighty-two days). Substantial concessions were gained by the strikers. In Algeria and Tunisia, the formal right to organize trade unions was granted in 1932, but membership was initially restricted to those literate in French and possessing an elementary school diploma. In 1944, the literacy requirements were abolished, opening the way for the larger-scale organization of workers. In Morocco, although indigenous workers were secretly organized during the 1930s, it was not until after the war that trade unions were made legal.[53]

The African trade union movement had great difficulty in asserting its independence from the French unions. During the late 1940s and early 1950s, French unions developed their own policies and their own affiliates in Africa.[54] Up until 1955, for example, the pro-communist CGT claimed half of all African union members in the French colonies, the Catholic CCFTC 18 percent, and the Socialist CGT–FO 10 percent. The African unions were represented in the metropolitan union and, through it, in the appropriate international body. But these were reluctant to recognize independent African trade unions.

In 1946, the French secretary-general of the World Federation of Trade Unions (WFTU) rejected the application of the newly formed General Union of Tunisian Workers, which had links with Bourguiba's Neo-Destour Party, because, he argued, "unity must be achieved around the traditional organization already integrated in the WFTU."[55] In the Maghreb, the French unions had a controlling and moderating influence over the strategy and tactics adopted by the local trade unions in their conflicts with employers and the colonial state. Much of the emphasis on legislative action rather than on direct confrontation and conflicts with employers derived from French union experience, particularly that of the CGT.

In 1954, the Algerian National Movement, on taking over control of the unions, accused the CGT and the Communist Party of "making their attitude towards the Algerian movement dependent on the exigencies of French internal politics"; and Harbi notes[56] that in Algeria nationalist trade unions were founded only as late as 1956. The French unions, like the members of the various French left-wing political parties, were concerned to emphasize the primacy of class struggle over the increasingly important struggle for national independence on the part of African workers. In 1952, the CGT–FO adopted a resolution affirming that "the mission of the trades unions is to emancipate workers of all countries, its action being in the field of class struggle and not within the narrower and dangerous field of nationalism."[57]

In this, the position of the French unions was little different from that of the British. The British TUC regularly recorded its belief that the anti-imperialist struggle had little or nothing to do with the development of "genuine trade union activity." Indeed, in 1957, the General Council of the TUC attacked the Ghana Industrial Relations Act as "a departure from the conception of independent trade unionism held in this country."[58] In the Belgian colonies, labor legislation dates back to the 1920s, but from the very start there was a clear distinction between the laws for European employees and those for African workers. The Congolese white unions, authorized by decree in 1921, like those in South Africa and the Copper Belt of northern Rhodesia, strongly resisted African trade unionism. It is not surprising that, despite the Congo having a labor force with one of the highest proportions of wage-workers in Africa, local unions were slow to develop there. African workers were not allowed to organize until 1946 and even then only under severe restrictions; it was not until 1957 that African unions were allowed to federate; and not until 1959 that an African delegate was able to attend international meetings. Political activity by unions was banned and, although strikes in the private sector were permitted, government employees were forbidden to strike. It was not until 1959, however, that private industry recognized the rights of unions to organize and represent workers.[59]

The growing strength and organization of the African working class during the first half of the twentieth century, despite entrenched resistance from the colonial authorities, and even more so from white settlers and white workers, is undeniable. This, it must be recognized, was in a context where many African workers remained migrants[60]—often caricatured on the left as inevitably reactionary strikebreakers. Also, despite efforts by colonial governments to keep them rooted in the rural areas, a significant proportion of African urban workers had established themselves definitively in the towns and were now effectively organized in trade unions. Despite the high level of mobility of labor, and the legal and other restrictions on workers' organization, the emerging African trade unions were active and increasingly political.

Given the fact that wage labor was employed as much by the public sector as by private enterprise, it is not surprising that many struggles and conflicts were centered around the state, giving even the most mundane of industrial disputes a "political" character. This served in turn to strengthen them. Working-class actions became inevitably associated with a collective struggle against the colonial state, and thus were increasingly compatible with the broad political struggle for the overthrow of the colonial state and national independence. During the 1950s and 1960s, the efforts of the colonial regimes in Africa were increasingly focused on controlling the trade unions and trying—unsuccessfully—to prevent them from linking their economic struggles to the wider political movements that had emerged around the vision of national independence, and that were growing in strength and militancy.

Nationalism and class struggle

In class terms, it was neither the peasantry nor the working class but the "new" petty bourgeoisie that for the most part spearheaded African nationalist movements. Although there were exceptions—in

Morocco, for example, where the indigenous bourgeoisie and "feudal" elements led the nationalist movement, and in Egypt, where the landowners and bourgeoisie predominated in the Wafd—this was the case generally, even in South Africa. But the working class was everywhere also closely involved in the nationalist movement; so too were the rural masses, and without the weight and commitment of the popular classes generally the various nationalist movements would not have achieved the successes they did. It is certainly the case that there were, in many parts of Africa during the colonial period, periodic rural uprisings and revolts, and movements based in the countryside (the *maquis*) certainly came to be very significant toward the end of the colonial period in broader nationalist struggles. In some colonial states, particularly in the settler regimes, the nationalist struggle was perhaps most bitter in the rural areas, where agrarian settler capitalism had its strongest roots, its most committed defenders, and some of its strongest opponents.

Allen has argued for sub-Saharan Africa that

> while the different territories varied greatly in level of urbanization, the extent of labour migration, the size of the educated elite or of wage employment, etc., the basic constituents of their social structures were similar, as were the political histories that began in the 1940s with the development of mass nationalism, especially in areas with relatively large towns and an organized workforce. Within many of the nationalist movements there developed a division between a conservative wing, drawn from African elites, and a radical wing, led by members of the elite, but taking its support more from trade unionists, ex-servicemen, students, women, labour migrants, and other subordinate groups.[61]

He cites as an example the difference between the United Gold Coast Convention (UGCC) leadership—prepared to cooperate with the colonial authorities in return for a gradual and peaceful transfer of power—and the supporters of Nkrumah, later the Convention Peo-

ple's Party, who demanded a far more rapid transfer, and were prepared to adopt a militant strategy employing strikes, demonstrations,
riots, boycotts, and agrarian conflicts.

The working class gave its support generally to the more radical
political parties, but the instances where the trade unions allied themselves unambiguously with the leading nationalist parties and continued to do so until independence were relatively few: Guinea, Ghana,
Tanganyika, Kenya, Tunisia, Algeria, the Ivory Coast, and Mali. In two
of these territories—Kenya and Tunisia—the unions acted for some
time as the basis of the nationalist movement and as substitutes for
political organizations when these were forced underground. In others, notably Nigeria, Morocco, and Cameroon, the unions at one time
appeared in the vanguard role of the nationalist movement, only later
to move into opposition. This occurred to some extent in most of former French West Africa. But generally, the unions remained carefully
separate from the leading nationalist political parties, playing an important part in the political struggle, working closely with minority
parties, or conducting campaigns and strikes that furthered political
resistance, without becoming affiliated or subordinated in any way to
a leading party. In Northern Rhodesia, the relationship between the
unions and the nationalist parties was ambivalent but highly political;
in Dahomey, between 1956 and 1960, the relationship was even more
problematic, but reflected similar problems arising from both issues
of class and issues of nationalist strategy and politics. The relationship
between the working class and trade union movement and the predominantly "new" petty bourgeois-led nationalist parties often remained ambivalent in the immediate postcolonial period.[62]

Class and the postcolonial state

Broadly, the more dominant the indigenous elites in the nationalist movement, the less violent and protracted the transition; where the
struggle for independence was more protracted, the greater was the

involvement of the popular masses (workers and peasants) and the greater the commitment to a revolutionary "war" of liberation. Left politics of the European kind, explicitly based on class politics, were constrained in an overwhelmingly colonial context, but in most countries some form of national "socialism" based broadly on the Soviet model inspired the ideology of the left and led, after independence, to a wide range of new states in which various versions of "African socialism" prevailed. More rarely, and particularly in the case of states where the nationalist struggle had been particularly protracted and bitter, Marxism-Leninism was officially espoused.[63]

While in a very few African states (notably Morocco and Egypt), the indigenous landowning classes and the bourgeoisie led the nationalist movement and effectively dominated immediate post-independence politics, the widespread coincidence of political independence with the coming to power of a fraction of the new petty bourgeoisie (often from the army) is remarkable. The young "Free Officers" coup of 1952 in Egypt led the way. During the late 1950s and the 1960s, many newly independent states adopted a radical populist rhetoric and initially made real efforts to break with the European-dominated capitalist path of development. A distinctive combination of state capitalism and the one-party state with various national socialist ideologies became increasingly pervasive through the late 1960s and the first half of the 1970s.[64] Debates on the nature of this distinctive "post-colonial state in Africa"[65] during the 1970s were part of the wider struggle by left intellectuals both to provide a theoretical critique of "underdevelopment" and to give concrete support to progressive regimes and movements in the Third World.[66]

Although some have referred to regimes of this kind as "radical bourgeois nationalism,"[67] the general absence of a strong indigenous capitalist class ensured the political predominance of the new petty bourgeoisie and often also an initial willingness of the working class and the trade unions to support such regimes, where they espoused a radical populist rhetoric. In one interpretation, these new regimes were characterized during the period immediately after independence by an intra-class struggle (within the petty bourgeoisie) as to the direction of development and over the kind of role that the popular classes would be encouraged to play. Amilcar Cabral—leader of the radical nationalist movement in Guinea-Bissau—argued that, in those cases where the petty bourgeoisie had been effectively radicalized by its involvement in a revolutionary mass movement or armed struggle for independence, it could take on the role, after independence, of a revolutionary class or at least open up the way for a genuinely popular worker–peasant regime.[68] Claims in support of such a possibility being realized in practice have been made for Eritrea, Mozambique, Algeria, Libya, Benin, Guinea-Bissau, Zimbabwe, and Namibia (at various periods), among others. Von Freyhold argues that such an outcome could also have been realized in Tanzania in the 1960s,[69] and Tom Mboya, the Kenyan trade union leader, even went so far as to declare that "most of our governments are working-class governments."[70]

An alternative interpretation would see even the "socialist" impulse in such regimes as a self-interested expression of petty-bourgeois hegemony,[71] which could lead eventually to the consolidation of class power, and possibly the emergence (via an intermediate state bourgeoisie) of a capitalist class and the development (via state capitalism) of a capitalist economy. Recalling the "Bonapartist state" described by Marx in the *Eighteenth Brumaire*,[72] the "radical populist" regimes of Africa could be characterized by a situation in which no indigenous class was effectively dominant and the state was therefore relatively autonomous at the national level, while remaining effectively subordinate to foreign capital (notably that of the former colonial power) at the international level. Insofar as the state—government and bureaucracy—was then largely responsible for orchestrating and managing the process of capital accumulation, it became possible to talk of state capitalism and even of a state bourgeoisie. From this perspective, the widespread harassment and suppression of left-wing political parties in the name of national unity, the banning of independent trade unions in the name of "African" (Tanzania), "Arab" (Egypt), or "Islamic" (Libya, Mauritania) socialism, the suppression of the peasants and workers, and even the very idea of class struggle all become explicable in terms of class conflict—between the popular and working classes and an emergent (or would-be) bourgeoisie. Sender and Smith see the impasse in African development as deriving in part from "an astonishing absence of any coherent, analytical/ideological framework within which to formulate state interventions of an effective and suitable kind"; they suggest that "in particular, the denial of the existence of a working class, and the absence of an analysis of rural class structures, has resulted in the ideological dominance of a 'classless' nationalism, albeit expressed in the language of socialism."[73]

Damagingly, in this context, denial of a role for a progressive working class (proletariat) became a feature not only of the political rhetoric of radical and authoritarian populism, but also of many left analysts in the immediate postcolonial period. In the late 1960s—less than a decade after independence for many African states—Saul and Arrighi argued that the economic interests and political affinities of the African working class on the one hand and post-independence elites on the other were becoming increasingly complementary.[74] Both, it was argued, were implicated in the appropriation of the economic surplus generated by the peasantry (seen from this perspective as the main productive force and the poorest, potentially most revolutionary class in African societies). The key distinction to be made in class political terms was, it followed, not between workers and petty bourgeoisie/bourgeoisie, but between the mass of unskilled laborers in African cities (who were to be regarded as peasants temporarily engaged in wage employment rather than part of the urban proletariat proper) and those skilled workers with higher incomes and more secure jobs. "These [latter] workers enjoy incomes three or more times higher than those of unskilled labourers and together with the elites and sub-elites in bureaucratic employment in the civil service and expatriate concerns, constitute what we call the labour aristocracy of tropical Africa."[75] Far from acting as the vanguard of the proletariat and a force for revolutionary or even signifi-cant political change, it was suggested, the "labour aristocracy" was divi-sive of the popular working classes and essentially reactionary.

It was remarked that, while the trade unions might have the poten-tial to challenge and even overthrow a government, in most cases they had failed to do so: nowhere, it was suggested (with the possible excep-tions of Congo Brazzaville and Mali), was a trade union–sponsored government in power. Davies, for example, argued that

> where the ruling elites are precariously maintained in power, the unions may precipitate a showdown by staging a successful strike, as recently occurred in Upper Volta and Dahomey, only to find that their efforts have removed a civilian government and paved the way for a military dictatorship. But where a nationalist government is well entrenched, union action may result not in the overthrow of politicians but in the absorption of unions into the party machine. Ghana, Guinea, Tanganyika, Tunisia, Egypt, Algeria, Ivory Coast, Mali, Senegal and several smaller states all have one federation in close relationship with the ruling party.[76]

He adds how, even while his book was in preparation, the Kenyan government had dissolved the major trade union federations and es-tablished one national organization under the control of the govern-ing Kenya African National Union (KANU). He saw the increasing subordination of African trade unions to the one-party state as funda-mentally undemocratic: "the idea of a trade unionism emanating from the policies of ruling elites suggests a variation of 'guided democracy' and 'scientific management' theories found elsewhere."[77]

But there is little support historically for the thesis of the reactionary "labor aristocracy," and any alliance between the organized working class and the ruling elite in the postcolonial period derived from a com-mon commitment for some time in many newly independent states to nationalism, anti-imperialism, "radical populism" and African social-ism. Even at the end of the 1960s, when the "documentation of the growing African working class [had] barely begun," Davies was obliged to admit that the workers and their unions had become

> one of the major foci of political power.... Unions have been involved in several major political crises. In Sudan, a general strike precipitated the downfall of the Abboud regime; in Nigeria, another general strike provided the occasion for a major trial of strength between the state and workers; in Dahomey, Congo (Brazzaville), Upper Volta, the Central African Republic, Ivory Coast, Guinea and Tanganyika, trade unions have been identified with attempts to overthrow governments; in Algeria, they became a battleground for both the Ben Bella and Boumedienne regimes.[78]

Also, if some left analysts were concerned at the failure of the organized working class to match up to expectations of its role as a revolutionary class, others recognized that, usually, the struggles by the better-off, better-organized workers were, in fact, struggles by the "advance guard" of the working class on behalf of the working classes as a whole. Jeffries, for example, taking the case of the 1961 strike in Sekondi-Takoradi in Ghana as an example, points out that it was the skilled railway and harbor workers of Sekondi-Takoradi who initiated and led the 1961 strike in response to the perceived failure of the TUC to respond to the July austerity budget; he suggests that "railway workers throughout Africa have tended to display a quite exceptional level of militancy and radical political consciousness."[79] He also points out that the generalization put forward by Arrighi and Saul was based on East African (Kenyan and Ugandan) experience, where the difference in wage rates between skilled and unskilled workers tended to be very high. In Ghana, by contrast, where the wage differentials were not so great, skilled workers, while admittedly part of the better-paid, relatively secure section of the manual working class, had consistently proved "the most radical 'mass' force in Ghanaian politics." Moreover, militant trade unionism in Ghana "was extremely popular not only with the unionised workers themselves but also with large sections of the non-unionised urban masses who looked to it for expression of radical criticism of government in the absence of an effective representative opposition party."[80]

Again, it was argued by some on the left during the 1960s and early 1970s that the lack of a democratic left-wing revolutionary tradition (or the suppression of any such groupings) was a major factor in the supposed failure of the working-class movement in Africa to capitalize fully on its evident strength. Certainly, the need for genuinely radical political leadership of the working-class movement was often recognized by trade union leaders. At the time of the general strike of 1964 in Nigeria—in which the Joint Action Committee of labor leaders, backed by over five hundred thousand workers, successfully defied the federal government—one of the strike leaders argued that "although the cause of the strike was based on economic demands, yet in its development it has raised possible political action which, with a developed Marxist-Leninist party, could have led to a proletarian revolution."[81] In fact, in many African states during the 1960s and 1970s, the working class and trade unions usually sought explicitly to link themselves with the more radical, often minority parties—as they had tended to do in the late colonial period. But in many states both trade unions and minority left-wing parties, representing the popular and working classes and the more radical sections of the "new" petty bourgeoisie, came increasingly into conflict with the regimes in power and often suffered extreme repression. External support for repressive regimes with a variety of political ideologies and state forms throughout Africa during the 1970s further undermined the capacity of the popular and working classes to organize and express their interests democratically.

As regards the role of the peasantry—by implication considered by the proponents of the "labor aristocracy" thesis to be the truly revolutionary class—despite the general arguments put forward for the role of the peasantry (and particularly the middle peasantry) in Third World revolutions,[82] there was little evidence to indicate this in terms of concrete class struggle. Bernstein argued that, in objective terms, "there is no single and essential 'peasantry'" and that "there can be no uniform 'model' of class action by peasants nor any single and abstract formulation of the relation of peasants to revolutionary politics, whether such a formulation expresses a blanket optimism or a blanket pessimism concerning their 'revolutionary potential.'" In fact, such historical accounts as exist of rural class struggle in the post-colonial period tend to refer to the struggles of petty commodity producers and the rural petty bourgeoisie against the various constraints (exerted by private traders or by the state itself) on their profitability and survival as the producers of commodities for the market. Relatively little has been written on the struggles of those poor "peasants" who are, in effect, disguised wage-workers, or of agricultural wage-workers more generally.[83] Nevertheless, the continuing links between the rural poor and the urban masses ensured a real alliance of interests among what might be termed the popular classes. The rapid growth of rural-urban migration in the 1960s and 1970s and the massive expansion of the shantytowns and slums across Africa shifted the emphasis of popular class struggle increasingly to the urban areas.

Conclusion

In historical reality, across Africa, the working class played a key role in the struggle of popular and working classes against capitalism, during the colonial period and in the immediate post-independence period. This "working class" should be seen as it is—a heterogeneous combination and evolving configuration of fractions and strata. The debates as to whether the working class or the lumpen proletariat would be "more revolutionary," or whether the better-paid workers of the formal sector constituted a "labor aristocracy" and were essentially therefore reactionary or at best uncertain allies in the progressive struggle, were misplaced, misguided, and misleading. The reality of class struggle throughout the colonial period and indeed from independence onward in most African states has been a constantly shifting constellation of different elements, which can be seen broadly as popular working-class struggle.

GLOBALIZATION, IMPERIALISM, AND POPULAR RESISTANCE IN EGYPT, 1880–2000

Anne Alexander and David Renton

For the late Victorians, the process of imperialism had an air of inevitability. The inexorable march of progress had by 1900 filled the blank spaces on the map of Africa with neatly drawn borders. The "dark continent" had lost some of its mystery, but most Europeans assumed that the "natives" would one day be grateful for the introduction of railways, telegraphs, and sanitation.

In the century since the "scramble for Africa" ended, a more critical opinion of the effects of colonialism has emerged. Universal faith in "progress" has not survived the horrors of the twentieth century. The colonial empires broke up under the pressure of the relative economic decline of the European powers and through the success of the national liberation movements of the 1950s and 1960s. Since then, policies of "structural adjustment" imposed by the World Bank and the International Monetary Fund (IMF) have been contested by an emerging generation of African writers,[1] and by radical critics of globalization in the G8 countries.[2]

Yet portrayals of Africa in the western media still cast the continent's people as victims of forces they cannot control. The sense of optimism has evaporated, but it has left the same images of Africans behind, impoverished victims of famine, war, and natural disasters such as the HIV epidemic. The aim of this chapter is to use the example of Egypt to show how the impact of imperialism on the lives of ordinary people has always been contested, and that this struggle has in turn shaped the actions of the Great Powers. We examine three key moments in the history of Egyptian popular protest, the 'Urabi revolt of 1880–82, which precipitated the British occupation of Egypt; the mass nationalist movements of the 1940s and the revolt against Anwar al-Sadat's policy of economic liberalization in 1977. A final section of the chapter will explore more recent developments and offer a critique of the forces that may lead resistance to imperialism and globalization in the future.

It is worth anticipating some possible reservations at the outset. First of all, some critics will ask whether there is a place for Egypt in a history of Africa. This question finds an echo in political debates within the country itself. Most often Egyptian leaders have claimed a place in the Arab world. The argument here is that it is impossible to understand the continent as a whole without saying something about the countries of the north. More than this, we would argue that events in Egypt over the last 120 years have had a profound impact not just on the Middle East and North Africa, but throughout the continent as a whole. The British occupation of Egypt in 1882 marked the beginning of the "scramble for Africa," while the uneven development of capitalism in Egypt foreshadowed developments throughout the Third World. In particular, the dependent role of the Egyptian economy prefigured by a century the problems of most African countries today. Resistance to imperialism in Egypt has played a crucial role in shaping the political landscape of Africa. The Suez Crisis of 1956 marked a turning point around the world. For the first time, one of the major imperialist powers was forced into retreat by one of its own former colonies. For a brief period, it seemed that by following the example of Gamal Abd al-Nasser, African countries could end western domination.

Today the dreams of the independence period are in tatters. Only a tiny minority of Egyptians have gained from the economic developments of the last thirty years. Just as the economic gap within the country has widened, so has that gulf separating these people living at the periphery of the world economy from those living in the core nations.[3] Opposition movements are stifled by repression, political meetings are routinely closed, dissidents tortured or killed. The results of Egyptian presidential elections are effectively decided in advance by the ruling party.[4] The ruling class relies on the passivity of the masses for its survival, but the recent history of Egypt is a history of struggle. As we shall argue at the end of this chapter, the lid cannot be kept on for ever.

Debt and annexation

Contemporary descriptions of the crisis in Egypt in the 1870s have a surprisingly modern ring to them. Profligate spending on grand infrastructure projects brought a "Third World" government to the brink of bankruptcy. The creditors, who advanced the loans at ruinous rates of interest, demanded payment but the country was already mortgaged to the hilt. A "hit squad" of negotiators representing international financial institutions imposed European control over the country's debt. A program of economic reform was finally agreed upon. In order that the shareholders might receive their dividends on time, taxes on the peasantry increased. Meanwhile, crop failures devastated the countryside, and export prices for key primary goods slumped further as the world trade depression intensified.[5]

The experience of Egypt in the nineteenth century shows clearly that indebtedness and development have gone hand in hand. It also demonstrates the intimate link between capital in the advanced capitalist countries and the military power of those nations. The immediate outcome of the Egyptian debt crisis was a revolt against a system that put bankers' profits before human need. It was in order to crush the uprising that Britain sent an expeditionary force to Alexandria in the summer of 1882. It would be more than seventy years before British troops left Egyptian soil for the last time. Debt crisis was a stepping stone to annexation.

The roots of Egypt's bankruptcy lay in the relationship between countries on the periphery of development and the heart of European capital. Despite the patchy nature of European development, the advantage gained by countries that had started to industrialize during the eighteenth century was enough of a lever to hold back the development of potential challengers. This is clear in the case of Egypt, which under the rule of the Ottoman vice-regent Muhammad Ali had emerged as a military and economic threat to European domination of the Mediterranean. Muhammad Ali attempted during the 1820s and 1830s to seize control of sections of the Ottoman Empire from his overlords in Istanbul. He also tried his hand at an early form of import substitution, introducing modern cash crops such as cotton to Egypt, and importing factory techniques to produce goods for the local market, which were protected by tariffs on imported products. As Muhammad Ali's troops approached Istanbul, the European powers intervened to destroy the Egyptian fleet. The peace treaty both dismantled Egyptian military power and also demanded the removal of tariffs.[6]

Over the next thirty years Egypt's rulers found that their attempts to benefit from the expanding world economy did not lead to independence, as Muhammad Ali had hoped; instead the country slipped further into debt. Rosa Luxemburg argued that this process was part of a global pattern of capital accumulation and expansion powered by international loans.[7] She described how French banks loaned money for the construction of the Suez Canal and then persuaded the vice-regent, Khedive Ismail, to buy £3.5 million worth of shares in the venture. These shares formed a large proportion of Egypt's national debt, as they remained under their issue price until 1875, when the British government bought out the Egyptian stake in the canal. Soon after the value of the shares began to rise, so that by 1900 they were worth around six times their 1875 price.[8] In order to buy modern machinery during the short-lived cotton boom of the 1860s, Ismail mortgaged the vice-regal family estates. The end of the American Civil War and the return of the American South to international trade sent cotton prices crashing, so Ismail raised another loan, this time for investment in sugarcane production. Egyptian peasants paid twice for these schemes, first as forced labor in the plantations and irrigation projects, and second through ruinous taxation that left thousands in starvation. According to Luxemburg, the process culminated in the domination of European capital:

> European capital has largely swallowed up the Egyptian peasant economy. Enormous tracts of land, labour and labour products without number, accruing to the state as taxes, have ultimately been converted into European capital and have been accumulated. Evidently, only by use of the kourbash [whip] could the historical development which would normally take centuries be compressed into two or three decades, and it was just the primitive nature of Egyptian conditions which proved such fertile soil for the accumulation of capital.[9]

Finally, the Khedival family ran out of money and Egypt defaulted. Representatives from European banks arrived in Alexandria in October 1878, and established in 1879 a Commission for the Egyptian Public Debt, wholly under their control. The entire Egyptian economy was put at the disposal of European creditors, despite wide-scale misery in the countryside and rising levels of poverty in the towns. Even the *Times* correspondent in Alexandria admitted to feelings of guilt at the brutal administration of the debt. The produce collected on behalf of the banks

> consists wholly of taxes paid by the peasants in kind, and when one thinks of the poverty-stricken, overdriven, under-paid fellaheen [peasants] in their miserable hovels, working late and early to fill the pockets of the creditors, the punctual payment of the coupon ceases to be wholly a subject of gratification.[10]

The first sparks of resistance were revolts by the peasants facing starvation. They resisted the demands of the ruling class, as the poor had done for centuries, by taking to the hills as outlaws. As Juan Cole describes, there was an edge to their protest: "The bandit gang operating between Sohag and Girga [in Upper Egypt] employed a rhetoric of social justice, vowing to unite those peasants oppressed by the state's overtaxation and brutal treatment of its subjects."[11]

In the towns, protests were shaped by a growing political consciousness across wide sections of Egyptian society. By 1880 this had coalesced around a group of junior officers in the Egyptian army, led by Colonel 'Urabi. Their discontent acquired a nationalist content. The naked greed of the Great Powers provoked widespread anger. Also, many of the demands of the popular movement were directed against the ruling Khedival family. As Alexander Schölch describes, "'Urabi's revolt raised the cry 'Egypt for the Egyptians!'"[12] The movement quickly pulled a wide spectrum of Egyptian society into political arenas previously reserved for the ruling elite.[13] A radical press developed, which was critical of the Khedive and the European advisers in his cabinet. City dwellers from small traders and artisans to Azharite shaykhs and radical intellectuals took part in protests. In the countryside, peasants invaded the estates of absentee landlords and redistributed the land.

'Urabi's movement was also influenced by European political ideas, which activists attempted to synthesize with appeals to older loyalties. According to Juan Cole, the techniques of the movement followed European practice, including petitions and organized demonstrations that forced Ismail's successor, Khedive Tawfiq, to invite 'Urabi into the cabinet as minister for war. Protesters convened an assembly to ratify a common law government and depose Tawfiq in alliance with urban and rural notables.[14] They received backing from the Islamic and Coptic clergy. In addition, they appealed over the head of the Khedival family to the Ottoman sultan in Istanbul for support, and reaffirmed Egypt's loyalty to the Ottoman Empire.

A decisive role was played by the urban and rural poor. Peasant farmers, the fellaheen who formed the backbone of the Egyptian agrarian economy, were forced to become day laborers on cotton plantations through the combined impact of debt and drought. In the cities, artisan society began to develop into a modern working class. Joel Beinin and Zachary Lockman argue that the first strike movement in Egyptian history took place in April 1882 among coal heavers at Port Said and Suez on the canal.[15] As the political crisis deepened in Cairo, tension exploded on to the streets of Alexandria with a massive urban uprising on June 11, 1882, which began after European troops fired at a crowd. More than 250 Egyptians and fifty Europeans were left dead by the rioting that followed. This "anarchy," which left Alexandria "in the power of a mob," according to the *Economist*, provided the final link in the chain linking debt to occupation.[16] Once British troops arrived in Egypt, the strategic and economic considerations of empire kept them there for seventy more years.

The British occupation of Egypt was not justified by a formal agreement or treaty until 1914. For thirty-four years Egypt was not a British protectorate, colony, or dominion. As P. J. Vatikiotis puts it, "Britain in Egypt was simply, though significantly a *presence* astride the Suez Canal and the route to India."[17] This ambiguity reflected a number of competing pressures. Strategic considerations required a balancing act between the need to secure the route to India and the desire to avoid antagonizing rivals, especially France. In this context, the claim that the occupation was about restoring legitimate Ottoman power gave a veneer of respectability to the British presence. The economic forces driving the development of imperialism played a key role in transforming the short-term demands of political strategy into a permanent connection between Britain and Egypt. For instance, the initial impetus for British intervention was justified by the need to protect British bondholders. The Executive Committee of the Anti-Aggression League argued in an open letter to the *Times* in June 1882 that this decision would inevitably have long-term consequences:

> The sole British interest specified by the Prime Minister is that of the bondholders. Beyond the general plea that the Egyptians cannot govern themselves, and therefore we ought to govern them (a plea which might similarly be urged for entering any ill-governed country), the

reason is that otherwise certain speculators will not get their dividends. If, that Egypt may be so administered that it can pay its debts, we are to maintain on its throne our nominee, agent or middleman, then for indefinite periods, a British fleet will have to parade before the forts of Alexandria every time a Khedive of our choosing happens to find himself in a ministerial crisis in Cairo.[18]

The logic of the situation compelled the British to install troops in the "forts of Alexandria" and to maintain Evelyn Baring, Lord Cromer, as consul-general in Cairo, to remind the "Khedive of our choosing" where his loyalties should lie. The fact of British military control accelerated economic trends that cemented Egypt's dependence on Britain. In turn, however, this dependence also gave British capital a substantial material interest in Egypt, which represented a far greater investment in the occupation than just the dividends of a handful of shareholders.

British occupation coincided with a period of increasing internationalization of trade. British firms were beginning to exercise greater control over the entire production process. Actual military occupation of a key primary goods producer, such as Egypt, was a logical extension of this trend. As Roger Owen describes, the journey of Egyptian cotton from the fields beside the Nile to the mills of Lancashire was almost entirely controlled by British or French capitalists.[19] British occupation had another significant effect on the economic development of Egypt. As a small cog in the greater machine of imperial trade, Egypt had two interlocking roles to play, first as a producer of primary goods for British industry, and second as a receptive market for the finished articles. Muhammad Ali's dream of self-sustaining indigenous industrial development was little closer to fulfilment by 1900 than it had been in 1832. Indeed it could be argued that the Egyptian economy in this period was distorted by the dictates of the imperial economy, as the sectors of production, processing, or distribution advanced, and the rest stagnated. In the words of Egyptian writer Salama Musa, "The reign of Cromer has transformed the entire Nile Valley into a gigantic cotton plantation."[20]

National liberation or social revolution?

The nineteenth century crushed Egyptian aspirations of independence. The first half of the twentieth century saw these hopes take shape again, eventually building into a mass movement for national liberation led not by the Egyptian bourgeoisie, but by the working class. Yet the weakness of leadership in the working-class movement opened the door to the Free Officers' coup, led by Nasser. The long boom of the 1950s and 1960s and the decline of British power provided the backdrop to Nasser's early successes. The nationalization of the Suez Canal proved that liberated colonies could take on their former masters and win. Yet the conditions that allowed the "Nasserist" model of development to dominate the Middle East and parts of Africa were only temporary. By the 1970s, Egypt was again deeply in debt to western governments and banks, and had been reabsorbed into the orbit of the United States, which had replaced Britain as the major power.

One significant effect of the British occupation of Egypt was that it stunted the growth of an Arabic-speaking native bourgeoisie. European businesses encouraged the development of a non-native layer of middlemen and agents, many of whom began to invest for themselves. As in many Ottoman and former Ottoman states, these entrepreneurs were often of Armenian, Syrian, Greek, or Jewish descent, and they remained distinct from the rest of the population. Protected by law, these religious minorities were exempt from Ottoman laws and taxes. The presence of this group of "foreign" capitalists left little room for the emergence of a native capitalist class. It was only at the beginning of the twentieth century that such a class began finally to emerge. Egyptian capitalists were chiefly wealthy through their vast land holdings, but they made tentative steps toward investment in industry and played an important role in founding the Wafd, the first nationalist party.

The number of these resident Egyptian businessmen remained small. Throughout the 1920s, the reins of colonial control were loosened, but British business retained a firm hold on Egyptian economic life. Into the 1930s, British firms continued to prosper from the underdevelopment of the Egyptian economy. Growth was also hampered by crippling debts to British banks. Before 1939, up to 30 percent of annual revenue was taken by debt charges.[21] The *Economist* estimated that of the £200 million of shares in Egypt in 1947, just 10 percent were owned by indigenous capitalists.[22] Underdevelopment shaped the political forces that could challenge British domination. The Wafd had led the nationalist mass movement, particularly during the revolution of 1919. But the Egyptian bourgeoisie was not yet confident to challenge the British for power. During a ministerial crisis in 1942, a handful of British tanks removed a Wafd government from office.

The Second World War transformed the Egyptian economy. Whole new branches of industry were created to fill the gaps in supplies.[23] Production grew in textiles, food, chemicals, glass, leather, cement and petroleum. The British Middle East Supply Centre (MESC) gave help to industrialists wishing to expand. The war opened up new markets in the Middle East. Yet the suspension of foreign capital was not continued after 1945. Agriculture was weakened and unable to meet the demands of a growing population. Wartime industrialization actually intensified the pressures on the Egyptian bourgeoisie. Workers began to articulate class demands against native capital, as well as opposing British occupation. During the 1940s, the Wafd vacillated between its desire to push for Egyptian independence from the UK and its fear of the working class.

Under wartime conditions, the number of industrial laborers increased to over 1,500,000 in 1946.[24] Trade unions were legalized in 1942, and the textile workers of Shubra al-Khayma in Cairo built independent unions. There were strikes over pay, conditions, and trade union recognition, which became politicized through the experience of repression. In December 1945, Shubra came under military occupation as wage disputes spiraled into a full-time confrontation with the government. In 1946, plans were laid for the formation of a national trade union federation. A general strike was planned for June, but the transport unions pulled out and the strike collapsed.

On September 6, 1947, strikes broke out at the huge Misr spinning mill in the Delta town of Mahalla al-Kubra, the very heart of Egyptian capitalism. The left Wafdist daily paper, *Saut al-Umma*, listed messages of support from all over the country and also reported a stoppage by textile workers in Shubra in solidarity with their sacked colleagues. *Saut al-Umma* announced that workers' organizations had sent a delegation of lawyers to represent the arrested strikers, and published letters of support from various unions, including the Port Workers' Union of Port Said and textile workers in Alexandria.[25] Although walkouts were not yet successful, they led to further struggles throughout the winter and spring of 1947–8. There were mass strikes again in 1950 and 1952. As elsewhere, workers looked to existing parties for leadership, and communists found themselves at the head of the movement.[26]

Although there was no single communist party, different communist cells played a role in the workers' movement. New Dawn and the Egyptian Movement for National Liberation (EMNL) were both influential in the unions. The EMNL merged with other communist parties to form the Democratic Movement for National Liberation (DMNL), which had 1,500 members and an influence out of all proportion to its size. There were also dissident non-Stalinist Marxists on the Egypt left, although their forces were far too small to have an impact on events.[27]

Since the rise of Stalin in the late 1920s, the strategy of the Communist International had been to instruct their colonial comrades to seek power not through the workers' movement, but in alliance with their own bourgeoisie. Liberation was seen as a process that would take place in stages. In their plan, first the Egyptian bourgeoisie would emancipate itself from British rule, and only much later could workers' issues come to the fore. The Egyptian communist groups, including the DMNL and New Dawn, adopted this model wholeheartedly. In a typical draft program from the early 1950s, one of the communist groups argued that "the people's democracy we want to establish in Egypt is not a form of the dictatorship of the proletariat. We aim to establish a democratic dictatorship of all the classes struggling against imperialism and feudalism."[28]

Inside the unions, communist groups argued that the most immediate issue was national liberation. Following the Free Officers' coup of July 1952, the DMNL and the trade union leadership called off planned transport strikes. That August, a strike broke out in the mill town of Kafr al-Dawwar near Alexandria. Despite workers' support for their coup, the Free Officers hanged two strikers. Large meetings demanded action, but the workers' leadership failed to give any focus to the movement. The DMNL and the unions opposed sympathy action in support of the strikers. The protests were halted, and the Free Officers banned all rival parties in January 1953.[29]

Rapid but uneven economic development had created a bourgeoisie that was too weak to confront imperialism, and the 1940s were years of decline for the Wafd. Other political forces such as the Muslim Brotherhood, which had grown to five hundred thousand members by 1948, were paralyzed by the lack of a clear social base.[30] Workers challenged both imperialism and the Egyptian bourgeoisie, but lacked an independent political leadership that was capable of realizing the revolutionary potential of the situation. As Tony Cliff argues in his book, *Deflected Permanent Revolution*:

> While the conservative, cowardly nature of a late-developing bourgeoisie is an absolute law, the revolutionary character of the young working class is neither absolute nor inevitable...the last, but by no means least factor in determining whether the working class in backward countries is actually revolutionary or not is a subjective one, namely the activities of the parties, particularly the Communist parties, that influence it.[31]

The communist groups were far too small to change the balance of forces in the mass movement. The largest force, the DMNL, argued that the Free Officers represented a progressive national leadership. Faced with the new regime, the network of solidarity that had been built up out of the struggles of the previous eight years fractured. Over the next few years, the Free Officers repaid the communists by smashing their organizations, banning their press and torturing their activists.

The expansion of the world economy during the long boom helped to build mass support for the new regime. Nasser constructed a welfare state, providing jobs in the state-owned industries. Across the world, it seemed possible for new states to catch up on their advanced rivals through state intervention, import substitution, and public works. Nasser promised to govern according to the rules of a new "Arab socialism," which were expressed in the National Charter of 1962: "Freedom today means that of the country and of the citizen. Socialism has become both a means and an end, sufficiency and justice."[32] The first task was the extension of industry. As late as 1952, manufacturing accounted for just 10 percent of Egyptian GNP. New factories were built, and the Aswan high dam was begun to provide electricity and water for irrigation. The size of farms was limited to fifty *feddan*,[33] and some surplus land was redistributed.

"Hero of the crossing—where is our breakfast?"

By the mid-1960s Nasser's state capitalist project was beginning to run aground. The first Five-Year Plan (1957–6?) produced impressive growth, while reforms to land ownership, rents, and widespread subsidies on basic goods raised the standard of living of ordinary Egyptians. The second Five-Year Plan began as an attempt to consolidate some of these gains, but serious economic problems emerged. The balance of trade deficit grew alarmingly, prices rose and shortages began to bite. The economic slowdown tipped into decline following the catastrophe of the 1967 war with Israel. Although military defeat shattered Egypt's pride, the economic effects were longer lasting: Egypt lost control of the Sinai desert and with it 70 percent of national oil production. In addition the Suez Canal was closed, depriving the regime of vital income.[34]

Egypt's economic problems were not only driven by internal factors. By the late 1960s the long boom was grinding to a halt. State intervention and high levels of arms no longer generated increases in production at a level that could keep the world economy expanding. The flagging Egyptian economy was suffering the same disease that plagued the rest of the world, slowing rates of growth, expanding external debt and rising prices.[35] Across the advanced capitalist countries, the slowdown in economic growth prompted a major ideological shift away from state intervention toward a new liberalism, a "monetarist" orthodoxy championed by Milton Friedman and the Chicago Business School. In the West this translated into a sustained attack on public services, wage controls, job cuts in state industries, and a shift towards privatization. In the Third World, the imposition of neoliberalism was made possible by a combination of external pressure and internal repression. Augusto Pinochet's massacre of the organized working class turned Chile into a private laboratory for free market economics. Resistance from below was crushed by the military dictatorship; the poor were made to pay for the crisis.[36]

Within this international context Nasser's successor, Anwar Sadat, turned the Egyptian economy toward *infitah*, economic liberalization.[37] This decision was motivated by strategic factors, including the desire to reorient Egypt toward the United States, and to disengage from dependence on the Soviet Union. Sadat expelled Soviet advisers from Egypt, to acclaim from western governments. The flagging economy would be revived by Washington cash. His choices were also shaped by the power struggle within the Egyptian ruling class following Nasser's death. Sadat hoped to weaken the grip of factions associated with Nasser.[38] His first public moves toward infitah were dressed up in the language of defending Nasser's legacy; later pronouncements were far more critical of what Sadat called the "stupid kind of socialism" of the 1960s.[39]

The centerpiece of infitah was Law 43 of 1974, establishing a "General Authority for Arab and Foreign Investment and Free Zones" (GAAFIFZ). This body offered enticements to prospective foreign investors: profits were exempted from taxation for five years, or forever with projects located within the Free Zones. Foreign companies did not have to comply with the 25 percent profit-sharing requirements that applied to Egyptian firms. Exchange controls were loosened and labor regulations were abolished for projects within the Free Zones.[40] Article 7 of the law made a solemn promise to investors that none of their profits would ever be reclaimed for the Egyptian people: "Projects may not be nationalized or expropriated, nor may invested capital be confiscated, seized, or sequestered except through lawful process."[41]

For many on the Egyptian left, Sadat was the betrayer of the revolutionary gains of the Nasser years. Communists who identified Nasser as a member of the "progressive bourgeoisie" saw in Sadat's rejection of the Soviet Union, and the privatization of the Egyptian economy, an authentic counterrevolution. Yet Sadat was just as much a part of the Free Officers' movement as Nasser. Infitah appealed not simply to an external capitalist class, but to large sections of the ruling elite. The people who benefited from the process of liberalization were those linked to the existing structures of power. According to Ghali Shoukri:

> The Egyptian writer Abbas Mahmud Al-Aqqad often said: "God only knows if Lucifer's revolt was revolution or counter-revolution."... If he had lived (he died in 1964) he would certainly have found a reply to his sarcastic question about Lucifer's revolt. Nasser's putsch would have suggested this reply to him: Lucifer's revolt is a revolution and a counter-revolution at the same time. The fact is that Nasser led the stage of revolution up to the day it failed, 5th June 1967. Sadat, who had accompanied him throughout the first period, is today leading the counter-revolution.[42]

Despite Sadat's hopes, infitah did not solve Egypt's problems. A small layer of state officials, contractors, and speculators became rich, while

the mass of the population struggled against rising prices and deteriorating conditions of work. In 1976, average income stood at just $280
per capita—less than Thailand or the Philippines. During the same year,
the newspaper *Al-Tali'ah* estimated that the purchasing power of 80
percent of the population had declined since the October War of 1973.[43]
The psychological consequences of infitah were profound: conspicuous
consumption by the elite and the widening gap between the lifestyles of
the new millionaires and ordinary people fueled a sense of betrayal.
Even moderate commentators such as Muhammad Hasanayn Haykal,
editor of *Al-Ahram*, describe the years of infitah as corrupt: "Not since
the days of Khedive Ismail had Egypt been the scene of looting on
such a massive and organized scale as it was during the last years of
President Sadat. Corruption spread from the top of the pyramid of
Egyptian society to the bottom."[44] The comparison with Ismail Pasha
is apt. The liberalization of export policies accelerated the accumulation of debt. The balance of trade grew, particularly as the terms of
agricultural trade deteriorated. Ten years after the beginning of infitah, Egypt had to import 25 percent of its foodstuffs. External debt
rose from $3 billion to $24 billion.[45]

The tempo of strikes and demonstrations increased throughout
the 1970s. Sadat's promises had raised expectations that ordinary
people would benefit from an economic miracle. In 1975, large
protests by workers on New Year's Day first raised an ironic slogan
referring to Sadat's exploits in the war with Israel: "Hero of the cross-
ing—where is our breakfast?" The same year, the Egyptian government turned to the IMF for assistance in plugging the spiralling
budget deficit.[46] The mass of the Egyptian population was now set on
a collision course with the regime.

As 1976 drew to a close, a general transport strike shook Cairo.
However, the new year opened quietly, reassuring press headlines con-
firming that the government would provide a pay raise for state sector
workers.[47] Over the next few weeks the government revealed the out-
lines of its plans for economic reform: the priority would be reducing

the £E1.3 billion (Egyptian pounds) budget deficit. The weekly paper *Akhbar al-Yawm* disclosed on January 15 that the driving force behind the economic reforms was the IMF.[48] Three days later, press headlines announced the government's decision to remove £E228 million of subsidies from basic goods, including flour, maize, sugar, tea, and rice.[49] From one end of Egypt to the other people took to the streets. Riots broke out in Alexandria—more than three hundred were arrested after crowds attacked the governor's residence and burnt the furniture. Protestors in Mansoura burned down the ruling party's buildings and the headquarters of the security forces. In Suez, demonstrators seized weapons and ammunition, then opened fire on the police.[50]

Cairo was shaken by huge demonstrations, buildings were set on fire and the protestors tried to cut the railway line linking Cairo with Alexandria. The ruling party's headquarters on Midan Ataba was set on fire. Pictures of the aftermath of the uprising show that the rioters chose their targets carefully—the casinos and night clubs of Pyramid Street, the sleazy heart of Sadat's Cairo, were smoldering wrecks.[51] Rhyming chants attacked the president and his wife Jehan directly, while others raised the cry of "Nasser, Nasser". Protesters shouted:

> Down with Sadat's palaces!
> Jehan, Jehan, the people are hungry.
> They dressed us in jute, now they are taking our money.
> They drink whisky and eat chicken while the people die of starvation.
> The Zionist is on my land, and the secret policeman is at my door.
> America: take your money away, the Arab people will crush you.
> Students and workers against the Government of Exploitation.
> Nasser always said: "Take care of the workers."[52]

For two days the crowds controlled the streets. Sadat flew back from his "rest-house" in Aswan, not knowing whether his plane would be able to land safely. Army units eventually restored order, and the regime unleashed a campaign of repression. According to the pro-government press, the entire crisis had been a communist plot, and secret documents were discovered proving that the disturbances had been caused by left-wing agitators.[53] Yet before Sadat ordered troops on to the street, he reinstated the food subsidies. The main demands of the protestors were met within two days of the outbreak of the uprising. The government was careful to stress that there would be no changes to the wage rises promised at New Year.[54]

The uprising of 1977 was not directed by the tiny communist underground. But the left had grown during the 1970s. Influenced by Moscow and Libya, a succession of "broad left" oppositions were formed. Ex-general Saddedien Shazli broadcast into Egypt, promising a return to the Nasserism of the past. An Egyptian Communist Party claimed a direct link to the movements of the 1940s. The smaller Communist Workers' Party received some important support in the factories, before it was pushed underground. Today's legal left-wing party Tagammu (the National Progressive Union) derives from the politics of such groups. Yet, the left failed to offer a genuine alternative. The whole tradition of socialism in Egypt had been warped by Stalinism. Opposition to Sadat was based around a nostalgic longing for the return of Nasser. Rather than building a mass base, parties like Tagammu looked toward an accommodation with "progressive" sections of the regime. Tagammu originated within the ruling party as a left faction around Khaled Mohi al-Din.

The main beneficiaries of the political degeneration of the national liberation movements of the 1950s and 1960s were not in the end left-wing groups. Instead, the crisis of the 1970s provided fertile ground for the rebirth of the radical Islamist movement. During the 1950s and 1960s, the Muslim Brotherhood had faced repression from Nasser and the Free Officers' regime. However, the organization was able to rebuild itself toward the end of the decade. The Muslim Brotherhood turned against revolutionary action, organizing instead along constitutional lines and with a semi-legal magazine, *al-Dawa*. According to Chris Harman, the Brotherhood "set its goal as reform of Egyptian society along Islamic lines by pressure from within.… This meant, in

practice, adopting a 'reformist Islamist' orientation, seeking an accommodation with the Sadat regime."[55] When radical Islam was re-
born in the 1970s, both the Muslim Brotherhood and the Islamic
Association publicly sided with the state against the "communist con-
spiracies" of the radical sects.

In Egypt, it was the Sadat government that began the process of direct encouragement for fundamentalism. In the 1970s, the Brotherhood's paper, *Al-Dawa*, became freely available across Egypt. Newer
and more radical organizations including Jihad (Holy War), which
would be blamed for Sadat's murder, Gama'at Islamiyya (the Islamic
Group) and Tafkir wal-Higra (Repentance and Atonement) were originally armed by the state and allowed to recruit a generation of politicized militants. There was a double advantage to the regime. The ideas
of Islamism served as a counterweight to left-wing ideas: the funda-
mentalists could be relied on to act against the socialists as ruthlessly as
the government. Meanwhile, the Islamists also whipped up communal
tensions with the Copts, providing a useful diversion for frustrations
that might have been directed elsewhere. Yet in manipulating the Islamists, the ruling classes were riding a beast, over which they had no
control.[56] This became clear with Sadat's murder by members of Jihad
in 1981 and has become even more evident since. Over the past twenty
years, the government has found itself more and more the ideological
prisoner of fundamentalism.

In the 1980s, the government allowed the Egyptian Brotherhood to
build schools, clinics, and welfare organizations. Under the leadership
of Hosni Mubarak, Sadat's successor, the ruling National Democratic
Party, supposedly made up of secular nationalists, has made concession after concession to the Islamist agenda, partly out of a desire to
recapture the political initiative by showing itself as the true guardian
of Islamic identity, but also because of the increasing bankruptcy of its
own ideas. The collapse of secular nationalism has done more than
deprive a section of the ruling class of its rationale for holding power.
It has also led large sections of the population to look elsewhere to

find some kind of voice for their discontent. The left's close association with Nasser opened up huge opportunities for the Islamists to pose as a radical alternative to the communists. Thus Islamist student groups have massively expanded over the last two decades. Islamist dress, in particular the head scarf worn by women, has become increasingly popular. The Islamists' criticisms of Egypt's dependence on the West have reached a wide audience. Even such media as radio and film are compelled to respond to the agenda of the Islamic groups.

Yet despite all the dire predictions of Western commentators, the Islamist movement in Egypt has failed to take state power, in the way the Muslim Brotherhood in the Sudan has managed to do. Nor have they even come close, as the Front Islamique du Salut (FIS) in Algeria did through the months of crisis in 1991. Instead they have oscillated between reformism, using front parties and working in semi-legality around elections and campaigns, and terrorism. Neither strategy has so far brought significant success. "In spite of the expansion of Islamic ideology over the past few years," Hani Shukrallah argues, "it cannot yet be said to have achieved hegemony within the dominant ideology." Although bourgeois nationalism is in crisis, the outcome has been "despondency, apathy, the absence of a common direction," not the victory of political Islamism.[57]

The revenge of the market: infitah in the age of structural adjustment

Between 1977 and his assassination in 1981, Sadat avoided a further confrontation over economic issues. His visit to Jerusalem in the autumn of that year neatly deflected attention from the ailing economy with promises of U.S. dollars as a reward for making peace with the old enemy. At the same time, a ferocious campaign of repression against first the left and then the Islamists undermined organized opposition to the regime. The restoration of the Sinai oil fields as a result of the peace deal, combined with an increase in workers' remittances from the Gulf and rising numbers of tourists, provided a new impetus to economic growth that took the edge off popular anger for a while.[58]

However, this temporary respite could never have compensated for the underlying weaknesses in the Egyptian economy. In particular, as in many Third World countries, foreign debt began to spiral out of control. By 1986, the Egyptian state owed $32 billion to foreign creditors. As oil prices began to fall, the economy tipped into recession during the late 1980s. Despite the agreement of a structural adjustment loan with the IMF in 1986, the crisis steadily deepened. The ratio of foreign debt to GNP stood at 150 pe cent by 1990. Real wages of unskilled workers had dropped by 40 percent in four years. In these circumstances, the outbreak of war in the Gulf in 1990 had a devastating effect. Nearly four hundred thousand workers flooded home from Kuwait, ending the precious flow of foreign capital into the already weakened economy.[59] However, it was the impending default on American military loans—and therefore the automatic suspension of all U.S. aid—which paved the way for the IMF's rescue package.[60] Restructuring was only made possible by a generous level of debt forgiveness, particularly for the crucial military loans. For the last ten years the poorest people in Egypt have been paying the price for this generosity as agriculture, manufacturing and public services have been reshaped in the interests of international and local capital. The 1990s have been indelibly marked by the struggles of ordinary people to resist the neoliberal onslaught against their jobs, services, and homes.

The process of structural adjustment has created a crisis in the Egyptian countryside. Far-reaching changes in legislation have removed the framework that gave small farmers, sharecroppers, and the rural poor limited protection from the pressures of the world market. State subsidies in the form of access to credit, fertilizers, and basic social services have all been withdrawn or cut back. In many cases, undiluted market forces have had a catastrophic impact on crop production. For instance, in one area the cost of fertilizer stood at £E26 per sack in July 1995. By

September a severe shortage had pushed prices as high as £E80, a 350 percent increase over just three months. Faced with the risk of losing between one-third and two-thirds of the year's sugarcane crop, the government intervened to ensure the distribution of fertilizer.[61]

During the 1990s, the regime slowly dismantled the 1952 land reform law that limited land ownership to fifty feddan per person and one hundred feddan per family. This reform had played a crucial role in the consolidation of the Free Officers' regime: it pacified the countryside at a time when the Free Officers were dealing with pressure from a rising tide of strikes and factory occupations. The new law was passed in 1992, but was implemented gradually over the next five years, with the final provisions taking effect in October 1997. According to the Land Centre for Human Rights, the law has been a disaster for more than seven hundred thousand tenant farmers who have seen rents increase fivefold in the space of a year. In 1993 the rent per feddan rose from an average of £E120 to £E660, or £E160 more than the average crop return.[62] The beneficiaries of the reform in the short term have been the large landowners, who have been able to increase their landholdings above the old limits, and in many cases rebuild family estates that were broken up by Nasser's reforms in the 1950s. The psychological impact of this has been immense: for the tenant farmers this was a return to the days of feudalism. Even the *Financial Times* commented "the reversion to pre-Nasserite agrarian capitalism has been abrupt."[63] In the long term, the likely winner will be multinational agribusiness. Egypt now produces a diverse range of cash crops for the European market, such as strawberries, mangos, avocados, and peppers.[64]

The losers in this process have been the hundreds of thousands of tenant farmers who are struggling to pay higher rents, or who have been dispossessed entirely and who are now swelling the ranks of the urban unemployed. The accelerating decay of the Nasserist welfare state has hit rural areas hard. According to data collected for the Family Budget Surveys, by the mid-1990s a greater proportion of the rural population were living in poverty than in 1974.[65] Yet health services have become ever more inaccessible in the countryside: rural health centers and basic health units accounted for only 14 percent of government-funded hospital beds in 1995.[66]

The centerpiece of the structural adjustment program was meant to be the privatization of government-owned enterprises. Government statisticians in 1991 calculated that out of 1.33 million workers in the public sector, 30 percent were "surplus to requirements."[67] Changes in the law allowed managers to sack workers in loss-making firms and to determine wages, bonuses, and conditions on a local basis. As the social value of the factory worker's wage remains stagnant or declines, these "fringe benefits" are crucial to working-class families' survival. Already by 1995 manufacturing workers accounted for 31.3 percent of the urban poor.[68] In addition, urban workers faced further pressures with the piecemeal removal of state subsidies on housing and basic goods, and the further deterioration of public services. In 1996 rent controls were abolished and protection from eviction ended. During the previous ten years consumer prices had increased fivefold.[69] The introduction of a new sales tax further shifted the burden of taxation on to the poor, while spending on both health services and education continued to decline.[70] By 1996 the urban poor were spending nearly 60 percent of their household income on food.[71]

In the meantime, state restructuring of the financial sector has generated a number of artificial booms, which have facilitated the "complicated adjustment of existing relations between the public sector business barons and their partners in the private sector."[72] Property speculation and phony privatization programs have made a very small number of the already rich even more wealthy. Large companies, such as the Osman, Bahgat, and Orascom groups, have benefited from the tax-free loans offered by the revitalized banking sector in order to cement their links to the multinationals. The most lucrative parts of the Egyptian economy are now firmly in the hands of a small number of these companies. For instance, the Orascom group consists of Egypt's largest private construction company, cement makers, natural gas supply companies, tourism developments, an arms trading company, and exclusive rights in mobile phones, Microsoft franchises, and McDonald's. The close connections between this elite band of speculators and powerful interests in the regime are underlined by the web of open and hidden subsidies enjoyed by the conglomerates. As Timothy Mitchell points out: "The state has turned resources away from agriculture, industry, and the underlying problems of training and employment. It now subsidises financiers instead of factories, speculators instead of schools."[73]

Despite the difficulties, the 1980s and 1990s saw significant resistance to the effects of economic reform. Workers' protests are one of the key factors that have slowed the pace of privatization and forced concessions from the government, which still lives in terror of a repeat of 1977. Attacks on conditions and wages have sparked off dozens of strikes, sit-ins, and workers' demonstrations. On September 30, 1994, seven thousand evening shift workers at Misr Spinning in the mill town of Kafr al-Dawwar occupied the plant in protest at cuts in production incentives and the introduction of a harsh new disciplinary code. Riot police and the army surrounded the factory to prevent other workers joining the strike and pitched battles raged across the town for two nights, leaving hundreds injured and hundreds more arrested.[74] In 1998 a wave of strikes and occupations hit Egyptian factories. Four thousand workers at the Transport and Engineering Company in Alexandria occupied their factory for three days in protest at management's failure to offer significant bonuses despite posting a £E17 million profit. A rash of strikes broke out in the steel plants of Helwan near Cairo, and there were protests by young women workers at the Bisco-Misr factory in Sawwah, also in Cairo. As *Al-Ahram Weekly* reported:

> Young women gathered in the street after a long day's work. "The incentives have been cut from 30 days' pay to four or five days' pay in the past four years. They call it privatisation, I think," said Reem, who

has been with the factory since 1992. "It is going from bad to worse, and I wish someone would feel our misery."[75]

The volatility of workers' struggles has been increased by the declining influence of the state-run trade unions.[76] Trade union leaders, who are appointed by the ministry of the interior, have rarely opposed privatization on principle. On occasions they have spoken out to criticize workers' exclusion from profit-sharing schemes, or against job losses, but for huge numbers of rank-and-file workers the trade union leadership is as much part of the enemy as management. Most strikes have demanded the dismissal of local union officials for failing to represent the interests of union members.[77] The decline of the trade unions' officially sanctioned role as a conduit for distribution of benefits and services to members, combined with a rising level of attacks on workers' living standards, is fatally undermining the trade union bureaucracy's ability to contain workers' militancy.[78]

Strikes in the factories have intersected with continuing street protests against cuts in subsidies, rising prices, and collapsing services. In 1986 the regime faced its most serious crisis since 1977 when policemen from the Central Security Forces rioted in Cairo and a number of different provinces including Sohag, Assyout, and Ismailia. Trouble started at the police camp near Dashour, on the outskirts of Cairo, and quickly developed into massive violent demonstrations by policemen. Shops and businesses in the plush suburb of Ma'adi and along Pyramid Street were wrecked by rioters, hotels destroyed, and private cars torched.[79] The state was forced to rely on the weight of the army to crush the protests, which centered around pay and conditions for rank-and-file policemen. After two days the death toll stood at thirty-six dead (thirty-two police, two soldiers and two civilians), and more than three hundred wounded.

The issue of solidarity for the Palestinian intifada has also been a radicalizing factor in Egyptian street protests. Huge demonstrations by students at the outbreak of the uprising were quickly joined by workers. Slogans in the demonstrations moved on from demands for the expulsion of the Israeli ambassador to chants against price rises, government corruption, and state repression. Workers also took part in solidarity action including strikes and occupations. The renewal of the intifada in October 2000 confirmed this trend: thousands of students from Cairo University fought pitched battles with the police, who attempted to stop them breaking out from the university compound. Banners and chants on the protest attacked the Mubarak regime for its links to Israel and the United States, and a group of students, possibly inspired by the anticapitalist protests in Prague a few days earlier, smashed up a KFC restaurant.[80]

Land reform has not been accomplished without a struggle either. Skirmishes between tenant farmers and landlords backed up by the police have been commonplace. Tagammu's paper, *Al-Ahali*, reported a bitter struggle in the village of Komshish when members of the Fiqhy family attempted to force a number of tenant farmers to leave their land. The police were called to the dispute and responded by arresting a large number of tenants. According to one local farmer, the landlords called the local people "dogs," and said, "if they won't do what we want now, they'll certainly move when the government makes them." Since 1992 dozens of tenant farmers have been killed and hundreds injured.[81]

The program of structural adjustment has only been made possible by immense repression. Egypt is still governed under state of emergency laws. Strikes are banned; political parties face harassment and repression. Torture and detention without trial are commonplace. Opposition parties find elections weighted against them—in rural areas, soldiers guard the polling booths to stop opposition supporters registering their votes.[82] During the mid-1990s the southern provinces of Egypt witnessed a brutal war of attrition between state forces and armed Islamist groups. Army units regularly destroyed crops to stop Islamist gunmen from hiding among the fields, and harassed and arrested villagers thought to be sympathetic to the Islamist cause. After a number of attacks on tourists, repression appeared not only to have smashed the radical armed factions, but also to have targeted more moderate electoral organizations such as the Muslim Brotherhood. Human Rights Watch reported in 1999 that Muslim Brotherhood activists had been arrested simply for possessing the organization's leaflets; the authorities "showed no sign of loosening the tight grip of the security apparatus, and documentation of its impunity—including torture, deaths in custody, 'disappearances,' and abysmal prison conditions—filled the pages of reports published by Egyptian human rights organisations."[83]

Anger and bitterness at the Egyptian regime show clearly throughout all of the significant protests and strikes of the 1980s and 1990s. However, the political currents that have attempted to give expression to this frustration have been unable seriously to challenge the state. Hani Shukrullah's judgement from 1987 still holds true a decade and a half later: "the growing weakness of the existing political system has not been transformed into the power of an alternative political force."[84]

Groups like the Muslim Brotherhood have maintained a mass base and some representation in the People's Assembly. The network of mosques, clinics, and schools supported by the Brotherhood has solidified their support, but the level of state repression has prevented the emergence of a mass Islamist party. None of the liberal opposition parties has been able to break out from the same trap. As for the communists, the remnants of their organizations emerged from the 1970s weak and disorientated. The collapse of the Soviet Union only finalized a process of decay that had started years before. By identifying the "progressive bourgeoisie" around Nasser as the key agent of change in Egypt after 1945, the communist groups dedicated their support to social classes that were ultimately hostile to the workers' cause. As the world economy stagnated, the local bourgeoisie ceased to shield its people from the demands of capital. The left had established a strategy that was local state capitalism, and once this strategy began to unwind, it had no second plan. The communists consigned themselves to share in the collapse of the nationalist dream. As Phil Marshall argues:

Stalinism had fetishised the state as a means of bringing change and was…crushed by the same capitalisms it had helped bring into existence. Joel Beinin's epitaph for the Egyptian Communists could serve for the left across the region. "Caught up by the embrace of the national movement," he comments, "they [were] destroyed by it."[85]

Conclusion

So will the bankers and bondholders have the last laugh? Has Egypt simply come full circle, back to the heyday of imperialist expansion, only this time the occupiers are sporting the colors of McDonald's, Coca-Cola, and Microsoft instead of British redcoats? "Globalization," to use the buzzword of the early twenty-first century, is after all simply a later stage in the old-fashioned process of nineteenth-century "imperialism." Both describe capitalist expansion, in particular the intensification of the restless search to find new markets, new avenues for investments, and new profits. As Karl Marx wrote over 150 years ago, "The need of a constantly expanding market for its products chases the bourgeoisie over the whole surface of the globe. It must nestle everywhere, settle everywhere, establish connections everywhere."[86] Both in the late nineteenth century and today, economic expansion has been underpinned by ruthless military force. Gunboats and British troops eventually followed Khedive Ismail's steam plows and cotton gins to Alexandria. Or as *New York Times* columnist Thomas L. Friedman put it: "the hidden fist that keeps the world safe for Silicon Valley's technologies to flourish is called the U.S. Army, Air Force, Navy and Marine Corps."[87]

However, despite a more than passing similarity between the Commission for the Egyptian Public Debt and the International Monetary Fund, the answer is clearly "no." The reason is simple: international capital has wrecked millions of Egyptian lives but it has transformed the country in the process. The Egyptian working class is potentially the strongest force for change throughout the entire Middle East and

North Africa. It is the biggest working class in the region, and has an inspiring history of struggle against both international and local capital. And the process of globalization is accelerating the growth of the working class, particularly by pushing huge numbers of tenant farmers off the land during the last few years alone.

The long decay of the dreams of state-led development and national liberation has laid bare the real forces in the world economy: an international ruling class that has its representatives in every society on Earth, and an international working class that is increasingly bound together across national and regional boundaries. The problem, as Egyptian history clearly shows, is that realizing this potential power depends on the subjective political judgements made by the organizations that hope to lead the working-class movement. Yet there was nothing inevitable about the defeats of the past. Both in the 1940s and in the 1970s, the workers were held back by the dominance of Stalinist ideas. It is an immense advance that the Soviet Union has gone, and with it the base of the old Egyptian communist parties. The decks have been cleared for an open struggle within Egyptian society. Events will test whether Egyptian socialists can meet the challenges to come.

The wave of protests that swept Egypt over Easter 2002 is a clear sign that people's mounting anger can suddenly explode onto the streets. The trigger for the protests was the Israeli offensive in the Occupied Territories, which first detonated huge demonstrations among university students and then spread to high schools across Egypt. As in September 2000, hundreds of thousands of school students organized protests in solidarity with the Palestinians. Their slogans were openly directed at the government, declaring that Egyptian society must be overturned before Palestine can be liberated. One activist explained, "The road to Jerusalem runs through Cairo." These teenagers face a future in a region scarred by economic crisis and imperialist war. It is they who will shape the battles of the next few years.

INTERVIEW WITH AHMAD HUSSAIN

Ahmad Hussain is a human rights activist living in Egypt. He has carried out research for a number of different projects, including community development work and trade union rights (Cairo, August 2001).

What was it that politicized you?

A lot of my political ideas stem from my relationship with my father. He was a local official in the Arab Socialist Union under Nasser. He was one of those who really believed in it, but after the catastrophe of 1967 and Sadat's betrayals he felt quite bitter toward the regime and gradually dropped out of politics altogether. For him, the fifties and sixties were a time when the whole world was up for grabs—they were building up industry, creating a welfare state and connecting with the struggle of other Third World peoples—but 1967 snatched all his dreams away. We used to talk a lot, and he always encouraged me to read widely, and more importantly to be wary of leaders with too many promises.

For me, the catalyst was the outbreak of the intifada in 1987. Before then I was quite cynical, but I got caught up in the demonstrations on the campus in solidarity with Palestine. The way that the police smashed the protests suddenly made me aware of what kind of a state we are living under.

In Egypt, just as almost everywhere else, economic liberalization is the order of the day. How has this process affected ordinary people?

One of the characteristics of Egyptian society is its unevenness. For instance, as far as economic development is concerned, some sectors of the economy are developing extremely quickly. If you have the money, you can be connected to any kind of technology you like: internet, mobile phones, and so on. Private investors have borrowed huge sums from the banks to create a superficial boom in some sections of the economy, particularly in property speculation. Recently a property developer started offering luxury apartments on the outskirts of Cairo which would be "totally digitized"—in a country like Egypt where the majority of people can't afford the basics, this kind of lifestyle is only a dream. If you go out into the countryside you could be stepping back hundreds of years. And it is not simply the case that people are running to stand still: in reality, huge numbers feel they are falling behind in the race to survive.

Unemployment is a huge problem, and even those who have jobs feel insecure and unfulfilled. The problem is worst for young people, and having a degree or a good education is no guarantee of work. Many graduates wait for ten years before getting a job. There was an outcry recently when the government announced that it would open up 170,000 public sector jobs and places on training schemes to graduates under the age of twenty-eight. For many people it was too late, and after waiting so long they simply saw their dreams snatched away from them again. So in the midst of all the internet cafés in downtown Cairo there are a lot of angry young people, wondering how all this modernization is going to benefit them. To add to this generation's disappointment, the government has made a lot of promises that economic change would bring prosperity for everyone. Egypt was supposed to be a "Tiger on the Nile," following the model of Southeast Asia. Now, even the ministers sound more cautious about globalization, although they are still pushing ahead with plans to privatize more of the economy.

Have workers been able to defend themselves against the effects of liberalization? What role have Egyptian trade unions played?

Trade unions in Egypt are both very powerful and very weak at the present time. The problem is that what power they have is often used against the interests of ordinary workers, because the official trade unions are part of the state machinery. This setup goes back to the days of Nasser, when trade unions were given legal recognition, but at the same time were incorporated into the structures of the state. As a result, officials at the top of the union bureaucracy have a vested interest in maintaining the status quo, and they act to stop any independent organization among workers at a grassroots level. Some trade unionists are now calling for an end to the old style of state-led trade unions, especially since the private sector is growing in size.

Privatization shows how globalization can be a double-edged sword for trade unionists. On the one hand, whenever public industries are sold off, management is bound to see workers' organization as a barrier to "modernization" and thus trade union organizations come under attack, with union committees being dissolved and so on. However, on the other hand, the attack on the official trade union structures actually weakens the grip of the trade union bureaucracy on the workforce, so workers have a chance to push for more radical action. In fact, there have been a lot of strikes and even factory occupations as a response to privatization. If you look back in Egypt's history, before 1952 there was a big independent trade union movement, which was very active in the fight against British occupation, as well as over economic issues. The problem for trade unionists who want to challenge union policy is that now it is illegal to organize a trade union outside the official trade union federation. It is also illegal to strike.

What about other grassroots campaigns? Have other nongovernmental organizations (NGOs) been able to fill the gaps that the official trade union movement has left empty?

It is extremely hard work trying to organize any kind of NGO in Egypt at the moment. For years there has been no letup in the pressure from the government. New laws, which came into effect last year (2000), mean that NGOs have to register with the Ministry of the Interior, and there are very strict rules concerning funding from abroad. Many well-respected human rights organizations have faced years of harassment for their work, and activists are regularly imprisoned. There are certain topics which are definitely taboo. In particular, any organization which takes up the issue of the Copts is bound to run into trouble. For instance, when the Egyptian Organization for Human Rights published an investigation into sectarian violence in the village of al-Kosheh, including well-documented allegations of police torture, the response of the Interior Ministry was to prosecute the campaigners not the police. Anyone who publishes information about these matters runs the risk of being dragged before the courts on a charge of endangering state security, or "damaging Egypt's reputation." It is not just a matter of political persecution; the police routinely use torture against people suspected of ordinary crimes. Last year two men died in police custody in the Kafr al-Sheikh area in suspicious circumstances. The response from their villages was to build barricades in the streets and attack government buildings.

How has the outbreak of the Palestinian Intifada affected the political situation in Egypt?

During the first few weeks of the intifada there were significant protests all over Egypt in solidarity with the Palestinians. However, these were mainly led by students and tended to die away quite quickly in the face of police repression. Since then, the level of protest has been much lower. There have been some important initiatives from the People's Committee for Solidarity with the intifada of the Palestinian people. The Committee organized two food convoys to Palestine. Officially, the convoys had the blessing of the government, and in the demonstration in the town of al-Arish there were officials and bigwigs leading off the march. But everyone could see that the authorities were uneasy. There are Egyptian companies selling cement to Israeli settlements, and the Egyptian government is tied to U.S. policy on Palestine, they don't want any movement which will jeopardize that cozy relationship. In any case, as the students found out, once you push a little bit too far, the state will use any amount of force necessary to stop you.

What do you feel are the prospects for the opposition at the moment?

Egypt lacks any kind of democratic culture. Opposition parties feel that the system is stacked against them by the overwhelming weight of the ruling party. Each time elections take place there are complaints about vote-rigging and intimidation. Of course, a small number of tame oppositionists are allowed to take their seats in Parliament. After all, that small concession to democracy can be an important safety valve to release people's frustration. At the same time, the government is pushing ahead with structural adjustment programs which leave people with even fewer social and economic rights. That's why some people find the idea of returning to Nasser's ideas attractive. They see Nasserism as a way of softening the blows from the market by providing a welfare system and guaranteed jobs in public industries. At a time when the current government is stripping all that away in the name of progress, many people can start to feel nostalgic for Nasser. They also identify Nasser with an Egypt which was confident to stand up for itself, and provide leadership for other Third World countries, instead of following slavishly everything which the United States demands. Despite this, the Nasserists are no stronger than any of the other opposition groups—they don't have the same kind of mass base, or relationship with ordinary people which Nasser himself developed in the 1950s.

Has the anti-capitalist movement, which has become so prominent at the summits in Europe and the United States, found an echo in Egypt?

The protest movement which has emerged to challenge the world's most powerful countries is comparable in its size and sophistication to the movements of the late '60s. Although there is no direct equivalent in Egypt to this movement, there is a growing sense that globalization can only benefit those who are already rich. The Egyptian economy is feeling the impact of structural adjustment and chronic debt, so many are beginning to question whether the market really does hold all the answers. The arrogance of the leaders of the richest countries to the anti-globalization movement mirrors their attitudes to the poorest countries. It was very significant that the forty-nine least developed countries felt they had to hold their own summit in Zanzibar at the same time as the G8 in Italy. If countries actually organized together, they could command a significant bloc of votes in the UN and the World Trade Organization. Yet the world leaders simply dismissed their concerns about globalization as naive. George Bush said at the Summit of the Americas in Quebec, "liberty is not negotiable," but his brand of liberty appears to mean simply the freedom to plunder the Third World. In the Middle East we can see very clearly that much of this talk of freedom is backed up by brute force. You only have to look at what George Bush's father did to Iraq to see exactly what U.S. domination means in practice. And, Bush has so far given unstinting support to Ariel Sharon's butchery of the Palestinians.

People are just beginning to wake up to some of the issues which the anti-globalization movement has highlighted. For instance, the issue of TRIPS (the Agreement on Trade-Related Aspects of Intellectual Property Rights) suddenly came home to people in Egypt when the major pharmaceutical companies took some local manufacturers to court for breaching intellectual property rights by producing cheap generic brands of popular medicines. Before that case, many people had no idea what TRIPS was. What we have to do is find issues like this so that people in Egypt can see that the question of globalization is not just an abstract one, but something which is having huge effects on their lives.

4

"THERE SHALL BE NO PROPERTY": TRADE UNIONS, CLASS, AND POLITICS IN NIGERIA

Jussi Viinikka

Nigeria is the most populous country in West Africa. It has a population of over 100 million and it has a working class that, while low in proportion to the population in western terms, is nevertheless around 5 million people, employed in capitalist workplaces of ten or more workers. However, the working class has more leverage than its size might suggest. The Nigerian working class has on many occasions in the past shown that it is capable of stupendous courage and valor in adversity.

From the 1930s onward, successive governments—both colonial and nationalist—made efforts to incorporate labor representatives into the state machinery. Through the bureaucratization of labor in "moderate" unions and union federations, the state hoped that it could wield some power via legal sanctions and threats of sequestration of funds. For their part the union bureaucrats would receive salaries far higher than their members' wages and would be willing to listen to the state when it threatened their personal interests as union employees.

However, these periods of (sometimes state-sponsored) labor unity in single union federations also saw some of the highest levels of class struggle—in 1945, 1964, 1970, and the early 1980s. The extended struggles of 1974–83, overseen by the state-sponsored united Nigeria Labour

Congress (NLC), noticeably overrode the ethnic and regional differences present in other areas of society. The working class seemed reluctant to heed laws and legal sanctions against industrial action. Strikes have consistently gone ahead in the face of bans. As an official of the NLC explained in October 1983: "The only language that the government and private employers understand is the strike. Let them make more decrees and Acts, they cannot stop workers from going out on strikes."[1] The Nigerian working class clearly must have enormous power if it is able to act with impunity under colonial, nationalist, and military governments alike. The central question is not whether a working class exists in Nigeria, or even the extent of its internal divisions, but its homogeneity as a class when it is defending itself as a class.

This chapter is an attempt to give snapshots of the high points of the Nigerian working class at its strongest and most combative, particularly when it has challenged state power, to set these in a historical, political, and social context, and to establish from this that such a combativeness is structured into the nature of the Nigerian working class. No attempt is made to present a history of Nigeria or of Nigerian labor movement intrigues (of which there are many tales),[2] or to locate the Nigerian labor movement in the sociology of the Nigerian state.[3] Nor is it the purpose of this chapter to provide a survey of past theories of the Nigerian and broader African working class,[4] or to present a social-anthropological monograph.[5]

Nigerian resistance in the 1940s

In the late nineteenth and early twentieth centuries, territorial conquest of the Lagos colony and the formation of a united Nigeria stimulated the growth of Lagos into a busy administrative center, with improved communications and expanded commercial activity all increasing the demand for labor. However, successive governors continued to regard local labor as poor quality and overpriced. Fear was still rife that any rise in urban wages would reduce the total quantity of labor available due to the "finite needs of the African."[6] Extensive use was made of personal taxation as a method of forcing Africans into waged labor.[7] Taxation was not easily accepted and was widely evaded and rebelled against.[8]

In addition to "free" waged labor, forced labor could be found in the mines and on the railways until at least 1944.[9] Nigeria's coal mining industry, only begun in Enugu in 1909, experienced its first strike in 1924.[10] This is especially impressive as much of the colliery labor was bonded or slave labor supplied by local chiefs acting as contractors to the colonial government.[11]

In 1949 at Enugu coalfield, twenty-three striking miners were shot dead by armed police. "The Enugu Shooting Incident," as it is euphemistically known, also left over one hundred miners wounded.[12] News of the massacre was greeted with such bitterness and resentment that Governor Macpherson was forced to set up an inquiry. Criticizing the colliery management and individual police officers, the report reserved its greatest scorn for Nigerian trade unions and the miners' leader in particular.[13] Sadly the massacre at Enugu was not unprecedented in colonial industrial relations.[14]

Communism and nationalism

The interwar years saw not only the first attempts to build nationalist movements in Nigeria, but also a modest influence for international communism. The *Negro Worker* was a paper set up in 1928 by the Profintern (established by the Communist International, Comintern) to act as an organizer for African workers. It was influential enough to be banned in Nigeria in 1930 for the incitement of "Bolshevism among the natives."[15] The *Lagos Daily Record* went to great pains to assure the Nigerian bourgeoisie that the governor's fears of Bolshevism were unfounded: "Marxist propaganda cannot flourish or vegetate under West African soil. What is really needed is sympathetic liberalism in the treatment of the natives, especially the progressive ones."[16]

Although it gave full formal support to the Allies in the Second World War, there was ferment in the nationalist camp on the question of "fighting for democracy" in principle while in practice being refused any democracy at home. The heightened political and economic profile of Nigeria within the empire and a growing questioning of the UK's colonial policy contributed to a postwar nationalist sentiment. In 1944 Herbert Macaulay and Nnamdi Azikiwe, two veterans of Nigerian nationalist politics, formed the National Council of Nigeria and the Cameroons (NCNC), declaring itself for home rule under British mandate.[17] Formed in the wake of the brutal suppression of a students' strike at the exclusive King's College, it was the first political organization to try and bring together nationalism and the nascent working-class movement, even giving its support to the 1945 general strike.[18]

This "labor nationalism" lasted only as long as the late 1940s, but these were a remarkably fecund few years. The honeymoon ended when the newly federated state fostered by the British Richards Constitution of 1947 created formal regional divisions and so encouraged political mobilization along the previously politically impotent lines of ethnicity.[19] In line with this division, the Northern People's Congress (NPC) was formed to lobby for the "north" and to counter the perceived "southern" NCNC demands for national independence. The Action Group was formed for the "west."

The general strike, 1945

The war years produced something of a boom in production and trade in Nigeria.[20] The closure of the Mediterranean sea lanes to the Far East led to an increased importance for West African exports, and infrastructure was built up to cope with these developments. As a result, domestic prices increased, but wages remained low.[21] In response, trade unions and their memberships multiplied during the war. Even though most unions were small there were extensive walkouts, demonstrations, and marches, resulting in a 50 percent cost-of-living allowance (COLA) award in 1942.[22] After this a Nigerian General

Defence Regulation was issued, banning both lockouts and strikes for the duration of the war.

The year 1945 saw the first general strike in Nigerian history. In June workers in all essential services struck for higher wages across the board for all Nigerian wage earners. The strike lasted over six weeks and succeeded in paralyzing the country. Immediate causes of the strike were the recognized fall in real wages since the last COLA in 1942, aggravated by the fact that postwar cash allowances were only given to European civil servants in Nigeria.

Even before the strike began, Lagos was fully aware of its implications and was preparing to fight it out without paying a COLA.[23] The government went to great lengths to break the strike, repeatedly threatening wage forfeits, arresting ringleaders, hiring hundreds of scabs, and banning pro-strike papers. The hiring of blackleg labor was not in itself an easy task, as both ex-servicemen and the registered unemployed solidly refused to scab.[24] The strike itself won all of its main demands: there was to be no victimization, the newspaper bans were to be lifted, and a commission should substantially raise wages.

The Zikist Movement

In 1946 Azikiwe's NCNC spawned a "left" opposition, the "Zikist Movement"—a radical anti-imperialist organization opposing both the UK and those Africans seen to be upholding the colonial state.[25] It drew support from all areas of Nigeria at a time when the NCNC was coming to the conclusion that its future lay with the new Nigerian middle class and southern bourgeoisie.[26] The movement came to advocate strikes, boycotts, and non-payment of taxes as its political weapons. In 1948–49 political talks given by members of the Zikist Movement led to a series of arrests on charges of sedition. One Zikist, Raj Abdallah, stated, "I hate the Union Jack with all my heart because it divides the people wherever it goes. It is a symbol of persecution and brutality."[27] The British government saw the Zikists as a communist threat, and included them in its political intelligence reports.[28] After the Enugu colliery massacre, Zikists organized demonstrations in many towns, with popular anger leading to rioting, and police retaliation causing death and injury.[29] Following an assassination attempt on Sir Hugh Foot, the colonial secretary, the Zikist Movement was banned in 1950.[30]

The general strike and the industrial action around the years 1945–49 demonstrated the problems of nationalist politics rather than the strength of working-class politics. The first Nigerian general strike helped build Nigeria's first "modern" nationalist movement, the likes of which were seen in many African and Asian countries in postwar years. Despite the massive popularity of its ideas, however, Zikism failed to capitalize fully on its potential. It could boast among its leadership trade union secretaries, prominent individual ex-servicemen and newspaper editors. But apparently unable or unwilling to create a "centralized national" organization, it could not coordinate the large number of activities that it initiated. Furthermore, it did not seek to use the power of the national trade unions, or to mobilize the large number of radical and disaffected ex-servicemen in the country.[31] Given the social turmoil, the willingness of the working class to confront the British colonial state, and the actual revolts that occurred, it is possible to suggest that Nigeria could have been saved from the mire of regionalism and taken a different road into the second half of the century.

The legacy of the strike was not, then, a long-term national labor organization but a short-term nationalist movement. It did, however, bring home to European and African rulers the potential power of organized labor. Nigerian workers were shown able to defy the colonial administration, take control of strategic communications centers throughout the country, and force the government onto the defensive: the Nigerian working class had come of age.

Independence and civil war

The years 1945–51 marked the birth of the modern-day Nigerian state. A constitution and moves toward a federal elected government and an African civil service probably better exemplified the beginnings of the later postcolonial state than the end of the prewar colony. The British spent the postwar years grooming a Nigerian political class in response to labor militancy and the threat (imaginary and real) posed by violent nationalism.[32] For any such policy to be effective, there had to be something to attract "moderates," and one of the main ways to do this was to provide administrative and government jobs. Therefore a "Nigerianization" policy began in the civil service. In addition, newly devolved regional government encouraged a scramble for constituency and the formation of regionalist parties. Exempt from elections, during the 1950s salaried "traditional" emirs and chiefs from the north consistently argued against independence and even home rule in the regional and federal assemblies.

Labor attempted to counter this with new trade union bodies using overtly socialist language. The Nigerian National Federation of Labour (NNFL), formed in 1949, produced a paper with the motto "Towards the creation of the socialist republic."[33] The All-Nigeria Trade Union Federation (ANTUF), inaugurated in 1953, declared the need "to organize and unite the trade unions of Nigeria irrespective of creed, nationality, religion, sex and political conception." In addition, it called for the creation of a socialist party "with a view to realizing a Socialist Nigeria."[34] Indeed, there were a number of socialist/Marxist groups in the early to mid-1950s. One, the Nigerian Youth Congress, spread communist ideas across the country and helped form the Socialist Workers' and Farmers' Party, which was banned after the coup in 1966.[35] However, none of these organizations undertook the work of building a base in the working class, despite the apparently sympathetic reception that Marxist agitation received.

The end of colonialism in 1960 marked more a technical than a substantive change in the everyday life of the majority of Nigerians. Most waged employment was still through the state, and most employment in the private sector was by European, predominantly British-owned firms. Colonialism left behind a legacy of a bureaucratically controlled economy geared primarily toward extraction of primary products for foreign markets. While it is important to acknowledge the great political significance of independence, it was not lost on the ordinary workers that they were still poorly paid and largely ignored.[36] The United Labour Congress (ULC) stated in a policy document in May 1962:

> Independence Day, October First 1960, freed us from colonial domination. It did not, unfortunately, free us automatically from colonial institutions. The edifice of privilege remains; only its proprietors are different.... The United Labour Congress of Nigeria will fight against the continuation of this exploitation of class by class as fervently as it fought against imperialism.[37]

The general strike, 1964

On the first day of June 1964, after over a year's brinkmanship with the government, the Joint Action Committee (JAC) pulled the Nigerian working class out on general strike. It was to be two weeks before the government was forced to concede to the workers' demands. Significantly, these were to be binding in the private as well as the public sector. Many individual employers refused to accept this, and in the private sector, strikes went on for another two months. Involved in the strike action were up to 750,000 of the estimated one million wage laborers in Nigeria. Importantly, many of these workers were not initially unionized.[38] Moreover the number of wage earners in workplaces employing over ten workers was only three hundred thousand.[39] The strike therefore pulled behind it many who traditionally had less propensity to take industrial action—domestic servants refused to work and the unemployed joined in the mass political rallies and meetings.[40] Even the police were sympathetic to the strikers' demands.[41]

The labor-nationalist honeymoon of the late 1940s had eventually collapsed in the mire of ethnic/regional factionalism sponsored by the 1947 Richards Constitution.[42] In contrast, 1964 witnessed a general strike against a nationalist government and as a consequence political radicalization took a very different form. Nkrumah in neighboring Ghana had recently taken his left turn toward "African socialism."[43] This began to take root in the unions, although the general strike ensured that an active role was assumed by the working class.[44] It is in this socialist context that the demand for salary restructuring was made. In and of itself it challenged the very existence of the Nigerian state, requiring as it did a more than 90 percent cut in income for some salaried members of the ruling class.

Over the course of the strike, political demands and political understanding grew, as did confidence to challenge the government. When on June 9, the prime minister declared that the strike was a stalemate—"the present position cannot be tolerated any longer"— the western regional branch of the JAC agreed. It suggested that the prime minister should therefore "resign within 48 hours."[45] This exchange helped ensure that the success of the strike was seen as a personal defeat for the prime minister. Calls for political change grew, and one month after the strike as many as 30 percent of workers were calling for some sort of labor party.[46] The JAC enjoyed huge popularity because its militant stance allowed it to represent the whole labour movement and to symbolize the success of the strike.

Over half of wage labour (54 percent) was state employed, and the low wages for workers and contrasting high salaries for top civil servants were seen as deliberate government policy. Also, as over 30 percent of workers were employed by European capital, the government was open to charges of supporting "neo-colonialism" by not supporting workers' demands on (mostly British) foreign employers.[47] The ideology of "development" and "national interest" acted as a brake on working-class activity, but like the colonial administration before it, the nationalist government became known as representing an alien class and possessing interests antagonistic to those of the working class and poor.

After the strike's success the actual increase in real wages was short-lived, as was the generalized interethnic solidarity that the strike had provided. The majority of Nigerians were tied to the land, and thus to state and ethnic political squabbles and competition between regions owing to the federal nature of Nigeria. Communal rioting in the autumn, resulting directly from a dispute over census figures (which would affect levels of regional grants), led to a fiasco in the December elections. The working class was not insulated from these events. The unity of the Nigerian labor movement was, for the moment, over. At the same time, the intelligentsia longed for a "Nkrumah," and the military saw the weakness of the government in the face of the general strike. The field was open for the military to take power, which it did in January 1966.

The civil war

Labor unity collapsed with the disintegration of Nigeria into civil war in 1967. At the time of the Johnson Aguyi Ironsi coup in January 1966, many had supported the military: "populist" in character, the coup appealed to those who opposed the graft and mismanagement of the civilian republic, and who supported Decree 34, which created a unitary state. Believing that it was solely the country's regionalist structure that kept labor from power, labor leaders welcomed the coup as a potential ally for labor—an end to regionalism and the start of labor's march to government.[48] However, the unitary state was a red rag to the politicians and military who were trying to carve out constituencies in the east. Killed in a counter coup attempt in July 1966, Ironsi was succeeded by Yakubu Gowon, who attempted to placate the easterners with the creation of twelve new states.

Blaming ethnic conflict in the north of the country, the oil-rich eastern states seceded under Lieutenant Colonel Ojukwu in June 1967. Often wrongly characterized as a war of Christian Biafra against Muslim Nigeria, the civil war was more about the failure of the federal constitution, political corruption, and, fundamentally, oil wealth.[49] The Biafra secession was trumpeted by the eastern politicians as the only recourse from national oppression by the north and the south. The federal politicians described it as the division of an inseparable nation. More important, however, was the growing value of oil exports and the financial opportunities this money presented to those who could control it. For the federal government the possibility of its loss was inconceivable. By 1967 oil already made up the vast majority of the country's earnings.

Manipulation of ethnic fears and prospects of a northern pogrom of migrant eastern Igbos encouraged parts of the organized labor movement to go along with the secession. Similarly, the federalist labor movement did little to stop the ensuing carnage of the war over Biafra. After mass starvation and military defeat, the erstwhile Biafran government leaders were brought back to the trough of a "national" government, while Biafra lay in ruins.

Mass strikes in the 1970s
The Adebo and Udjoi Commissions

The cessation of the civil war in January 1970 lifted the lid on the pent-up grievances of the Nigerian working class. The Adebo Commission recommended pay raises in the public sector, and smaller Nigerian private employers followed suit. However, many European-owned plants refused their workforces the increase. The new year was ushered in with a train of industrial disputes that led eventually to a government climb-down and a full implementation of the report's findings in the private sector by government fiat. Despite the small size of the working class and the fragmented nature of the labor federations in 1971, the geographical concentration of the working class fostered the cross-fertilization of ideas and boosted workers' confidence.[50] Crucially, the conflict overrode the communal ethnic and religious tensions of Nigeria. Most notably, as secessionist leaders had been welcomed back in Lagos, eastern workers were included in the strikes.

The industrial action itself took many forms. Given that strikes were still illegal, many workers took action that enabled collective self-defense (occupations), or secretiveness (Luddism), and there was also a variety of individual incendiary activities as well as outright coercion of management. Workers ransacked three textile mills, bus drivers deflated bus tires in the depot, and managers were attacked and kidnapped, among other activities.[51]

The events surrounding the implementation the Udjoi Report of 1974 were similar in many respects to those of Adebo. Another commission on wages was required so soon because, in real terms, the Adebo award had been eroded by the customary price rises imposed by market traders and landlords. However, as Diejomaoh points out, the big manufacturers of fuel, tobacco, drinks, and food all chose to put up their prices drastically immediately after the Adebo and Udjoi awards.[52]

There was much debate in the 1960s about whether private sector unions had the potential to lead and initiate strike waves.[53] In any case, the academic debate over the precise role of private sector unions was curtailed by the events of 1975 when private sector unions did indeed lead the struggle.[54] Thus it was demonstrated that the pattern of public sector unions leading those of the private sector was a historical rather than structural pattern.

Labor and economic growth

During the 1970s the oil industry became the main source of Nigeria's wealth, as agriculture had once been. Nigeria's economy thus became based primarily on exploitation of labor involved in oil production. By 1976 Nigeria was the world's seventh largest oil producer at two million barrels a day, and by 1978 it was the world's third-largest exporter of crude oil.[55] It is significant that, of all the mushrooming profits, enough was set aside as investment capital to allow Nigeria to process only half of its domestic petroleum requirements. This can be seen as a symbol of the government's reluctance to invest in a thought-out program of national development. Increasing dependence on oil meant that Nigeria's domestic economy swung with the pendulum of the world price of oil. Just as its receipts quadrupled during the 1973–74 oil price rises, so they would collapse with oil price falls. In the oil boom years, Nigeria embarked on a program of large-scale infrastructural and commercial development, inducing labor migration into vacant manual and civil service jobs as private and public employment increased.[56] The International Labour Organization (ILO) estimates that there were 9.6 million workers in employment in 1981.[57] In any case, it would appear that numbers in waged employment rose dramatically during the 1970s.

Resistance in the 1980s

During the existence of Nigeria's Second Republic (1979–83) every section of the working class was to engage in major strike action, from university lecturers to nurses, from oil workers to magistrates. The two-day general strike in May 1981 represented a departure from previous general strikes in its brevity and intensity. Otobo estimates that between seven hundred thousand and one million workers were involved.[58] Indeed, the Nigerian Labour Congress (NLC) in 1983 publicly called on the state governments of the federation "to surrender voluntarily to the working people of this country if they can no longer govern."[59]

It is with hindsight perhaps a moot point whether the Congress, as representative of the working people, would have actually accepted such power if it had been offered: a power taken by the military in that same year. Nevertheless the working class does appear to have felt able to break state laws with impunity, such as those banning strikes in the oil industry and other "essential" services. Not only was this law little known among rank-and-file oil workers, but those who did know of it generally felt that its imposition would have been industrially counterproductive.[60]

Activities of the Nigerian Labour Congress

While busily issuing decrees limiting working-class self-activity, Obasanjo's military government, anxious to incorporate a labor bureaucracy into the political framework of the state, established the Nigerian Labour Congress as the central labor federation in 1978.

The chief of staff attended the NLC inauguration and said: "I regard this event as a watershed between the 'old unionism' and the 'new unionism' as well as between the disruptive old traditions which had characterized our past trade union development and a new era of constructive trade unionism."[61] This pedigree did not guarantee that everything went the preferred way of the military. Alhaji Sunmonu, previously jailed for his union activities, was elected president of the NLC. Within a year the NLC and the federal government were moving rapidly toward collision.

In February 1980 the NLC published a "Workers' Charter." Widely read by workers, it gave them a window on the political economy of Nigeria. It demanded workplace democracy and a welfare state. It pointed out that the recent "indigenization" policy for industry only served to expand the ranks of "Nigerian exploiters" at the expense of foreign ones.[62] As a result of the charter's publication and a string of May Day rallies, union leaders were denounced as communists and enemies of the state. They apparently accepted the charge. In his May Day address, NLC President Sunmonu had declared:

> The great lesson of May Day is that workers will not achieve anything except through struggle, unity and solidarity. Our objective is to ensure that class and property will be wiped out of our society once and for all time. In the final end of the struggle, there should be no property because there will be no capitalism.[63]

Some concessions were wrung out of the recently elected civilian president, Alhaji Shehu Shagari, in negotiations during March–April 1980, but in practice they were ignored and a strike began on May 11, 1981.[64] In the weeks before the strike, the government-controlled mass media attempted to split the class by claiming the strike was "political"—communist—rather than "economic," and in any case blaming the working class for the galloping inflation and their own poverty. The strikers included in their ranks "essential service" workers banned from striking, and oil workers who faced the death penalty or twenty-one years' imprisonment under Decree 35 of 1975. The state's immediate response was repression, arrests of union leaders, and media misinformation. During the strike, most economic activities were brought to a halt. Most cities were without water and electricity, and transport was impossible as buses, trains, and even taxi drivers joined the strike. The strike was called off when the government agreed to award a substantial pay raise across the board.

For all of 1982 the country was paralyzed by strikes and industrial action consistently supported by the NLC.[65] At the end of 1983 the Manufacturing Association of Nigeria (MAN) described the year as the worst in two decades. If anything, disputes intensified during 1983, as state governments either would not or could not pay their employees. The situation was such that in July the NLC was obliged to threaten a national general strike.[66]

The Buhari coup

The military coup of December 31, 1983, led by Brigadier Sani Abacha, was again generally welcomed as a preferable alternative to the redundant and corrupt civilian republic. The following day it was announced that the head of state was Major-General Muhammed Buhari. *West Africa* wrote: "the mood of the country now is anybody-but-the-politicians."[67] In the first few days, the military scored points on a number of issues. In response to the widespread shortages, soldiers were ordered to break open warehouses thought to contain consumer goods, and doorstep auctions were held of household essentials. Prices in shops and markets fell as soon as it became known that armed soldiers were intervening to force down exorbitant prices. The Nigerian Union of Railwayman even suspended its planned strike as a mark of "respect" to the new regime.[68]

In 1979 the military had handed government back to an elected civilian administration under President Shagari. Initially the military government's austerity plan was dropped as oil wealth began to fill the Treasury coffers. In contrast to the first years of the republic, "retrenchment," the closing of plant and the sacking of workers followed just a few years into the regime. In the labor-intensive textile industry, for example, more than half of the workforce of two hundred thousand was retrenched between 1980 and 1984.[69] By 1982 it had become common for lowly government employees to be up to six months or even a year in wage arrears.[70] A depressing scene is documented for the working class: poor, often homeless, and with family members at each other's throats.[71] The 1981 strike brought into focus the direct connection between "business activities," government policy, and the miserable lives of the working class. The mass retrenchment of workers in various industries was directly traceable to specific government policies and the considerable financial mismanagement and official corruption that dominated the private sector.[72]

The broadly favorable response to the new military takeover in December 1983 is a clear indication that the civilian government was held responsible for the economic collapse. The sole reliance on oil meant that, as a result of the precipitous decline in oil production, exportation, and revenues in the 1980s, the government was unable to mediate class contradictions effectively and keep development projects afloat. The first casualties of declining oil wealth were the workers.

The experience of the NLC leadership during the Second Republic demonstrates the failure of too mechanical an approach to the question of bureaucratizing labor—the way trade union leadership can become a conservative force cut off from the rank and file. There are always tensions between the leadership and the rank and file, and a union federation of such recent formation, thrust into the experience of "retrenchment" under Shagari, was in no position to exercise the strongly moderating influence over the working class that its sponsors had hoped; it did not have the necessary residual respect gained over years of struggle. Indeed, an early attempt it did make at moderation had no resonance. It could be argued that Sunmonu's NLC did play a largely unrecognized role in keeping revolutionary declarations merely at the level of rhetoric, but the NLC nevertheless offered significant support to labor struggles, while at the same time presenting no practical political critique upon which to base a serious bid for state power.

The struggle for democracy

Babangida and the economy

On taking power in 1985 the central issue facing the new military leader, General Ibrahim Babangida, was the servicing of Nigeria's foreign debt. The International Monetary Fund (IMF) proposed a structural adjustment program (SAP)—a stiff set of measures designed to cut living standards for the bulk of the population in return for a rescheduling of current debt and an extension of loans. Babangida gained popular kudos for going out of his way to reject the SAP package as neocolonialism before going ahead with many of the very same measures under the guise of their being Nigerian. And just as with the IMF SAP, it was the poor and the working class who had to pay for the restructuring and the rich who were to gain. The Naira was devalued, the financial sector was deregulated, subsidies were cut, taxes were increased, and overall government spending was slashed, especially on health, education, transport, and communications. By 1993 the economic crisis was hitting hard. In August that year, the chairman of a transnational company complained, "at the moment nobody is looking after the economy."[73] Or as the Nigeria Employers' Consultative Association (NECA) put it, "the economy seems to have been abandoned."[74]

The 1991 World Bank report put Nigeria at thirteenth lowest per capita income in the world; per capita income dropped from $1,000 in 1980 to just $300 in 1993. The GDP in U.S. dollars fell from $99 billion in 1980 to $37 billion in 1990. By 1993 Nigerian workers typically took home 20 percent of their 1983 wages in real terms. Labor costs in the textile industry were lower even than in India.[75] Concomitant with this, between 1986 and 1992 Nigeria was a net exporter of some $4 billion per year in debt repayment.

The pro-democracy strikes, 1993

From July 5 to 7, 1993, Lagos and other principal cities in Nigeria erupted in massive pro-democracy demonstrations calling for an end to military rule and the installation of the civilian president-elect. The financial centers and the civil service were closed down, as were gas stations and most markets and factories. The pro-democracy demonstrations were mostly good-natured and appeared to enjoy widespread support. One eyewitness reported that "the bonfires lit by unemployed youths may have given the wrong impression of the nature of the protests, the fact is that they enjoyed the support of the nation's middle and upper middle class.... They featured the working class, students, market women and youth."[76] But on July 7, under the auspices of senior army commander Sani Abacha, the federal army waded into Lagos to "restore order" and began by shooting dead around 150 people, while hundreds of others were arrested by the State Security Service (SSS).

The demonstrations had been convened by the recently formed Campaign for Democracy (CD) and other civil rights groups, which called on citizens to block the roads and stay away from work as a means of forcing Babangida to release the results of the recently held presidential election. The polling had been on June 12, 1993, and the Social Democratic Party (SDP) candidate, Moshood Abiola, had been the front runner when the poll results were annulled on June 23. Multimillionaire businessman Abiola later distanced himself from the pro-democracy demonstrators, who had chanted pro-Abiola slogans and were shot for their troubles by troops called in by his fellow SDP member, the state governor of Lagos.

From August 12 to 14, to achieve a "passive dislocation of civil society" a renewed stay-away was called by the CD.[77] The protests were well organized, with leaflets supporting the stay-away circulated throughout Nigeria, even inside military barracks.[78] The protest was a complete success in the South and East, and confounding the machinations of the government, protests were also seen in the northern towns of Kaduna and Kano.[79] While the information secretary, Chukwumerije, claimed that the protest was a complete failure, another minister was issuing a warning of dismissal to those civil servants refusing to go to work.

The street protests and the widespread stay-aways from work involved state and federal employees but also private sector workers. This section of demonstrators could have been far more powerful if the NLC had from the beginning developed a policy of collective strike action organized from workplaces to oust the military—in other words, a political general strike. Instead the CD was left in the driving seat. That there were several excellent responses to the stay-aways and pro-democracy street demonstrations only serves to show the anger that existed. It was not until the protests began on July 5 that Babangida was forced to concede that he would leave office. An Interim National Government of nominated civilians was to take office on August 27. On July 7, the same day as the army was sent in to retake the cities, the Social Democratic Party and the National Republican Convention agreed to participate in the proposed interim government.

The NLC strategy

The National Executive Committee (NEC) of the NLC met on August 17, 1993, to consider its next move, given that information had been circulated anonymously that three union leaders were to be included in the interim government. In order to regain the initiative from the military, a strike ultimatum was issued for the immediate release of the election results. It stated that, were military rule to continue past August 27, "in the circumstances, trade unions will resume their historic role as during the anti-colonial struggle."[80] Noticeably, Abiola did not feature in the plan and power was to be handed to the Senate leader.[81] Wary of previous sellouts, on August 24 around two thousand workers invaded the NLC offices to ensure that the NEC decision to strike was upheld. Haruna Yakub of the Dock Union said, "we are here to ensure that our strike is not sabotaged this time around."[82]

For good measure the fifty-thousand-strong Nigerian Union of Petroleum and Natural Gas Workers (NUPENG) made a more overt announcement for an indefinite strike if Abiola were not sworn in as president by August 27. Most oil workers walked out. Civil servants began their strike on the first day back after the long weekend of Eid-el Mahlud. Airports shut down and military air-traffic controllers were drafted into Lagos International Airport. Oil companies claimed that export production was not affected, but Bonny oil terminal could only load during the day because skilled workers were on strike. Sadly the strike was not as successful in parts of the north, and the Katsina state NLC chair actually instructed his members to work as normal.

Babangida announced his resignation on August 27, and on August 29 the acting head of state, Chief Ernest Shonekan, felt forced to release imprisoned civil rights campaigners and to promise cancellation of fuel price increases. These three facts provided a cover for the NLC to call off the strike after September 2 without any movement by the government on the question of democracy. There was considerable dissatisfaction with the outcome of the strike and many delayed their return to work.

With this outcome the NLC managed to appear almost wrong-footed over the general strike. The demand for Abiola to be sworn in was not in the strike ultimatum, and once Babangida had resigned, the demand for the Senate leader to become president was not one that inspired the popular imagination. At the time of the June presidential elections, most people were not particularly concerned with Abiola as long as Babangida went, hence the low electoral turnout—whichever way you voted was against Babangida. It was only in the intervening period that a strong national pro-Abiola current had developed.

Military regimes are unstable in recession, especially when they are trying to play cat-and-mouse with an electorate. Due to their very political exclusivity they are vulnerable to counter-coups from within, but unlike in social democracy where there is a plurality of elected parties, from without they are vulnerable to little other than a genuine mass movement. It is only during periods of crisis, when the military is appearing vulnerable and there is no established or credible parliamentary force, that an outcome involving one or both of these options, a mass movement or a counter-coup, is possible.

In 1993 the Nigerian working class was the force that swept away Babangida. But it did not go far enough. With a strong and militant general strike across Nigeria, an organizational pole of attraction would have existed for the population to rally around. If workers had occupied their workplace and organized on that basis, there might well have arisen a demand not only to get rid of the military, but also to sweep away the whole edifice of state and army that gives rise to the corruption and oppression facing workers under both military and civilian regimes. In the medium term, only if working-class anger could be defused by the NLC could a democratic solution be avoided for the incumbent military.

The Abacha coup

On November 17, 1993, Sani Abacha, now a general, announced a coup against the Interim National Government. On the following day, all elected bodies and political groupings were dissolved. Military or police chiefs replaced the elected state governors. A military Provisional Ruling Council (PRC) was announced, including a smattering of civilians. Some human rights campaigners even endorsed Abacha as a pro-democrat who would re-civilianize Nigeria. Meanwhile, the NLC called an indefinite general strike to begin on November 15 in protest against punitive 700 percent rises in the price of fuels. There was a general belief that the strike was going to last for some time, and some panic buying occurred. The strike was well supported, as organizers had been dispatched from Lagos across the country to explain the issues and the necessity for solidarity. As the strike progressed, more and more of the states that had initially not joined the strike walked out in the face of government indecision. The strike was finally called off after the new military government under Abacha promised to limit the fuel price rise to "only" 400 percent. With the dissolution of parliament and the two political parties, and with Abacha's center of government at Doddan barracks in Lagos, the military was firmly in charge.

The pro-democracy strikes, 1994

In the weeks leading up to the anniversary of the June 12, 1993, elections, Abacha arranged the arrest of hundreds of pro-democracy demonstrators, and declared that he would not stand for "confrontation or subversion" from any quarter.[83] As it turned out, pro-democracy demonstrations were modest. Nevertheless president-elect Moshood Abiola declared himself president of Nigeria. He was soon arrested and charged with treason. Demands grew to have him released and installed as head of state.

In pursuance of this aim, on July 4, 1994, NUPENG began one of the most bitter and economically painful strikes in Nigerian history. It was to last almost nine weeks and at times included almost all of the onshore oil and associated industry workers in Nigeria. Wariebe Agameme, NUPENG president, had earlier replied to government claims that a strike would be illegal and politically motivated by pointing out that, on the contrary, "the government itself is illegal"; "And is the seizure of power by the military not politically motivated?"[84] Fellow oilworkers in the technical and white-collar union PENGASSAN joined the action on July 12. By the end of that week, bank workers, nurses, teachers, and others had all joined the strike. For good measure the Lagos NLC chapter came out of the national federation unilaterally.[85] There was even a pro-democracy demonstration by farmers in Oyo state. Over the next few weeks the strike wave spread sporadically across the country. On August 3, 1994, the NLC leadership was pressured by its members into calling the Nigerian working class out on an indefinite political general strike against the military and in support of Abiola. Despite this the strike was called off after only two days, the leaders having received no guarantees or assurances from the government.

Abacha's regime applied a sophisticated cocktail of bribery, intimidation, and trickery to try and break the oil strike. By the end of July an estimated twenty-five million Nigerian naira had been spent just on breaking the strike of the PENGASSAN members at the key Nigerian National Petroleum Corporation.[86] This proved a short-lived victory, as both NUPENG and PENGASSAN chapters rejoined the strike in mid-August. As in 1993, the propaganda machine went into full swing, with press releases occasionally finding their way into the lazier foreign news reports.[87]

In frustration, on August 17, Abacha decreed that all national and state bodies of NUPENG, PENGASSAN, and the NLC were dissolved, and placed them all under his nominees.[88] Abacha later threatened all oil workers with instant dismissal if they were not back at work by August 25. Some 10 percent of the two hundred thousand oil workers were scabbing during the strike, but on the day that Abacha made the threat almost nobody went to work. In the evening the labor minister, Ogbemuda, ordered them all to be sacked en masse. The move was a pointless measure, as everybody involved knew that if the oil fields were to return to full production, sooner or later the striking oil workers would have to be reinstated as the only skilled labor available. Tackling the problem from the top, on the following day it was announced that the boards of almost all state-owned companies and federal agencies were henceforth dissolved, including the Nigerian National Petroleum Company.

The oil strike and the state

"Nigerian politics is chiefly about getting access to a share of the oil money. Now that money is under threat," explained the London *Economist*.[89] As long as oil keeps flowing, the rest of the economy can be overlooked. A general strike and consequent collapse of everyday services affects the working class, and the middle class, and can even on occasion bring inconvenience to members of the ruling class and junta, but an oil stoppage is totally crippling. Oil accounts for about 60–70 percent of Nigeria's GDP, and around 98 percent of its exports. The problem Abacha faced with the oil strike is that the stoppages on the onshore fields began to bite both abroad in terms of exports and at home in terms of having funds to distribute around the country. Access to, and manipulation of, the government spending process had by the 1980s and 1990s become the "golden Gateway to fortune."[90] However, the oil strike itself had less effect than might have been expected, for the simple reason that much of the capacity for domestic fuel was already offline.[91]

When it became clear that oil production was continuing apace from offshore rigs, on July 25, 1994, in a demonstration of internationalism, PENGASSAN and NUPENG called on the expatriates working the offshore rigs to join the strike. Shell's onshore wells produced very little oil during the strike and accounted for a large part of lost production. For oil that was lifted, four out of seven export terminals were strikebound by July 15. Shell was forced to declare force majeure, enabling it legally to default on oil supply contracts.

The Nigerian economy was in free fall during 1993–94. Even before the renewal of the pro-democracy demonstrations, non-oil exports fell from $16 million in January to $5 million in March 1994. Government revenues were kept going by the simple expedient of printing more money.[92] This helped push inflation to 60–70 per cent. Real food prices doubled or tripled in the few months before the oil strike. In industry, by the middle of August 1994, 60 percent of factories were closed either because of the strikes or for lack of fuel or power, or both.[93] Ironically, leading financiers were often in favor of the aims of the oil strike despite themselves. One was quoted as saying: "Some people are saying that the workers are making political demands, but the workers are right. There is no way you can solve the economic problems without resolving the political crisis."[94]

Recent protest movements in Nigeria

The widely condemned execution of environmentalist Ken Saro-Wiwa and eight colleagues in 1995 demonstrates the violence endemic to the Abacha regime. There was little to commend Abacha:

when he died on June 8, 1998, a columnist described him as "the most ruthless maiming and killing machine Nigeria has ever known in peacetime."[95] Abdulsalami Abubakar, his replacement, immediately released a number of political prisoners: CD leader Ransome-Kuti, two oilworkers' leaders and ex-president Obasanjo. It was former President Olusegun Obasanjo who in May 1999 became Nigeria's first elected head of state since 1983.

Nigeria must be the only oil-rich country where a government, not content with being enriched by a rise in the international price of oil, then attempts to further impoverish the population with punitive domestic fuel price rises. In December 1998 and January 1999, when fuel jumped from N11 to N25, there were widespread demonstrations. Again in December 1999, Adams Oshiomhole, NLC president, warned against any fuel price rises being tied to Obasanjo's privatizing budget for 2000, with a threat of a general strike, and rallies in January.[96]

On June 1, 2000, gas prices were raised to N30 per liter, leading to an immediate doubling of transport fares. The NLC gave an ultimatum for the rise to be reversed or it would call a general strike. Obasanjo kept the price rise and the strike began. Oshiomhole was frank in pointing out that, as the largest civil organization in the country, the NLC had a duty to provide leadership to all those affected by the rise, and to canvass the active support of market traders, area (street) boys, and the rural poor. Flying pickets went to non-unionized factories to give the workers confidence to join the strike. The upswell of support meant that soon even state governors joined the campaign. The aims of the strike were very well supported across the nation. It was widely known that the price rise, privatization, and spending cuts were all part of the package being demanded by the IMF. A public sector strike was actually called on the occasion of an IMF team visit shortly after.

Ethnicity, regionalism and national organization

"Muslim–Christian" violence has been widespread in Nigeria since the 1980s and more recently ethnic violence has erupted between many communities, including some in the oil states of Itsekiri, Urhobo, and Ijaw, and in June 2001 in Nassarawa state between Hausa and minority Tiv-speaking communities. Thousands have died in these clashes. However, in 2001 alone over four hundred people died as a result of fires and explosions of poorly maintained oil facilities built in the middle of the villages and towns in the oil states.[97] Crime and violence are endemic, resulting in thousands of deaths each year. It is sometimes easier to blame another group with which you live rather than to scrutinize the corrupt politicians, officials, and international oil companies. Crime is so widespread that some state governments have become popular for actually employing criminal groups as "state" vigilantes. We can say that the state itself is the largest danger to public safety through lack of spending on health and sanitation. Nigeria is a very dangerous place to live.

Regionalism and ethnic strife are part of the Nigerian body politic. The state's original 1947 constitution enshrined this principle in its division of Nigerian administration into three competing regions.[98] Later, Babangida allowed only two parties, in an arrangement supposedly aimed at undermining the development of regionalist parties oriented toward "ethnic" politics. In previous republics, parties had mobilized ethnic divergences within Nigeria to their own ends, attempting to fuse an ethnic group into a mythical common identity of interest against "ethnicities" from other regions. Upon election and access to federal cash—"chop"—politicians could fund their own fiefdoms and disseminate patronage: the payoff for this political support. This type of politics rose to a pinnacle during the Second Republic, when huge amounts of money were looted from the state coffers.

The creation by governments of more and more states has been promoted as an attempt to cut away the basis of "chop" politics; the dismembering of larger regional states and the creation of many (now thirty-six) smaller ones was intended to preclude the creation of "ethnic" fiefdoms. In reality, however, these changes fueled continual demands by self-styled leaders of smaller and smaller "ethnic" milieu for their "own" states. The average state population today means that the number of voters needing "ethnic" mobilization to secure a place at the trough of federal "chop" has come within the grasp of more modest aspirants. Smaller states mean more, if weaker, contenders for federal power.

Football provides a fine example countering this turmoil. The whole country supports the Super Eagles without apparent regard for religion or ethnicity. The state is divorced from this support. Fans can cheer the Eagles, support the flag, wear the strip, and sing against the military and for democracy. Nigeria is otherwise bereft of pan-national organizations. The army structure itself is grounded in the north–south divide. The only sizeable national organization across Nigeria is the NLC. This is the reason why the federal government is wary of it and why the NLC plays a pivotal role in Nigerian politics.

Conclusion

The mass strikes in Nigeria's history have been frequent, effective and political. The November 1993 general strike is a case in point. It was called in protest against fuel price rises, yet it was held in a context of a high level of political mobilization and was clearly regarded as a threat to the state. A mass or general strike, which is of a subjectively economic nature, brings upon itself an objectively political character.[99] A strike in one workplace demanding higher wages is economic. A strike demanding a higher minimum wage, or lower fuel prices across the country, becomes political.

One of the perennial problems facing capitalist rule in Nigeria is the deep divisions between the various sections of the ruling class, in terms of core interests and regional and ethnic cleavages. It is in these spaces that the working class is able to wedge open huge gulfs in the ruling power of the state. It is in this direction that future struggle will succeed. Repeated military coups are usually justified as correcting regionalism and corruption. However, the army has proved itself at least as chauvinist and greedy as any civilian government.

Military government can be a very useful form of capitalist rule in a developing economy that is growing. Because of its access to coercive force, it can act in a more authoritarian manner toward both working people and individual capitalists than many other types of bourgeois government. Less constrained by political competition and censure, a strong military regime can to an extent ride roughshod over vested interests in the pursuit of generalized capitalist development. With hindsight business was happy with military control of Nigeria in the 1960s and 1970s. The Gowon and Murtala/Obasanjo regimes constituted a "modernizing" force, bringing in laws and regulations on banking, insurance, companies, and taxation, and generally laying down a legal foundation for a modern capitalist economy.

Those of us with a consistent interest in the working class should perhaps take the often-used labor rhetoric of taking state power more seriously. Time and again it has been shown that when popular anger has forced unions to foster good organization and militant political leadership, the working class has been able to act as a class. The rich history of class struggle in Nigeria has shown a class in the process of learning to know itself. There is a definite opportunity for revolutionary Marxist politics to learn from the Nigerian working class.

Some years ago Cohen wrote on the subject of African labor history that there is "more and more" agreement about the questions that need to be asked. Crucially, "we must attempt...to help bring about a tradition of analysis of the working class struggle."[100] Marx suggested why it is important to build a tradition of analysis, but only in order to encourage the tradition of working-class struggle: "The philosophers have only interpreted the world, in various ways; the point is to change it."[101]

INTERVIEW WITH FEMI ABORISADE

Imprisoned by military governments throughout the 1980s and 1990s, Femi Aborisade is an active socialist, trade unionist, and pro-democracy campaigner. He is the general secretary of the National Conscience Party (NCP), formed in 1994 in the wake of the nationwide pro-democracy demonstrations. A radical organization, it stands in total opposition to privatization and campaigns for free access to public services for the poor (Centre for Labour Studies, Ibadan, May 2001).

Can you explain what political activity you have been involved in since the 1970s?

As a student at The Polytechnic, Ibadan, in the late 1970s, I was a member of the Marxist Socialist Youth Movement and later its secretary-general. During my compulsory one-year National Youth Service Corps (NYSC), a national program for Nigerian graduates before engaging in any employment, I served with the Ondo state branch of the Nigeria Labour Congress (NLC) in 1982–83 as its education officer. After the service year, I was employed by the national headquarters of NLC—the central labor organization—as education and administrative officer.

I held that position till 1986 when I was sacked on the grounds of "liberating" education programs....The trade union bureaucracy felt threatened by the kind of questions which workers who attended the programs were asking in their various industrial unions.... In 1986, some political associates and I started the publication of a news organ called *Labour Militant*, of which I was the editor. In 1988 and 1989, I was detained for four months and nine months respectively by the military junta for publishing special editions of *Labour Militant,* which denounced state clampdowns on the NLC.

I have ever since been involved in the human rights and pro-democracy movement in Nigeria.... Many times I was detained without trial by the military. For example, in 1996, I spent ten months in detention for leading a mobilization against the undemocratic political transition program of the Abacha junta.

Can you say something about what the NCP stands for?

It was formed to campaign against continued military rule and for the actualization of the June 12, 1993, elections—meaning that the civilian winner of that election should be sworn in as Nigeria's president. Its program is essentially based on access of people to social services as a fundamental right. The party rejects privatization and insists that under its government, the privatized enterprises will be re-nationalized. Its chairman is an extremely well-known human rights crusader—Gani Fawehinmi. I am the national general secretary.

Is there any difference in how the NLC operates under Adams Oshiomhole, compared to the pro-democracy period under Pascal Bafyau?

Pascal's leadership was under military dictatorship. Adams' current leadership is under a civilian regime that has just succeeded the military. On the issue of Adams giving state chapters of NLC more responsibility in terms of strikes without worrying that they get out of control: no doubt, there are more activities, strikes, etc., now than under Pascal. But appreciate that, first, workers have gained increased confidence under the current dispensation, and second, more often than not, the leadership tails the movement rather than leading it. This was the case particularly during the 1998–99 strikes for a minimum wage, which dovetailed into Adams' leadership.

In other cases where struggles start at the initiative of the leadership, such struggles often end up being undermined by the intervention of the NLC leadership. Many workers and leaders of NLC state chapters complained that Adams' intervention made them accept something below what they set out to achieve.

The weaknesses of Adams' leadership are not clearly seen by many workers because they believe that the NLC under him [Adams] is better than under Pascal, forgetting that he was part and parcel of Pascal's setup. Besides, some gains are being made—no matter how minimal.

How did the state takeover affect the NLC in 1994 and since?

Simply put, the imposition of sole administrators on the NLC, NUPENG, and PENGASSAN [oil unions] meant the workers lost a collective voice. The NLC merely existed as a formality. In reality, it had collapsed and was of no relevance to the workers. The class enemy was running the organization.

The truth is that some ordinary workers argued that one of the most effective ways of resisting state takeover was for no official to hand over to the military-imposed administrators. That would have led to arrest and detention. That would have increased the number of activists in detention. But it would have also increased pressure on the military junta.

It was lack of readiness on the part of unionists to risk their lives and freedom that left the vacuum for human rights activists who were not in any unions. And without any mass base, the human rights activists are generally recognized to be the saviors of Nigerians in terms of the struggle to terminate military dictatorship. Of course, the outstanding role of the leaders of the oil workers was an exception.

What is your attitude to the nationality question in Nigeria that has seen recent and terrible so-called ethnic and religious divisions?

The organizations that I belong to and the unions where I have influence maintain that the right to self-determination, which includes secession, is a universal democratic right. However, the solution to the economic problems that make people demand a breakup of the country do not lie in dismembering the country. We therefore focus on access to social services being constitutionally recognized as a fundamental right. We appeal for the unity of the oppressed people from all nationalities against the oppressors from all nationalities.

We condemn violence on the part of all ethnic militias but we explain that the state should be held responsible for their excesses. In the absence of a democratic, people-oriented government, a breakup of the country will be inevitable in the long run. Political stability appears far from Nigeria.

How has the Nigerian labor movement responded to SAP and privatization in recent years?

The NLC leadership officially accepts privatization. In fact, Adams is a member of an official body, the National Council on Privatization (NCP). This is a body that supervises the wholesale privatization of public enterprises, leading to loss of jobs by several thousands of workers.

A counterrevolution has taken place. The ownership structure of the public sector of the Nigerian economy has been changed fundamentally—from state-owned enterprises to wholesale privatization. There is no resistance to this historic development. The [NLC] leadership opposes privatization only in selective non-strategic cases like the National Arts Theatre.

What attitude has been taken to globalization and the international institutions, the IMF and World Bank?

Globalization is being presented as a force operating beyond human control. This perspective must be combated. The unions ought to explain to their members that the processes leading to globalization are consciously designed out of the interest of multinational companies (MNCs) and their financial institutions. Unions must insist that production be for need, not profit. They must demand the global standards of respect for the right of unionization and access to social services as a fundamental right.

At every new phase of the relationship between the northern capitalist countries and the so-called Third World, the economic and political structure subsists only on the basis of alliances between forces. Globalization, or its reality in Nigeria, which is privatization, has taken root on the basis of the alliance between the Nigerian ruling class and international capitalism.

In fact, old-style imperialism would have been shocked at the ease with which they secured the consent of top labor leadership in pushing through the privatization program in Nigeria and across the world for that matter.... The challenge for trade unions today is to resist privatization.

For years people have thought of the African working class as some kind of labor aristocracy and therefore unable to successfully lead other oppressed groups to challenge political power. What do you think about this thesis?

The truth is that the other oppressed strata have never on their own opposed the demands of workers for improved conditions. They have never seen workers' demands as being in conflict with theirs. The ruling class usually whips up sentiments that the demands of the workers make it difficult for the state to attend to the needs of the other oppressed groups.

Historically, the ruling class in Nigeria engages in this divisive argument each time labor demands an increase in the national minimum wage. But over the years, others have come to realize that the lot of the workers determines their own lot and that indeed they have a common interest. When workers are not paid or are poorly paid, the poor peasant farmers and the poor petty traders (mainly women) know from their own experiences that their sales suffer. In an age of increasing unemployment, there are several dependents on the worker, and they have come to appreciate that their interests and that of the worker (who sustains their survival) are the same.

How important is international solidarity among workers?

This is absolutely necessary. The pro-democracy movement was strengthened by international support. Without trade union solidarity and direct worker-to-worker contacts and solidarity internationally, the confidence of the workers to fight is seriously undermined. Internally today, Nigerian workers have been coerced. With a fighting leadership, they will rise. But the current leadership is not inspiring on fundamental issues. The leadership fights the symptoms (opposition to price increases, de-unionization, wage cuts, etc.) but accepts the root cause of the problems—liberalization, privatization, deregulation, etc.

There has been some talk in the past about forming a genuine labor, workers' party in Nigeria. What do you think about this?

Any party must have a people's needs–driven program as opposed to the market-driven economic one. If the Adams-led NLC sponsors a party, it will most likely adopt privatization just like the NLC's official line. In such a situation, the appeal it may have among workers will not be sustained for long. There will be no fundamental differences between it and other bourgeois parties. A party sponsored mainly by the NLC will sooner or later disappoint the huge and revolutionary expectations of the masses.

After the collapse of Stalinism more then ten years ago, does left-wing politics appeal to ordinary Nigerians?

Yes, tremendously! From my own involvement in the National Conscience Party (NCP) I know that ordinary people want fundamental changes. It is the only party known to be in opposition currently in the country. The major problem is the determination on the part of the ruling class to commercialize the electoral process.

Perseverance and consistency in showing that there is an alternative worldview from the view of deprivation will rally forces for change in the long run, nationally and internationally. There is a need to build international support for local struggles in the labor movement. The collapse of the deformed workers' states in the former Soviet Union and other Eastern European countries has forced the leadership of the labor movement into the full embrace of imperialism. They lack confidence in the ability of the rank and file to fight and change society. They believe reaching an accommodation with the state and imperialism is the only pragmatic way out. If international support for local struggles wins some concessions, it will play a strong role in boosting the confidence of the working class and oppressed. It will facilitate the process of winning them over once again to the ideas of genuine Marxism and discourage them from looking up to their class enemies, the IMF/World Bank, etc., for salvation.

With the support of the NLC leadership for privatization, we should not envisage an easy resistance. The only option left is for a rank-and-file movement to develop nationally but also internationally. Rank-and-file workers' solidarity on a world basis offers the only effective way of resisting globalization. I know there are difficulties but they can be overcome with time in the process of practical attempts at collaborational activities. What is crucial at this stage is the will, the vision, the understanding to appreciate the need for building international solidarity. Marx's clarion call is more relevant today than ever before: Workers of the world, unite!

RESISTING THE STATE: THE TRADE UNION MOVEMENT AND WORKING-CLASS POLITICS IN ZAMBIA, 1964–91

Miles Larmer

In October 1991, Frederick Chiluba, the chairman general of the Zambia Congress of Trade Unions (ZCTU) and president of the Movement for Multi-party Democracy (MMD), was elected president of Zambia, ending nineteen years of one-party rule by Kenneth Kaunda's United National Independence Party (UNIP). As well as providing the new president, the trade union movement had been central to the organization of the successful MMD campaign. Trade unions were important to multi-party transitions in a number of African countries in the early 1990s, but nowhere more so than in Zambia, where they had emerged as the de facto opposition to UNIP in the early 1980s, and where the actions of workers had been central to resistance to Kaunda's policies throughout the one-party state era.

Many earlier writers had sought to portray the Zambian working class as apolitical and economistic; a selfish labor aristocracy that had failed to give sufficient support to the national liberation struggle, and which equally failed to support postcolonial nation building, partly because their immediate economic interests were opposed to those of the rural African poor. This thesis was applied to Zambia by writers from establishment and radical traditions alike.[1] Studies of postcolonial labor throughout sub-Saharan Africa tended to assume that African "socialist" governments were acting in the national interest and redistributing national wealth and power. Labor challenges to such governments therefore represented the narrow interests of an urban elite, which through their position in the economy were able to grab more than their fair share of a finite national economic cake, thus preventing their poorer rural cousins from receiving economic support from the state to develop their way out of poverty.

This study attempts to demonstrate that the Zambian working class has in fact been central to the political history of Zambia, because of its position in the economy, its awareness of this position, and its willingness to act upon it in ways that had demonstrable political impact. Workers and their unions struck against the low-wage system that was the basis of colonial exploitation, resisted constant attempts at co-option by the Second Republic one-party state, and played a major part in the transition to multi-party democracy in 1991. They were consistently identified by the representatives of state power and international capital as a major block on their attempts to reform the economy in their own sectional interests. Apparently lacking an explicit ideology, Zambian workers nevertheless acted in ways that demonstrate the enduring relevance of class to understanding postcolonial African political change.

Trade unions under colonialism

From the late 1920s, the colonial backwater of northern Rhodesia was transformed into a major global producer of copper, a vital component in emergent manufacturing and electronic industries. As multinational companies rapidly expanded production in the remote "Copper Belt" region, the recruitment of sufficient and appropriate labor supplies was a key concern. Skilled (white) labor was attracted only by relatively high wages from South Africa and elsewhere, while tens of thousands of unskilled miners were recruited from the African population, mostly subsistence farmers who were now drawn into the cash economy through taxation. The need to minimize labor costs was central to the separation of white and African labor, with the latter recruited on a migrant basis. A system, and ideology, of migrant labor was already well established in southern Africa: Africans were seen as essentially rural and tribal, and worked only for "target" wages. They were not allowed to settle permanently in towns, where they might become "detribalized" and develop identities based on national or class identities, which might subsequently threaten colonial or capital control. This migrant system had the happy (for capital) coincidence of passing the costs of labor reproduction onto rural African societies, and providing a justification for low single-male wages, which helped make Northern Rhodesian copper production among the most profitable in the world. However, the weak colonial state never fully enforced migration controls, and many Africans quickly established themselves as residents of the new towns growing up around the copper mines, where there were 26,023 African miners by 1940.[2]

Colonial complacence regarding native labor was decisively ended by African strikes on the Copper Belt in 1935 and 1940. An increase in poll tax sparked the 1935 strike, which was organized through the Watch Tower sect and Bemba dance societies, and was ultimately put down by force, with six miners killed. Although attempts were made to portray the dispute as an ethnically based riot, the subsequent commission of inquiry heard from a compound manager that "These people form a definite social group quite shorn of anything tribal, they live in a world entirely different to the other natives."[3]

The main focus of anxiety was initially the white mine workers, who brought to the Copper Belt the South African tradition of militant but racially based trade unions. They established the whites-only Northern Rhodesian Mineworkers' Union in 1936, and in 1940 carried out effective strike action, which substantially increased their wages. This provided an instructive example to African workers, who struck two days after the white dispute ended. Their demand for ten shillings a day was coupled with a demand that they should be given jobs reserved for whites and paid the same wage. "Tribal" representatives recognized by the mine companies were unable to control the dispute, which was led by a "Committee of 17" elected by the miners themselves. The strike was well organized and disciplined, but a confrontation between three thousand strikers and 150 working men was put down by troops, with seventeen being killed and sixty injured. This episode put African miners at the center of official concern; a mine compound manager told a further inquiry that "The skilled native is the man who stands on the threshold of the enjoyment of the luxuries of our civilization, he is the man who is most affected by any rise in the cost of living…he is also the person that we can expect industrial trouble from in the future."[4]

The post-war Labour government, influenced by new theories of industrial relations, sought to address and incorporate increasing African demands. In 1947, William Comrie of the British Trades Union Congress (TUC) was dispatched to help establish African unions along "British lines": that is, as non-political bodies that could negotiate over wages and conditions without recourse to industrial action. An African Mineworkers' Union (AMWU) was established in 1949, and a Trade Union Congress in 1951. The majority of the new AMWU officials were clerks and "boss boys", whose interests were not necessarily the same as those of the majority of unskilled miners. However, the reservation of "white" jobs frustrated the advancement of this aspirant group, who sought instead to advance their interests via a problematic alliance with the mass of ordinary miners.

The African union movement preceded the emergence of nationalist organization in Northern Rhodesia, which began in 1948 with the establishment of the Northern Rhodesian Congress (later the African National Congress, or ANC). The problematic relationship between African nationalists and trade unionists provided a foundation for the subsequent belief that organized African workers were an apolitical "labor aristocracy" who were only interested in their own economic position. The emergent nationalist movement protested against the introduction of the Central African Federation (CAF) in

1953, an attempt to ensure that revenues generated from copper mining and African labor were channelled to white settlers, primarily in
Southern Rhodesia. However, the union movement refused to fully
support nationalist protests. Bates argues that "Throughout the nationalist period, the union withheld a major resource from the nationalist parties; it refused to employ the strike weapon in support of
political objectives."[5] This claim is not supported by contemporary reports by the colonial Labour Department, which in 1951 stated that
"The leaders of the African trade unions were all to a greater or lesser
extent concerned with politics and there were periods when political
considerations kept union leaders from devoting a sufficient time to
normal trade union functions."[6]

Unionists were not, however, prepared to place their industrial
power unconditionally in the hands of nationalist leaders. Union culture was dominated by an emphasis on branch level and shop steward
organization and democratic accountability. Epstein described monthly
branch meetings attended by eight thousand miners where "rank and
file members are free to participate in the discussions."[7] The AMWU
demonstrated its power by a three-week strike in 1952, which led to a
subsequent commission awarding significant wage increases. In the
mid-1950s, increased concern about union militancy led the mine
companies to establish a separate white-collar African union, the
Mines African Staff Association (MASA). This was part of a general attempt to co-opt an African elite, which might form a counterweight to
rising mass African expectations of economic and political change,
and more specifically to split the skilled union leaders from their rank-
and-file membership. Despite attempts to make membership of the
new union compulsory for salaried staff, many remained in AMWU.
MASA members were isolated, and abused by women on the streets.[8]

An economic downturn in the late 1950s reduced union militancy,
but also undermined attempts to co-opt an African elite and spurred
the growth of mass nationalist movements. Union leaders and members provided conditional support to the most radical nationalists,

particularly the United National Independence Party (UNIP), which, unlike the ANC, established a successful grassroots organization,[9] with its strongest sections on the Copper Belt. The economic power of mine workers, and their unwillingness to allow all the copper revenues to accrue to the mine companies and white settler society, played a central role in undermining the financial basis for the CAF, which ended in 1962, and paved the way to Zambian independence in 1964.

Transition to a one-party state, 1964–72

Despite its traditions of autonomous organization, the Zambian union movement was relatively weak and divided in the years after independence. The new UNIP government legally established the new Zambia Congress of Trade Unions in 1965, and its first officials were appointed by the Minister of Labour, which led some observers to see the ZCTU as a hopelessly co-opted union movement.[10] Certainly, amid the optimism of the post-independence period and an economic boom, loyalty to UNIP was expressed, and sincerely felt, by union leaders and the majority of Zambians. This was, however, coupled with an expectation that the inequalities and injustices of the colonial era would be addressed. Under pressure from their members, the new Zambian Mineworkers' Union (ZMU) called for strike action to address unequal white and African wages. Under the new Trades Union and Trade Disputes Act, disputes in "essential services," including the mines, had to be approved by the registrar of trade unions. The registrar insisted that elections must be held for national and branch union posts before a strike could take place. With the Unilateral Declaration of Independence (UDI) in (Southern) Rhodesia in 1965, strike plans were called off in the national interest, but the union elections went ahead. UNIP saw these elections as an opportunity to gain control of the ZMU; as Kaunda stated, "We want loyal party leaders also to control the…labour movements. We cannot afford the luxury of calling this undemocratic."[11]

UNIP put forward lists of approved candidates in the union elections, and its regional secretaries attempted to pack meetings with their supporters. However, this attempt to influence the election backfired. UNIP candidates were shouted down in rowdy local meetings, and they won only twelve of fifty-three places available.[12] In defending their autonomy from UNIP interference, union leaders stressed (as they would consistently under UNIP rule) that they were only concerned with "industrial matters," a syndicalist discourse that observers sympathetic to the government cited to justify their argument that organized workers in general, and mine workers in particular, were selfish and unconcerned with political development.

The ZMU signed an agreement with the mine companies in January 1966 that awarded increases of 8–9 percent. This was not satisfactory to the majority of miners, and wildcat strike action broke out in March 1966, beginning at Nchanga and spreading to all four major mines by April 4. Kaunda announced that a commission would investigate pay issues, and there was a return to work by April 14. The subsequent Brown Commission recognized many of the miners' grievances and awarded an across-the-board 22 percent pay increase. The miners had learned that they could not rely on the new independent state and their union leaders to address their needs, and a pattern was set of unofficial strike action as the only way to get results. Subsequent pay awards were made to other workers, which established the "wage leadership" of the mine workers as part of the postcolonial political economy.

Many union leaders were incorporated into UNIP as MPs and ministers,[13] and their loyalty to the state and party was not in doubt at this time. As part of UNIP's corporatist approach, the ZCTU had been given representation on the UNIP National Council, but this body

> was used mainly as the platform for the announcement of policy or new policy initiatives by the President.... It neither served as a forum for debating public policy nor even putting forward alternatives. Yet membership of this body entailed clear obligations towards UNIP with or without participation in its decision-making.[14]

Thus, trade union officials were appointed, apparently as representatives of their members' interests in the new one-party state, yet had no real ability to influence policies. However, despite the loyalty to UNIP of union leaders, and the "genuine efforts"[15] of the ZCTU to educate its members, many workers were unable or unwilling to put the lessons taught into practice. Unconstitutional strikes continued to occur with little or no justification and with monotonous frequency.[16]

The minister of labor railed against union leaders in July 1968: "Why have you tolerated...wildcat strikes? Have you no control over your members? Have your members no respect for you?... If this is so you should not be where you are."[17] UNIP supremacy was undermined by the success of the ANC in the 1968 election, and by growing internal divisions. Kaunda centralized power by taking personal control of all major policy decisions. Partial nationalization of twenty-five major companies was announced in 1969, and in the same year Kaunda wrote to the United Nations Development Program (UNDP) to request help in developing a wages and incomes policy; the UNDP asked the International Labor Office (ILO) to produce a report in this regard. The ILO was highly influential in newly independent nations; the author of its subsequent report had previously claimed that "Probably the biggest single influence on official wage and labour policy in underdeveloped countries has been that of the ILO."[18]

In such countries, the ILO encouraged tripartite cooperation, and extended its remit from labor policy toward the developmental model of "Basic Needs," which accepted the notion of organized workers as part of an urban elite, and which claimed to put the needs of the unorganized, the unemployed, and the peasantry at the heart of national development planning. Kaunda, who regularly attended ILO conferences, was described in a 1970 ILO report as "A firm believer in a strong democratic trade union movement which could play an important role in the economic development of the country."[19]

Professor H. A. Turner, who was sent in 1969 by the ILO to produce this report, had previously identified the problem of rising wage differentials in developing countries, highlighting "the pursuit of orga-nized sectional interests by what may be, in local terms, an already privileged labour aristocracy."[20] Turner proposed that "the basic refer-ence standard for the actual level of minimum wages should...be an estimation of the actual living standards of cultivators in the tradi-tional sector of the economy."[21]

Like the ILO, Turner favored government intervention in em-ployer-labor wage relations and brought to Zambia his experience in advising the British TUC, at a time when its members, having been characterized as "affluent" and aspirational, were being urged by an in-terventionist Labour government to accept productivity deals and wage freezes as part of a "social contract."

Turner recommended the maintenance of wage and price controls, the linking of any wage raises to productivity increases, and the need for increased worker education, in which the ILO could play a promi-nent role. Turner saw the potential solution to these problems in the announcement, in Kaunda's speech to the UNIP National Council in August 1969, of a 51 per cent nationalization of the copper mines: "This initiative materially changed the context of my mission, and provided a basis on which it appeared that some of the solution of the difficult problem of incomes and prices policy might be possible."[22] For Turner, an advocate of state intervention in industrial relations,

> The development of state participation in the major industrial and distributive enterprises means that the Government now stands on the "commanding heights" of the economy, while the use of state stores to reduce the cost of living, and the announcement that work-ers' representatives are to be included in the boards of directors of the major enterprises, should help to create good psychological condi-tions for the acceptance of a national wages policy.[23]

The mine takeover had been widely predicted and was negotiated and implemented by the expatriate economists and advisers who dom-inated Zambia's state bureaucracy, and the mining industry. Although it was presented as a radical extension of national control of the economy, the *Economist* reported at the time that "the shrewdest businessmen in that part of the world have argued for some time that a 49 percent stake in a business whose success is underwritten by government participation may be more valuable than 100 percent of a concern exposed to all the political winds that blow."[24]

The copper price subsequently fell from £700 to £500 per ton in 1970. Management contracts were agreed with the private mine companies, RST and Anglo American, which formed a new joint marketing operation, and which continued to repatriate their share of the profits instead of investing it in Zambia, as the government had asked. Thus, the nationalizations did not deliver additional revenue or increased practical control over this vital national resource, raising the question of why nationalization took place at all. While Kaunda's need to outflank radical opponents within UNIP may have been one factor, more central motivations are revealed by Kaunda's speech announcing the mine takeover. Kaunda shared Turner's concern regarding Zambia's "dual economy":

> Here in Zambia we also face the danger of creating two nations within one. But not along the capitalist pattern. The important division in our society is not that which exists between trade union labour on the one hand and managers and property owners on the other, but between the urban and rural areas. These are the two nations we are running the danger of creating; these are the two parts of our dualism; urban and rural and not so much between labour and employers.[25]

Describing class consciousness as "one of the biggest dangers in Zambia," Kaunda went on:

> There must be no more irresponsibility among workers, among civil servants. Wildcat strikes, official strikes retard development and cause untold harm to the people's economy.... Zambian workers, therefore, must be convinced and committed humanists who, from now on, should know that the improvement of their well-being alone

is not sufficient; they must be concerned about the betterment of the well-being of their fellowmen, particularly in the rural areas where the majority of them find their livelihood.[26]

Kaunda criticized the high level of urban wages, arguing that "the gap between the Zambian in paid employment and his brother in the villages is proportionately greater than between the urban Zambian and the expatriate,"[27] and announced a wage freeze that would continue until Turner's wages and incomes policy was implemented. Kaunda approvingly noted the pledges made at the 1967 Labour Conference, and announced the establishment of works committees, the appointment of workers' representatives to the boards of nationalized companies, and the creation of productivity targets. Thus, it can be argued that the nationalizations are best understood as an attempt by an effective coalition of state and international capital to increase their control over the economy, and over the organized working class, by enabling the state to restrict worker demands in the interests of national development.

The nationalization announcement followed violent clashes on the Copper Belt between UNIP and members of the renamed Mineworkers' Union of Zambia (MUZ), which had declared a dispute following the 1969 budget announcements. The UNIP mayor of Kitwe was shouted down at a mass meeting: "When he warned that the Party would see that the workers lost their jobs if they went on strike, many shouted back, 'It is all right, we will go back to our villages.'"[28]

The strike was ended through conciliation. Union leaders offered support to government economic policy, and ZCTU president Wilson Chakulya pledged to support new productivity targets. The incorporation of the unions into the state was strengthened by the 1971 Industrial Relations Act (IRA). The IRA enforced a "one industry, one union" policy and a mandatory check-off system for the deduction of subs, both measures designed to strengthen trade union organization and finances. The ZCTU was legally recognized as the ultimate representative of Zambian workers. Its member unions had to pay 30 percent of their income to the ZCTU, and needed its permission before declaring a dispute. The IRA also introduced works councils and an Industrial Relations Court; and made strike action in "essential services" (mines, railways, etc.) virtually illegal. The IRA was presumably meant to provide a highly centralized ZCTU with professional organization and structures, which could exercise control over its membership and prevent the problem of unofficial strike action.

There is little evidence of the perspectives of ordinary Zambian workers during this period, but Michael Burawoy's sociological study of mineworkers gives a tantalizing glimpse of their discontent. One young surface worker told Burawoy, "Independence has changed very little on the mines. Though there is nationalization and Zambianization, all these are superficial because white men control everything."[29] Indeed, Kaunda's reforms were seen as making things worse:

> Nationalization has not made any difference. In fact work has become harder than expected.... The pay scales have fallen because the Company has brought in new grades, and when we complain management says our Government has taken all the money in the 51% and that we should not complain to the Companies but to the Government.[30]

Attitudes toward union officials were dismissive—one branch chairman was described thus: "He is a fat man, who moves in a green Zephyr. I don't know him because I just see him move in a car."[31] Regarding strike action, one worker told Burawoy: "When we want to go on strike we just go and without consulting the Union because their policy on strike action is difficult to understand.... They are not strong because they are part and parcel of management."[32]

Thus, the tripartite approach promoted by UNIP and its advisers, and welcomed by senior union officials as giving them a participatory role in national planning, was perceived by these workers as placing their representatives on the side of a hostile company. As one experienced miner put it, "We work harder than we did in the Federal days. Pay scales are low. The Union and the Company work together with the Government to bring in pay groups which have cut our categories and acting allowances."[33] Burawoy later identified the concept of "production politics,"[34] arguing that nationalization and the corporatist one-party state brought national politics into the mine or factory, and turned day-to-day economic struggles between capital and labor into challenges to the political hegemony of the state. Workers' response to the intervention of the state into their workplace struggles appears to have been, in turn, a close identification between economic unionism and political resistance.

In August 1971, a new political challenge to Kaunda emerged, when a previous UNIP vice-president, Simon Kapwepwe, broke with the ruling party to form the United Progressive Party (UPP). There is disagreement about the extent of working-class support for the UPP. Gertzel argues that "urban labour did not, in 1971–72, identify with UPP; their loyalty to UNIP and the Government remained" and that workers were only interested in economic issues.[35] Union leaders had declared their loyalty to UNIP in 1971, but the limited evidence of grassroots unionists' views appears more mixed. The UPP won only one of eleven by-elections in December 1971, in the historically militant mining seat of Mufulira. However, these elections took place amidst widespread repression and violence on the Copper Belt, with UNIP Youth League members stoning UPP candidates.

The UPP used socialist rhetoric (though this was not unlike that of UNIP) and Kapwepwe was regarded as a radical. However, for that very reason, he had as a leading UNIP figure spent much of 1969 trying (and failing) to persuade striking miners to return to work. He had also condemned absenteeism, which "involved an element of drinking."[36] Given their record of political autonomy, it would have been surprising if organized workers were prepared to give unquestioning support to the UPP. Nevertheless, the party was strongest on the Copper Belt, among organized workers and small businessmen. The UPP was banned in February 1972, with the detention of Kapwepwe and 123 others, at the same time as Kaunda confirmed his decision to declare a one-party state. In December 1973, the first one-party state elections were held, in which turnout fell from 77 percent in 1968 to 39.4 percent,[37] with the highest "no" vote against Kaunda being registered in the Copper Belt mining constituencies.

The profits derived from nationalized industries did not find their way to the rural poor, but instead served as the basis of patronage, which helped create loyalty to the one-party state.[38] UNIP's approach to rural development can perhaps best be summed up by the Rural Reconstruction Program (RRP), introduced in 1975, which forcibly relocated the urban unemployed to army-run camps in rural areas, in an unsuccessful effort to boost subsistence agricultural production.

Nationalization, the one-party state and the IRA comprehensively failed to deliver loyalty from Zambian workers. Works councils failed to undermine trade union representation in the state-owned companies, where workers continued to see trade unions as their representatives.[39] Most importantly, the state failed to prevent consistent high levels of unofficial strike action (no workers were prosecuted under the IRA for unofficial action in "essential services"), or to restrict pay demands significantly. This was apparently a reflection of the relative strength, independence and organization of the trade unions at shop-floor level. Rank-and-file workers were willing to take action independently of their leadership, and to remove leaders with whose policies they disagreed. The election of union leaders was a key arena of state–labor conflict throughout the one-party Second Republic. Union leaders regarded as too close to UNIP were regularly removed, and in the early 1970s a younger generation of union leaders were elected. Newstead Zimba, who had been detained in an earlier dispute, was elected ZCTU secretary general in 1971, and Frederick Chiluba became ZCTU chairman general in 1974, defeating the MUZ's pro-UNIP David Mwila. However, such electoral challenges were not always allowed.[40]

Frequently under attack by Kaunda for not stopping strikes, the new ZCTU leaders pledged their loyalty to the one-party state, while resisting further incorporation and defending their right to address industrial issues through syndicalist language. Mine workers' wages fell in relation to the international copper price, but stronger union organization meant that other groups of workers were able to challenge company and government pay restraint, particularly in the public sector. Chiluba, writing in *Workers' Voice*, the ZCTU newspaper started by Zimba, and (aside from church papers) the only independent editorial voice during the Second Republic, defended the unions' right to fight for wage increases:

> The ZCTU is not the alternative to the GRZ [government] so that if the latter fails to achieve its goals or its plans it should not cast its eyes on the former as if we caused the evaporation of jobs in the country.... Besides, there is no guarantee that any wage increase which is forfeited by the workers will be directed to the creation of jobs.[41]

What remained constant was, in Gertzel's words, "The willingness of workers to engage in action that ultimately implies mass confrontation with the government.... Economic discontent...when it relates to perceptions of unequal distribution of wealth, becomes a potential political issue, and a challenge to government policies."[42]

As declining copper and rising oil prices undermined the economy in the mid-1970s, the policies of the International Monetary Fund (IMF) forced the government to remove food price subsidies. The threat of widespread strike action, and what the World Bank subsequently described as "political pressure from the trade unions,"[43] led to the reversal of this decision. As the living standards of all Zambians, apart from those at the very top, declined in the late 1970s and 1980s, and government sought to solve the increasingly acute economic problems by imposing sacrifices on ordinary Zambians, this pressure led to the ZCTU emerging as "the only real opposition to UNIP."[44]

Economic crisis and rising opposition in the 1980s

In 1980–81, proposals to reform local government became the testing ground for the emerging union-state conflict. The reforms, which increased central control over local government and services, were criticized by trade unions as both a centralization of UNIP authority and a waste of money. The MUZ, which sought to defend the relatively high-quality services provided in the mine townships, refused to participate in the new structures, a position endorsed by the ZCTU. Union leaders were expelled from UNIP, which prompted a wave of strike action across the mines.

The extent of the strike wave, which made 1981 the year of greatest lost working days since independence, took union leaders by surprise. The leaders were readmitted to UNIP in April, and both union and party appeared to retreat from confrontation. However, a new mine-based dispute, combined with meal shortages on the Copper Belt, led to a new confrontation and to strikes on the mines and railways. In July, four union leaders (including Chiluba and Zimba) were detained, the first time this had occurred since independence. Calls were made in the ZCTU for a general strike, but instead appeals were made to Kaunda. The conciliatory attitude to UNIP seems to indicate that union leaders were unwilling to confront the one-party state directly at this stage, and instead combined expressions of loyalty to UNIP with a defense of their right to address economic (rather than political) issues.

In 1985, the introduction of Statutory Instrument No. 6 enabled the minister of labor to revoke "check-off" compliance of fees payment, to be used against unions engaged in "political" or "unofficial" strikes. This was identified as a significant attack on the union movement, in dramatic terms by *Workers' Voice*: "1985 will be recorded in the annals of Industrial Relations history in Zambia as the year the basic Trade Union freedom died at the stroke of a pen overnight."[45]

International intervention and advice now came from the IMF rather than the ILO, but the "problem" of urban workers remained at the heart of the discourse of the external advisers, on whom the government continued to rely. The IMF structural adjustment program led to the removal of food subsidies in December 1986, and to riots, starting on the Copper Belt and spreading to other urban areas, leaving fifteen dead. UNIP immediately revoked the food subsidy removal and in May 1987 Zambia broke with the IMF program. In contrast to those critics who seek to identify the ZCTU as managerial,[46] pro-capitalist, and structural adjustment, the ZCTU supported the break with the IMF, and opposed the reestablishment of the relationship with the World Bank/IMF in 1989–90. The subsequent World Bank report found that

> the early demise, in 1987, of the adjustment package imposed by the IMF resulted from an unrealistic (or unconsidered) assumption that the majority of middle and lower income urban Zambians would tolerate pauperization at the hands of a rapidly depreciating nominal exchange rate, notwithstanding the lesson and history of the previous decade,[47]

and that "wage rigidity"[48] was a significant factor in preventing the implementation of adjustment policies. Thus, the labor movement and wider working class emerged as leading opponents not only of UNIP, but also of the international bodies that played an increasing role in economic decision making, and which had devised and implemented an adjustment program subsequently acknowledged to be poorly designed and based on financial projections with little basis in reality.[49]

The role of the ZCTU in the Movement for Multi-party Democracy

In 1989, a return to neoliberal economic policies led to the removal of subsidies to basic foodstuffs, and to increasing discontent. But it was the collapse of state "socialist" regimes in Eastern Europe in late 1989 that was the impetus for Chiluba's widely reported statement to a ZCTU General Council meeting in December, where he called for an end to the one-party state: "This statement by the trade union movement leadership, also formulated as a General Council resolution, was the first public call from the union movement, or other social actors, for multiparty politics."[50]

By this time UNIP had abandoned its efforts to incorporate the ZCTU, and announced a new bill amending the 1971 IRA, further restricting the right to strike and removing the "one industry, one union" clause, thereby encouraging splinter unions and effectively derecognizing the ZCTU. This legislation was passed in 1991, too late to have any effect. Nevertheless, "The demand for the restoration of multi-party politics in late 1989 was directly related to the leadership's perception that the new IRA (1990) threatened the existence of the ZCTU and the organizational cohesion of the Zambian labour movement."[51]

Amid industrial unrest and student agitation, the UNIP National Convention met in March 1990, where calls for multi-partyism were heard. As attempts to pass a new constitution (which gave more power to top UNIP officials) failed in Parliament due to the non-attendance of MPs, the apparent unraveling of the one-party state led Kaunda to announce a referendum on multi-partyism in May 1990. The following month, the IMF program forced the removal of meal subsidies (then accounting for 10 percent of the national budget), leading to riots in Lusaka (where UNIP offices were targeted for attack) and a subsequent coup attempt, which was celebrated on the streets until its failure became clear. The price rise was effectively rescinded and a date for the referendum announced.

The riots were important in establishing the possibility of change, but it was the mass organized base of the ZCTU that served as the real basis for the Movement for Multi-party Democracy. Formed in July 1990, the MMD led a swift and peaceful transition to multi-party rule. Mass rallies (seventy thousand-plus in Lusaka, and two hundred thousand on the Copper Belt) demonstrated huge popular support for the MMD and the impossibility of defeating it with force (Kaunda's interview with Nordlund confirms that he abandoned plans to arrest Chiluba for fear of the consequent unrest). Simultaneously, strikes continued at a high level, with economic demands by the mine workers leading to a three-week strike in September. At this time, the referendum was abandoned; multi-partyism was legalized in December

1990, and a date for a multi-party election was announced. The ZCTU declared its official support for the MMD in October: "Local ZaCTU officials were by 1991 firmly established as local campaign-managers for MMD as the organizational structure of the ZaCTU constituted the MMD campaign organization."[52]

The importance of the union movement was also understood by the non-labor leaders of the MMD, who elected Chiluba as its president and presidential candidate in March 1991. UNIP continued to use legalistic means to detain MMD leaders and disrupt rallies, but to little effect. Chiluba and the MMD won an overwhelming electoral victory in October 1991, in both urban and rural areas.

There is no doubt about the centrality of the ZCTU to achieving political change in Zambia in 1991. One writer argued at the time, that "the ZCTU is today the most powerful non-state association in Zambia"[53] and that "the organizational autonomy of the union movement is one of the main reasons why the trade union movement spearheaded the transition to multiparty democracy in October 1991."[54] Nordlund goes further: "The arguably most powerful civil society actor in Africa throughout the one-party rule era was the Zambian trade union movement."[55] The ability of trade unions to resist co-option and defend their autonomy, often through the tactic of being "apolitical," enabled them to play a crucial role at the time when political transition became possible.

Conclusion

Even before it took power, the MMD (unsuccessfully) sought to restrain strike action in the interests of national development. The MMD portrayed itself as the friend of the working masses, but at its top levels it was increasingly dominated by business and regional interests, and rapidly implemented structural adjustment policies and price rises to an extent never tried by UNIP. The union movement, which had been so effective at resistance to UNIP corporatism, proved far less resistant to the MMD's embrace of the free market. In the context of falling copper prices and rising urban unemployment, it was unable to present an alternative ideology that would provide a rallying point for its members and the wider Zambian poor, whose numbers soared in the 1990s. Despite the MMD's slavish dedication to IMF policies, Zambia's economic decline has increased along with its international debt, while government expenditure on social services has declined rapidly. Zambia has also suffered terribly from the impact of HIV/AIDS.

In 1994, the ZCTU split over MMD proposals to privatize state-owned industries, with unions based in these industries, particularly the MUZ, arguing that it was necessary to engage in the sell-off process;[56] the union movement has subsequently reunited. The negative experience of nationalized industries meant that "workers do not…hold to nationalization as an innately progressive or worker-friendly project…. For the union activists, the bottom line is the protection of jobs and working conditions."[57]

Most labor leaders are not consulted, although the MUZ still appears to have access to the top levels of government. The union movement has withdrawn its support of the MMD, and the headline of the *Workers' Voice* of July 2000 declared, "Boot Out MMD in 2001 Elections."[58] ZCTU president Fackson Shamenda criticized the government for leaving education and health provision to the market, and challenged trade unions to "broaden their appeal to civil society…and form strategic alliances in order to fight injustices and poverty."[59]

As I have attempted to show, the economic importance of organized workers, and the desire of state and capital to control them, has forced their unions, often under pressure from below, to play an important political role at all stages of Zambian history, while maintaining that their role was essentially economic. This contradictory maintenance of an artificial division between economics and politics was in part a defensive reaction to authoritarian colonial and postcolonial governments, which constantly warned unions not to get mixed up in politics. It also reflects the contradictions that beset all union bureaucracies, which may challenge the ways in which economic power affects their members, but whose position rests on accommodation with it.

It is easy to conclude that the union movement's support for the MMD was a mistake and that workers' organizations should have maintained their syndicalist approach to politics. But rather than retrospectively condemning the role of the unions in achieving political changes that have subsequently proven not to have addressed the needs of the organized working class or their rural counterparts, it is more important to recognize that the Zambian union movement has, in repressive circumstances not of its own choosing, enabled the workers' voice to be heard throughout the last seventy years, and to have consistently challenged the power of state and capital. This history seeks to recognize the achievements of Zambian workers; to point to the inherent limitations of confronting this power while unequipped with an ideology that explains its underlying basis; and to suggest that in learning the hard lessons of these struggles, the Zambian working class may find new ideas and organizations that will further their cause in the future.

INTERVIEW WITH AUSTIN MUNEKU

Austin C. Muneku has been working for the Zambia Congress of Trade Unions since the early 1990s. He became involved in politics while he was at high school and was suspended for organizing a political demonstration. Austin continued to be active during Kenneth Kaunda's last decade in power. In the 1990s he was a forthright campaigner for trade union rights in the ZCTU. The decade saw the fall of Kaunda and the rise to power of the Movement for Multi-party Democracy, headed by the ex-ZCTU leader Fredrick Chiluba. This was a period of austerity and privatization that Austin calls "the lost decade for Zambia" (ZCTU National Centre, Kitwe, Zambia, July 2001).

What were the events that have shaped your political development?

I was born on October 13, 1963, almost exactly one year before independence. But what shaped my political background were my early years at high school, called Munali Boys Secondary School. I got suspended in the third form for my part in the school demonstration against poor administration that took place in 1979. When I completed high school my interest in politics continued while I was doing my studies at the University of Zambia. I actively participated in various associations. After university I joined a state-owned company where my interest to work with unions grew. Through a friend of mine who joined ZCTU my work and interest in trade unions continued. He was a major influence on me. In 1993 I joined ZCTU as deputy director of research and economics.

What have been the key moments for you in the struggles that have rocked Zambia and particularly the workers' movement since independence?

Even without an inspirational and visionary leadership, unions in Zambia continued to thrive during the First and Second Republics. At one time ZCTU was regarded as one of the best organized, strongest and most united labor movements on the continent.

Soon friction started brewing between the trade unions and the government. The beginning of this friction started in 1972 when Zambia was declared a one-party state. ZCTU started to resist some of the policies under the one-party regime. The decentralization program was greatly opposed by the ZCTU, leading to some of its leaders being expelled from party organs. In protest the mine workers went on strike. The key concerns were the local government decentralization, free medical services, expulsion of ZCTU leaders, and a deteriorating economic situation.

Another key moment in the trade unions was when they came out strongly against the structural adjustment programs the country was embracing in order to secure the IMF and World Bank assistance. These campaigns led to the 1986 food riots that witnessed mass protests on the Copper Belt against what was perceived as an IMF-imposed price increase on the local staple food, mealie-meal and bread. In 1987 there was another national strike throughout the country against structural adjustment programs.

In 1989 the trade unions resolved to spearhead the campaigns for the restoration of multi-party politics. In response the UNIP government in 1990 amended the Industrial Relations Act with the aim of weakening the ZCTU. The 1990 Industrial and Labour Relations Act removed the mandatory "one union, one industry" rule and automatic affiliation to ZCTU. In the same year the UNIP National Council forced out ZCTU delegates to the convention and consequently the links between ZCTU and the UNIP government were severed.

In the same year the trade union movement was in the forefront of organizing the famous "Garden House Conference" where people from a cross-section of society converged to form the Movement for Multi-party Democracy. ZCTU was the only formation in civil society with structures at all levels, which it used to promote the MMD's campaigns. They were the key element to the victory of the MMD.

Zambian workers play a central part in political developments throughout the Second Republic as an organized working class but without a distinctive class-based ideology. What do you think about this?

I agree that this is not only a weakness but also a major deficiency. The great weakness of the trade unions in Zambia is that in the past they have operated without an ideology of their own—a political ideology that they could use as a bargaining tool or determinant of their alliances with either political parties or civic groups and for their own purposes. Recently this realization has made the movement rethink its approach to issues including social, economic, and political questions. At present there are trade unionists looking into social and economic alternatives in Zambia, which will be the basis for their future engagement on broad national issues including political choice.

What has been the politics of the ZCTU and the Mineworkers' Union of Zambia (MUZ) since Chiluba's election in 1991? There is a split in the union movement over privatization—perhaps you could tell us more about this? Can you talk specifically about the effect on the trade unions?

Let's be clear about this—the rise to power of the MMD and the policies of liberalization did not benefit the trade union movement. The ZCTU membership declined drastically over the years due to unending retrenchments and redundancies as a result of the economic reform measures such as privatization. After 1991 the MMD saw the trade unions and the ZCTU in particular as a potential opposition and amended the Industrial and Labour Relations Act to deregulate the labor market so that it conforms with principles of liberalization. However, the underlying motive was to actually further weaken the trade unions.

Three years after the MMD took office—to be precise, in 1994—the ZCTU was plunged into internal crisis and leadership struggle, which was politically sponsored. The MMD felt it was losing its grip on ZCTU among other things. This climaxed at the 1994 ZCTU Quadrennial Congress. Two factions arose and accused each other of being pro-MMD and compromising the workers by failing to oppose and challenge unpopular MMD policies, in particular the structural adjustment programs, which included privatization and restructuring the public service. When the other faction lost elections at the 1994 Congress they decided to break away from ZCTU. Five national unions broke away, including the MUZ.

Following this loss of major affiliates the ZCTU relaxed its policy of "one industry, one union" as it openly accepted affiliation requests from new unions, hoping to compensate for its lost membership. And to be honest the ZCTU to some extent also contributed to the union fragmentation. However, it has now come to realize the dangers of this kind of approach—particularly the potential to further weaken the trade unions. Soon ZCTU went on a reconciliatory campaign and some unions have since come back.

Can you tell us something more generally about the experiences in Zambia and for the left since Chiluba was elected? Wasn't it regarded at the time as a victory for the movement?

Yes it was! Our involvement in the victory was huge. During the pro-democracy campaigns the trade union movement with others formed alliances with what seemed to be the most progressive political movement, the Movement for Multi-party Democracy. For the first time the trade union movement put all of its resources, structures, and infrastructure at the disposal of the MMD during the entire period of the pro-democracy campaigns before the election in 1991. It was therefore logical that the trade union movement had a lot of expectations with the ascending of the MMD party to government. This was more so since some of our very own comrades from the trade union movement assumed positions of national influence, including even the president himself.

Now, we were not unaware of the dangers. Past experience had shown us that trade unions were used when needed and then discarded or simply sidelined when the political end was attained, as was the case in the First and Second Republics, but the Third Republic brought renewed hopes in the trade union movement. However, what was hoped would be a positive change as far as the trade union movement was concerned, with the restoration of democracy and democratic institutions, proved to be the beginning of a nightmare for the trade union movement.

What was the cause of this nightmare?

It can be seen in different ways. It could be attributed to a large extent to the failure to subsume the trade union movement within the ambits of the ruling MMD party and the consequent fear and uneasiness by those in power to allow a strong and independent trade union movement to flourish. But I suspect that the resolve of the trade union movement to remain free and independent was not well appreciated by some within the political ranks of MMD.

This created a situation of uneasy truce for a while, a situation that worsened as the economic crisis deepened. The crisis cannot be overestimated and I suppose the greatest disappointment to the trade union movement was the manner in which a government that we struggled so hard to bring to power at great workers' sacrifice quickly turned around to create an environment aimed at weakening the movement.

What happened next was akin to a declaration of war against the trade union movement. The economic reform measures under the MMD regime became synonymous with retrenchments, redundancies, and joblessness for the majority of Zambia. The result was destitution and widespread poverty. It is estimated that about 70–80 percent of Zambians live in conditions of absolute poverty today—a record which surpasses even the colonial era. The gap between the rich and the poor is even greater than it was in the Second Republic. The Zambian worker is worse off today than he was ten years ago both in terms of standard of living and quality of employment. The economy is increasingly becoming informalized instead of being formalized. The massive retrenchments and redundancies witnessed in the formal sector have greatly reduced the trade union membership.

But what was the political opposition to these measures? What did the trade union movement do practically to challenge this?

The opposition was extremely weak, creating a de facto one-party situation in Parliament. The trade union movement was one of the main forces left to take on those in the corridors of power on national issues, especially unpopular policies. But a strong trade union movement was a thorn in the flesh of the political heavyweights and this had to be controlled. Therefore, the main reason behind hurried government action was to divide and rule the trade union movement. In so doing the trade unions will be weak and easy to manipulate. Our capacity to resist was hampered by these changes. Whereas in 1990 there were nineteen national unions with a total membership of about 350,000 members, in 2001 there are thirty-two national unions with a combined membership of less than 250,000 members. There are also two federations, namely the Zambia Congress of Trade Unions (ZCTU) and the Federation of Free Trade Unions of Zambia (FFTUZ). ZCTU has a total of twenty-eight affiliates with a membership of about 235,000 members.

The government claims that it was necessary to amend the labor laws so that they are in conformity with the dictates of a liberalized economy and to liberalize workers' organizations. However, what this has brought about is simply the deregulation of the labor market, thus removing the little protection workers previously enjoyed and restoring the employers' right to hire and fire at will. The quality of employment has also declined with the emergence of part-time, contract and casual employment as opposed to permanent and pensionable employment. There is increasing de-Zambianization in most of the privatized companies. Complaints of racism and slave conditions applied to Zambian workers are on the increase. Is this the kind of future we resolved to create for our movement in 1990? The answer is obviously no.

What are the lessons that need to be learned from this experience? What is the way forward for the trade union movement?

The last ten years are what one can simply call the lost decade for Zambia. More harm than good has been done to Zambia in the last ten years than the Kaunda regime managed to do during their twenty-seven years of rule.

The adaptation to the new environment and the resilience to survive against all odds has been one of the greatest achievements of the trade union movement. Attempts to destabilize and fragment the trade union movement have met with strong resistance from the general membership. Only a strong and united trade union movement could stand the harsh environment witnessed during the last ten years.

The working class has learned that you cannot assume that your own will always take care of you and we have learned to distinguish between genuine trade unionists and those bent on using the trade union movement as a launch pad to attain their personal desires and ambitions. What else have we learned? The trade union movement is now very cautious in engaging in political parties. The trade union movement will depend on its membership to appraise and assess the worthiness or unworthiness of any future political engagement. It is in this context that one has to ask the anti–third-term-for-Chiluba campaign what took them so long to realize that someone or some people were taking them for a ride?

Can you tell us about the recent elections [December 2001]?

The results of the recent elections in Zambia may have far-reaching consequences. It is an undisputable fact that the majority of the Zambians voted against the MMD and its presidential candidate. According to the final results, the MMD president got a paltry 29 percent of the total votes cast to claim the presidency of Zambia and return the MMD government for the next five years. In real terms, 71 percent of those who cast their vote did not vote for the MMD candidate.

Political analysts strongly believe that the presidential results, even in the face of a fragmented opposition, would have been completely different had the MMD government not tampered with the constitution in 1996. The opposition was severely divided into nine competing parties. However, a number of trade unionists have scooped parliamentary seats on opposition tickets, including Japhet Moonde, former ZCTU deputy president, who is now a member of parliament on the UPND ticket. Other notables are Austin Liato, also former deputy president of ZCTU, and Neddy Nzowa, former president of the National Union of Communication Workers. It remains to be seen whether this will make any difference to workers.

The consequences for the workers are obvious. The suffering that they have undergone during the last decade of MMD rule is bound to continue. Moreover, there was generally little support for the MMD government from the labor movement in general. Workers must now brace themselves for more hard times and be prepared for action if their welfare is to improve. Already, the price of the staple food maize meal has increased twofold, making it unaffordable for 80 percent of the population who are poor, and who now include a large proportion of the working people.

What do you make of the much talked-about globalization? How does it affect your struggles?

In Zambia the implementation of economic reforms with the support of the International Monetary Fund and World Bank has made our work more difficult. These bodies are the reality of globalization in Africa. The trade union movement in Zambia needs to come up with ways to face these challenges.

My strategy against these forces remains a strong, united, independent, and self-reliant trade union movement in Zambia and elsewhere. It is the task of us to help rebuild it. If the lessons of the past are learned and if we are prepared to take militant, mass action when necessary, the trade union movement can continue to champion equality and social change.

The key to this is for the trade unions to start thinking of merging into bigger unions to increase their strength. And alliances with other groups currently engaged in what is termed the "anti-globalization movement." The demonstrations at Seattle, Davos, and Prague are clear testimony to the hope for a worldwide movement; this movement must include trade unions and the working class.

6

SOUTH AFRICA UNDER THE ANC: STILL BOUND TO THE CHAINS OF EXPLOITATION

Peter Dwyer

Any attempt to understand and contribute to the social and economic processes unfolding in South Africa will be partial if it does not situate them within the context of Africa's economic crisis and that of international capitalism.[1] The roots of the current problems in South Africa go very deep. It is important to remember the international nexus to which South Africa has long been bound. By the early 1970s the post–Second World War international capitalist economic boom was beginning to falter, as it fell into an economic crisis from which it is still struggling to recover.[2]

Peer behind all the talk on globalization today and something else emerges. It is an ideological point, hammered home by politicians of both left and right, many academics and nongovernmental organizations (NGOs), with political implications that haunt workers, trade unionists, and the unemployed the world over. Very simply it goes like this: it is alleged that capital is now more mobile, multinational corporations (MNCs) can swiftly move location, and workers and others should not resist this process. What, then, is the point in fighting back against, say, privatization and deregulation? Workers must adapt to market conditions, be more flexible, cooperate with management and government, work harder, and moderate their wage demands. If they do not, business will simply move to where labor is cheaper and workers are more compliant.

This orthodoxy has trickled down and developed into a near unquestioning belief that globalization is all-powerful and something done to us by outside forces beyond our control. This myth has, to a greater or lesser extent, been uncritically swallowed by academics, political parties, many NGOs, and the media. It is not difficult to see who benefits most from such "ideological" concepts.[3]

Laboratories of democracy

Let us now look at South Africa. Although it is in some ways the exception in southern Africa, it is vital that any assessment of the prospects for radical transformation in the region and the continent includes a survey of it. Economically, politically, and militarily, South Africa is the most important country in the region and highly symbolic in the history of the African liberation struggle. It accounts for 44 percent of the total gross domestic product of sub-Saharan Africa and 52 percent of its industrial output, and as such it has a well-developed working-class and labor movement.[4] According to the International Labor Organization, the growth in South Africa's trade union membership since the early 1980s has been the fastest in the world: at 40 percent of the workforce it covers something like 3.1 million workers.

We will consider the changing social processes that have unfolded since the first free elections in April 1994 as they affect the working-class movement that developed, primarily after the early 1970s, in the fight against apartheid. This movement is best represented by the largest trade union body, which has just under two million members: the Congress of South African Trade Unions (COSATU), to which almost 50 percent of all trade union members are affiliated. The federation was founded in 1985 after four years of talks with other unions. Without downplaying the importance of other labor federations, COSATU warrants particular attention as it is part of a Tripartite Alliance ("the Alliance") with the ruling African National Congress (ANC) and the South African Communist Party (SACP). It epitomizes the development of the independent labor movement that carried on the fight against apartheid:

> It was principally Cosatu which kept the mass democratic movement's torch alive between mid-1986 and mid-1988.... Popular resistance continued but organization was seriously crippled. Cosatu acted as a centre in assisting the mass democratic movement to regroup its forces, and the unions' organised strength was central to the failure of the state of emergency.[5]

Several decades of rapid accumulation under state-led capitalism, enforced by a centralized authoritarian apartheid regime, resulted in a diversification from dependence on agriculture and mining to manufacturing, which in turn changed the nature of work. This industrialization meant an increase in economic dependence, by capital and the state, on African labor. It provided the platform on which to build independent unions, the development of which was central to the events that characterized South Africa from the 1970s onward: a period generally regarded as the turning point in the contemporary struggle against apartheid.[6]

In the new generation of trade unions that grew out of the strike waves, particularly around Durban, in the early 1970s, emphasis was put on rank-and-file organization. Shop-floor organization focused on greater worker participation, an increasing role for shop stewards, and a reduced reliance on full-time union officials, turning existing members into conductors for organization and recruitment. Workers were to be encouraged to develop each other as unionists and shop stewards in unions run by workers.

With this purpose the Federation of South African Trade Unions (FOSATU) was launched in April 1979, incorporating twenty thousand workers from across thirteen trade unions. They were organized on the principle of direct worker control through elected shop stewards and shop steward councils in order to develop shop-floor organization. FOSATU explicitly orientated itself around working-class politics and was committed to staying independent of the ANC, fearing that collaboration would result in workers' interests being subsumed under popular slogans and nationalism, so reducing the emphasis on class that was a central principle and strategy of the organization.[7]

Trade union membership exploded from 220,000 in 1980 to 670,000 in 1984, with African workers representing 43.4 percent of all trade union members, whites 33.9 percent, and Coloured and Asian workers 22.7 percent.[8] The epitome of this increase in working-class power was the organizational capacity that developed. By late 1985 there were 795,000 workers in 23 unions with 12,462 shop stewards.[9] So organized and rooted did these trade unions become that in the 1980s there were up to 150 union meetings taking place on any one night across the country.

As the fight against apartheid raged in the mid- to late 1980s, the trade unions asserted their power. Their activities were typified by mass stayaways (political strikes), such as the one on September 6–7, 1989, coinciding with white elections, that involved between two and three million workers. More labor days were lost through work stoppages between 1986 and 1990 than in the previous seventy-five years.[10] But the power, organizational capability, and resilience of the black working class stand out particularly when we look back at the fight against apartheid:

> We can say this with certainty: that in the 1980s hundreds of thousands of African workers began, slowly, haltingly and amid many setbacks, to begin controlling their own lives. They gained a new pride and a new voice and some acquired a new goal: to wrest power from the few and win it for the many.[11]

Such action was a practical expression of the strength of the black working class and it was this that primarily forced the apartheid regime to negotiate with the ANC, releasing Nelson Mandela and lifting the ban on the main liberation organizations in February 1990.

The rainbow that lit up the world

The end of formal apartheid was a victory against a racist regime and the MNCs that had done business with it, the banks that had financed it, and the imperialist governments in the West that had supported it. While the conflicts in Yugoslavia and Rwanda were being etched on our collective consciousness, South Africa cast a rainbow of hope across the world as we celebrated from Norwich to Nairobi in April 1994. The "Rainbow Nation," personified in Mandela, restored, in an increasingly cynical world, some hope that progressive political change was still a possible and worthy goal. It restored and demonstrated the belief that ordinary working-class people and peasants, the exploited and oppressed, could still bring about change from below despite being faced by powerful governments, a brutal state, the army, and MNCs.

Although the ANC leadership did not stand for socialism, many in the party and the South African Communist Party (SACP) did, and for millions of South Africans the fight against apartheid was also a fight for socialism. It was (and still is) common to see on marches and protests and at political rallies banners proclaiming "Phantsi [away with] capitalism," and television pictures of the time are strewn with socialist symbols, songs, and rhetoric. These were not an accessory to the struggle but deeply rooted in it, symbolizing the aspirations of many for a new South Africa, a socialist one. This is not merely an academic point. There is a danger that the history of the struggle will be depoliticized and sanitized for liberal consumption, to fit neatly into a pluralist conception of how to effect political change. One trade union activist joked to me that he feared, in years to come, that the red banners would be "air-brushed out" of pictures of the events.[12]

Long walk to freedom: quick step to neoliberalism

In the elections of 1994, the ANC received 62.7 percent of the vote and became the biggest party in the Government of National Unity

(GNU). The GNU was created mainly for conciliatory purposes, although the former ruling National Party walked out in June 1996. The ANC was set to call all the shots at policy level, having been elected on policies detailed in the Reconstruction and Development Program (RDP). Keynesian in flavor, it was the torch that was to guide the country out of the darkness of apartheid and to light up the lives of millions. Its significance lay in the fact that the vast majority of black people had heard of it, and that through their unions, community organizations, churches, youth, and women's groups, many had been party to its formation. It was a manifesto for a new South Africa.

I asked trade union activists to tell me what they and their friends and families in the townships expected from an ANC government. Leonard Maleokazi, a shop steward for the National Education, Health and Allied Workers' Union (NEHAWU) and an ANC member, gave a typical response:

> I thought that the ANC would deliver things that were previously denied to us. Like for instance I thought that the health would be free. I had thought that the education would be free. Those are the things that I had in mind.... People thought that first of all people would not be hungry, there would be jobs, there would be shelter, the doors of education and culture would be open...at your workplace in the townships, there were great expectations that everything was going to be great.[13]

Many activists whom I met and interviewed explained that their source of inspiration was the RDP—some could even quote it line by line! Such expectations lay behind the tears of joy when the ANC was elected. The level of hope and then the disappointment filtered down to even the youngest black people. A father heard his seven-year-old son, Osiame, singing to the tune of the national anthem: "*Nkosi sikelela I Afrika*, Mandela promised me a VCR and when I went to fetch it Mandela said *voetskek*! [go away] and never come back!" He told his father that kids in his township school sang it all the time.[14]

Although changes were to be made in running the country, in retaining the services of the National Party finance minister, Derek Keys,

Nelson Mandela "delighted investors, businessmen and white South Africans [with] his commitment to free-market economic and political moderation. Again and again, Mr Mandela has stressed the need to restore business confidence and attract foreign investment."[15] Shortly after he was released from prison in February 1990, Mandela publicly stated that he was still in favor of nationalizing the banks and the mines, which prompted the South African MNC De Beers to announce that it was moving part of its operations to Geneva. This dramatic example, and the gradual realization that capital was under no obligation to stay in South Africa, contributed greatly to the evolution of thinking in the ANC away from the RDP and policies such as nationalization, and toward the private sector and "fiscal discipline." In October 1994 the deputy president, Thabo Mbeki, announced that the GNU was committed to privatizing public assets as part of a range of measures to reorganize government finance.[16] Nelson Mandela, who had promised that "the nationalization of the mines, banks and monopoly industry is the policy of the ANC and any change or modification of our views in this regard is inconceivable," now said nothing.[17]

Such changes were not confined to Mandela. Those chosen to form the first cabinet included two of the twenty or so former leading COSATU activists. One was Jay Naidoo, of whom it was said: "with his well-cut suits and carefully tailored vocabulary, the new-look Mr Naidoo . . . is a figure of flawless economic orthodoxy. The firebrand trade unionist and militant socialist has become a persuasive advocate of fiscal and financial discipline." The other was Alec Erwin, formerly a leading official of the fiercely independent FOSATU and at the time deputy minister of finance and SACP member (now minister of trade): "To hear Mr Erwin…defend the need for discipline—with a fervour and passion few orthodox economists could equal—is to believe his conversion is genuine…once a doctrinaire socialist…he has made his peace with capitalism."[18]

The "New South Africa" had been reclassified as an "emerging market," thus further exposing it to the whims of international investors. The government was under pressure from the interests of capital to hook deeper into the global political economy. According to the World Bank, "to be fully effective, measures that liberalize trade need to be accompanied by complementary policies on foreign direct investment."[19] In March 1995 former members of the apartheid regime, Chris Stals (then governor of the Reserve Bank) and Chris Liebenberg (then finance minister), who had been kept on by the ANC, abolished the financial rand—an exchange control mechanism that attempted to insulate the country from the excessive movements of financial capital. Unsurprisingly money poured in, but it poured out just as quickly when incorrect rumors about the health of President Mandela led to investors taking their money out of the country in February 1996. This highlighted the herd-like character of the international investors whom the government would place so much emphasis upon attracting. Then when the so-called Asian miracle economies collapsed in 1998 (which some in the ANC and academia had touted as a model), South Africa felt the cold winds of hot capital leaving the country as investors panicked. The Central Bank poured a staggering $3 billion down the drain in a futile bid to defend the Rand.

In 1996 South Africa was placed forty-fourth out of forty-six developing countries in terms of international competitiveness.[20] This was underscored by an unemployment rate of up to 50 percent, with almost half of all unemployed people being under thirty; 2.5 million illiterate people, or 30 percent of the population; and 90 percent of workers not possessing any skills or training.[21] It is factors such as these that lay behind government and business talk of the need to "improve skills" and implement "changes in management techniques." Such talk is usually code for holding down wages, privatizing state assets, and cutting government spending (the neoliberal spin is "fiscal discipline"), always resulting in attacks on the living standards of the working class and the most vulnerable. Despite deepening social and economic inequalities, the government was encouraged to speed up the privatization of state-owned companies and to relax exchange controls in order to halt the persistent speculation on the rand. The glaring contradiction was noted by the conservative newspaper *Business Day*: "There is...nothing South Africa can do to insulate its markets from foreign economic developments such as rising interest rates. The fact is that the vagaries of international markets will take their toll, and we must pursue policies that will attract more permanent investment by foreigners."[22]

Did such calls tell on the ANC? In March 1996 the ministry in the office of the president overseeing the implementation of the RDP was closed. With constant pressure on the Rand the government made an epic about-turn in macroeconomic policy. Advised by the World Bank, without a word to its Alliance partners and practically all its elected members of Parliament, in June 1996 the ANC announced a new framework and set of targets called Growth, Employment and Redistribution (GEAR). GEAR, whose "cornerstone is fiscal discipline, tax concessions, moves towards scrapping exchange controls, sale of state assets and increasing flexibility in the labour market,"[23] was diametrically opposed to the ideas put forward by COSATU. In short, GEAR had all the ingredients of a neoliberal recipe that bore remarkable similarity to a self-imposed structural adjustment program. It was immediately condemned by COSATU; incredibly, the SACP remained silent for a year.

Privatization would become a major weapon in attempts to extend economic growth and to reduce the government's borrowing requirement and interest bill. With this major change in policy, showdowns between the government and its Alliance partners were predicted as the ANC was now clearly "espousing many of the modern principles of a free market economy."[24] By increasingly adopting a conservative stance on economic policy, the ANC was effectively agreeing that global markets dictate and are the final judge of government policies. Just as the black majority had elected a government, so that government moved closer to abdicating its responsibility by delegating it to "the markets." In this way it unwittingly acknowledged the Marxist adage that power resides not in elected parliaments but in the boardrooms of unelected and unaccountable businesspeople and bankers. It appeared to accept that redistribution of wealth would come through economic growth and the free market.

The ANC's record in office

The RDP envisioned economic growth as an outcome of the redistribution of existing wealth: for example, through progressive taxation and public sector job creation. The government now indicated that redistribution of wealth, in the second-most unequal country in the world, would come through economic growth—"trickle-down theory." Between 1996 and 1998 GEAR predicted that annual GDP would grow by 3.5, 2.9, and 3.8 percent respectively (although it needs to average 5 percent to make any dent in unemployment). It actually fell from 3.2 to 1.7 and then to 0.1 percent. Despite bold predictions of 126,000, 252,000, and 246,000 jobs being created over three years, there were job losses of 71,000, 126,000, and 186,000. In total a staggering one million jobs have been lost since 1994 in the agricultural and non-agricultural sectors, in a country where unemployment averages 40 percent.[25] Practically every target was missed and even much-needed private sector investment, instead of rising by the predicted 9.3, 9.1, and 9.3 percent between 1996 and 1998, fell from 6.1 to 3.1 to –0.7 percent.[26] But this was not all that GEAR contained. The trade liberalization so vigorously implemented by Alec Erwin, the trade and industry minister, had disastrous effects on the economy—particularly for the clothing, textile, and shoe-manufacturing industries, which, unable to compete with their giant global competitors or cheap imports from the likes of China, shed twenty-two thousand (predominantly women) workers in 1998 alone.[27]

No one disagreed with GEAR's objective of creating 833,000 jobs over four years. But this new strategy called for price and wage moderation, implicitly ruling out a national minimum wage, at the same time as ruling in greater labor market flexibility. Pressure is clearly being put on the government from many sections of the business community and the press to privatize state-owned companies in order to offset the danger of capital flight and entice foreign capital to invest in privatization projects. Lamenting the slow pace of the government privatization program, the hired prizefighters of the bourgeoisie continued with their advice: "If investors and owners of firms do not believe that the government has made a credible commitment, they will not invest and will simply move their money to a more inviting climate."[28] This kind of policy and GEAR, with its emphasis on tight control over government spending, contradicted the ANC's social equity proposals, with potentially damaging results: "Government needs to urgently reconcile its public investment policy with political and social priorities. Unless it does so, there is a real possibility that the social discontent reflected during student protests this week will find expression in society in general."[29]

No shift in gear as Mbeki takes the wheel

With Mandela standing down as party leader in December 1997, would there be any change in the direction of the ANC under new party leader, soon to be president, Thabo Mbeki? Previous internal critics of the party, such as Winnie Madikizela-Mandela, publicly said that Mbeki would be more radical.[30] The ANC increased its share of the vote, but the election could only measure the votes and not the manner in which they were cast. The day after the election, an ANC shop steward told me:

> sooner or later we are going to have to break the Alliance, there is a conflict of interest in many instances...at one stage or another we are going to have to say 'OK, ANC, go your way now. We as unions are gonna really start addressing the real issues and not consider you as government because you cannot continue with this privatization program.' Because if we don't do that I am telling you...the leadership of COSATU is going to have a huge problem.[31]

Within six weeks, a million public sector workers went on strike, in August 1999. At the center of differences over wages was the government's macroeconomic policy, GEAR, and its plans to "restructure" (read "cut and privatize") the public sector. Changes to the running of Cape Town metropolitan council could result in the loss of ten thousand municipal jobs as the council decreased its size and privatized services. The state-run train company Spoornet was sacking one thousand workers a month, and there were plans for a further twenty-seven thousand workers to lose their jobs in the run-up to its privatization; the number of workers employed by Spoornet had fallen by thirty thousand since the ANC came to office. In total the country had lost forty-two thousand non-farming jobs in the fiscal year 1998. A vivid indication of trouble in the mining sector was given when industry chiefs announced the sacking of a further twenty-eight thousand workers by the end of 1999.[32]

In his state-of-the-nation address in February 2000, Mbeki announced the government's intention to press ahead with its free market policies to redress the apartheid legacy. Taking a cue from the New Labour government in the UK, Mbeki, along with many social democrats and socialists, pushed the idea of an "African Third Way"— clearly pro-business, but moderated by a commitment to social justice. An International Investment Council (IIC) was to be set up to plot a foreign investment–driven economic revival. The IIC was handpicked by Mbeki and includes such rampant free market luminaries as financier George Soros and Niall Fitzgerald, co-chairperson of the British-Dutch MNC, Unilever.[33]

Although privatization is central to releasing funds for treasury coffers and appeasing foreign investors, Mbeki chose not to mention the speeding up of privatization on this most public of public occasions. This hesitancy reflected tensions in the Alliance, forcing Mbeki to keep an eye on COSATU and the SACP. It is notable that any criticism of the government is immediately denounced, one suspects from fear that any dissent may increase tensions further. Criticism of GEAR and the conservative direction of the ANC is what lay behind the expulsion of former ANC Soweto councillor Trevor Ngwane in 1999.[34]

Mbeki's frustration with COSATU was evident when in the same speech he stated that the country cannot be held hostage by elements that he described as holding back the economy. This was clearly a reference to the nationwide wave of public sector strikes in August 1999 by COSATU and other trade union federations.

Having laid to rest any fears that investors had about state interference with the market and assuring the markets of continuity in the macroeconomic policy that had characterized the first four years of ANC rule, Mbeki rejected any attempt by the state to create jobs and redistribute wealth. This was at a time when the IMF and World Bank had, under immense international pressure from trade unions, NGOs, and anti-capitalist protests, been forced onto the defensive. Clearly government policies toward employment and growth look set to stay in accordance with discredited neoliberalism: growth through privatization and wage restraint.

So since the ANC came to power in 1994, social change led by the government has been slow and fragmented. We can confidently conclude that there has been very, very little economic redistribution toward the poor, who made up the vast majority of people who voted ANC. A government census in 1998 showed that 73 percent of black people were in unskilled or artisan work, 9.1 million of them earned $90 or less a month, and 62 percent earned less than $248 a month.[35] A report looking into changes in income distribution between 1991 and 1996 showed that the new black middle class had become better off since democracy, with the rest getting poorer.[36] A small black economic elite has benefited most from democratization over the past ten years, while poorer black people have actually experienced a decline in income. The report shows that the economic elite is becoming significantly black and that economic class divisions bear markedly less correlation to race than is popularly believed. The proportion of black households in the top 10 percent of all South African households increased from 9 percent to 22 percent between 1991 and 1996. At the same time, the richest 10 percent of black people received an average

17 percent increase in income, while the poorest 40 percent of households actually suffered a fall in household income of around 21 percent. Such reports confirm what many black people know only too well: that racial inequalities of income persist, but have been exacerbated by class inequalities as the new black elite becomes part of the ruling class.

With one million jobs lost and every employed person supporting something like five others, the lives of millions of people are being destroyed. The unemployed and many workers cannot afford to pay for health care, in a country with 4.2 million people living with HIV/AIDS and a government unwilling to spend the money needed to buy drugs.[37] Health care is free to all children under six, but one senior nurse and shop steward complained to me:

> Our health is not accessible to everyone, as a matter of fact it is becoming more and more inaccessible as far as I am concerned. People are talking that you have free health for people under the age of six. So what! If you can't get into a hospital before 7 o'clock in the morning, it doesn't matter whether you are two months or whether you are 50 months, you will not get in because they have a shut-down point at a particular time. Is that everybody having free health under the age of six?[38]

"Shut-down points" arise because of GEAR-enforced social spending cutbacks that have seen the state budget deficit cut from 9 percent of GDP in 1993 to under 3 percent in 2000. Yet approximately 57 percent of South Africans live in poverty without income, water, electricity, food, or access to jobs and education. Children, the elderly, and the disabled suffer the most. The majority of the poor are women and their rate of unemployment is 50 percent higher than that of men. Women are also the first to be retrenched because of the jobs they occupy, such as in the textile and clothing industry in Cape Town and Durban.

It is true that houses have been built, but many are so small that township residents commonly refer them to as "Fiat Unos." The KwaZulu Natal-based Built Environment Support Group found that

70 percent of houses built with government subsidies between 1994 and 1999 were not of a suitable standard. Part of the problem, they argue, is that in spite of promising to spend 5 percent of national spending on housing, the government spends just 1.8 percent.[39]

The widely heralded water delivery program has initially connected three million people to water. But scratch the surface and a picture of "leaky pipes" and "shoddy workmanship" emerges, creating "fundamental flaws" as a comprehensive study found in 1999.[40] Where other services have been provided, the introduction of GEAR translates into the privatization of utilities such as electricity and gas, and services such as libraries, clinics, and parks. It is denying local communities funding and removing decision making from elected councillors and giving it to city managers and consultants, as with Igoli 2002 in Johannesburg, a project to reorganize the metropolitan council and its services. If services do not make sufficient profits for the private owners, they will increase charges for residents, offer inferior services, or withdraw them altogether. The ANC premier of the Gauteng province, which the metropolitan council falls under, is Mbhazima Shilowa, former general secretary of COSATU.

While not sufficiently funding social spending and bemoaning its limited resources, the government chose to reduce those resources further by cutting company tax from 48 percent in 1994 to 30 percent in 2000, so saving businesses more than $1 billion. At the same time, it planned to spend over $3 billion on the purchase of military hardware, the contracts for which are mired in a corruption scandal involving members of the government. This is seven times the yearly amount given by them to local government to provide municipal services.[41]

The political irony is that, should the ANC find the political will to deal with one of the most abhorrent legacies of apartheid, "apartheid debt," it would free up something like $9 billion. The Alternative Information Development Centre and Jubilee 2000 South Africa have argued that this money should be released. They have calculated that it could have provided 300,000 new homes, electrification of 2.5 million homes over five years, water and sanitation for 21 million people over five years, 1,060 new health clinics, the upgrading of 50,000 class-rooms, rehabilitation of 20,000 schools and the building of 77,000 new classrooms by the year 2000.[42] This measure, combined with increas-ing taxes on companies, eliminating corruption and reducing the high salaries of government officials and their consultants, would be more than enough to create sustainable jobs and provide the free health care and education that people thought would become a reality when they voted ANC.

Resistance of a special type

The intention of the government, through GEAR, was to encourage local and international investors and to convince them that the ANC was credible. To do so it had to discipline labor. The South African Mu-nicipal Workers' Union (SAMWU) and to a lesser extent the National Education, Health and Allied Workers' Union (NEHAWU) have shown consistent opposition to GEAR and are a constant thorn in the side of the ANC and the COSATU leadership. Outside the unions, struggles over rents, evictions, water and electricity supplies are being taken up by new working-class-based community groups in town-ships, and some, such as the Anti-Privatization Forum, are seeking to make links with workers' organizations.[43] The leaderships of COSATU and SACP have avoided the political and ideological thrust of GEAR and have been unwilling to tackle the class politics that are the basis of it. For the SACP and for a large part of COSATU, as practically all their national office bearers are SACP members, this stems from their polit-ical formulation of the state and the struggle against apartheid as a two-stage revolution.

The adoption by the ANC and the SACP in the early 1960s of the SACP theory of Colonialism of a Special Type (CST) guided the liber-ation struggle as waged by the ANC and SACP.[44] Briefly, CST argues that apartheid was an expression of monopoly capitalism in South

Africa, meaning that "black South Africa" was still a colony of "white South Africa." A corollary was a two-stage approach to the liberation struggle: the first objective was to carry through a national democratic revolution, in which the "colonized" would be liberated and apartheid abolished, and the second was a socialist revolution in which capitalism would be replaced. As not all classes had an objective interest in pushing for the second stage, the allotted role of the working class, with the SACP leading it, was to ensure that a post-apartheid South Africa became a socialist one—eventually. CST and the two-stage approach did not go uncontested, and it has been extensively criticized by people mainly outside the ranks of the SACP as effectively sidelining independent working-class struggle and organization.[45] Furthermore, the notion of a "national democratic revolution" covered the class antagonisms between a national petty bourgeoisie and the mass of the working class. Joining the "national" and "democratic" elements of the revolution into a single form obscured the predominant bourgeois "nationalism" of the ANC as a particular expression of the struggle against apartheid.

Class struggle led by the working-class movement, as a strategy for change, was in essence rejected by the ANC, whose strategy was predicated on a negotiated solution to a de-radicalized South African capitalism and not, despite its rhetoric, a radical alternative to it.[46] This theorization has practical implications today that can hamper workers' struggle and the fight against capitalist exploitation. For example, at a rally in Johannesburg protesting against plans by the metropolitan council to privatize services and sell off council properties, SACP spokesperson Mazibuku Jara referred to the council in these terms: "These are *our comrades*. It makes it difficult for us to use tactics that we used against the previous government."[47] The same politics and strategy that obscured class antagonisms during the liberation struggle continue to do so today.

Of course, there were other alternatives to this route, most notably that taken in the early 1980s by FOSATU and a diverse group of left-wing trade unionists and intellectuals—often labelled "workerists." As Friedman correctly notes, this did not involve merely a difference about union tactics; two very different political strategies were battling it out for the leadership of the biggest union federation in South African history, COSATU, and ultimately for the leadership of the liberation movement.[48] The result was of paramount importance, for it shaped the strategy and tactics of the major union and community groups in the fight for liberation. It was a debate that also reflected both the weaknesses and strengths of those opposed to apartheid. The outcome was also important, as it placed upon political activity (and theory) particular imperatives that conditioned the basis for mass mobilization and influenced the trajectory of the transition to liberal democracy and the struggle against exploitation today.[49]

Making sense of the clouds that shadow the rainbow nation

It might seem that the internal debates of the 1980s are of no relevance today—except that to gain insight on the present in South Africa we sometimes need to cast our gaze back through the window to apartheid. When we do so, we can say with certainty that no serious left, independent political organization was developed. Such an organization could have acted as a pole of attraction outside of what became the Alliance, inside the factories, schools, and townships. The lack of such an alternative surely limited the options that could contribute to the direction of the liberation struggle.

It was correct to argue that racial segregation and poverty could only be totally eliminated through a break with the social relations of capitalism in South Africa. However, the left, by concentrating their political work on the relationship between capital and labor, mainly trade union work, downplayed the contradictory nature of working-class consciousness and downgraded the political issues in the townships. It relied on trade unions to build a working-class movement, while not forming an independent socialist organization that could have united the political struggles in the trade unions and townships. This allowed the ANC to rebuild itself and attract workers and others by dominating COSATU from its inception, through groups such as the United Democratic Front and aided by material and logistical support from Moscow through SACP connections. The rallying call of the ANC was "national liberation" (invoking African nationalism), leading a broad political movement including workers, the unemployed, urban and rural township dwellers, church, youth and women's groups, white liberals and even the liberal wing of capital. The failure to develop a network and organization of activists politically independent of the ANC and SACP meant that from 1990 onward many of the best activists, such as Moses Mayekiso, saw no alternative but to join the SACP.[50]

With little or no independent socialist competition, once the ANC was elected its leadership could more easily pursue their historic, bourgeois class agenda. Former ANC president-general Dr. Xuma explained such an agenda with honesty: "It is of less importance to us whether capitalism is smashed or not. It is of greater importance to us that while capitalism exists, we must fight and struggle to get our full share and benefit from the system."[51] McKinley shows it was clear from the outset that the ANC wanted only to manage South African capitalism, not challenge it fundamentally. Instead of the ANC seeing the radical potential (embryonic in mass strikes, township boycotts, etc.) of the struggles waged by the working class to forge a different type of society, the potential they generated was used to gain strategic access to existing institutionalized political and economic power. This strategy was pursued regardless of the tactics involved, including left-wing rhetoric, armed struggle, and militant mass action.[52]

The use of mass action, turned on and off like a tap, was what fundamentally brought the apartheid regime to the negotiating table. Morris captures the severity of the compromises made with the former apartheid rulers at the Kempton Park negotiations in 1993, which paved the way to the transition to liberal democracy. He accurately counterposes not some idealized vision of change, but what was articulated in countless rallies, slogans, and proclamations by ANC leaders and supporters alike, during the fight against apartheid, in their bid to "make the country ungovernable":

> Instead of revolution, negotiation; instead of uncompromising transformation, compromising concession…instead of sweeping aside the old order and all who had implemented it, dismantling the old order jointly with its old architects; instead of radical exclusion of the old to the benefit of the new, inclusion of both old and new in a newly created social framework.[53]

This was never a foregone conclusion as debates raged inside the ANC both in exile and in South Africa, and among its trade union and other allies in civil society over the direction of both the struggle and a post-apartheid South Africa. So the tactical approach of the ANC leadership to accessing political and economic power twisted and turned over the course of the liberation struggle depending upon the type of pressure that was exerted upon them. But the necessity of looking for common ground with the "liberal wing" of capital for some kind of social contract in the drive to restructure an ailing South African capitalism was a constant theme. This resulted in their trying to contain mass struggle, as their objective was political change controlled by them from above and not by working-class people from below. The SACP gave this strategy a socialist coloring, and still does. The cumulative history of the ANC leadership's political practice reveals a tendency to strangle the self-activity of the working class. Today this translates into government ministers condemning "greedy workers" and the minister of public services and administration, and SACP central committee member, Geraldine Fraser-Moleketi, accusing striking public sector workers of "pursuing narrow trade unionism to the detriment of broader social transformation."[54]

The South African working class: the key to breaking the chain

The ANC did not waste any time in co-opting organized labor into the state. This started when leading COSATU activists were elected in 1994 on an ANC platform to provincial and national parliaments and councils and were given jobs in various state departments. Bargaining mechanisms were also put in place, such as a new Labour Relations Act (LRA) of 1995 that set up the National Economic Development and Labour Council (NEDLAC), a "consultative forum" between state, labor, and capital. While such new acts can be viewed as "pro-labor," equally it is not hard to see that they commit labor to a bureaucratic process of negotiations. Such legislation was welcomed as a victory by COSATU and many workers, although some say it is now harder to take both official and unofficial action, as one shop steward explained:

> because of this new LRA, which puts labour at a disadvantage, there is no way that you can strike unless a dispute has been declared. In the past you just go on strike. So people are scared because if there is an un-procedural action you are disciplined immediately. That is a way of keeping you in line.[55]

The Alliance serves as an important means by which the ANC has sought to subsume the working-class interests of the labor movement into the broader "national interest" (theorized by the SACP as the "national democratic revolution"), and so to defuse any consistent political protest. Long before the government came to power it was clear to business and the ANC that the attitude of organized labor would determine the ability to sail a steady ship in post-apartheid South Africa. It is clear that, as COSATU is the dominant federation, it will be the key to the success or failure of the corporatist structures set up after 1994.

The effect of these various pressures is that the leaders of COSATU and its affiliates pursue contradictory policies. They sometimes express workers' frustrations with the practice of the government, while channeling discontent into directions that continue the partnership with business and government through NEDLAC. In tolerating repeated snubs by the ANC, they claim that disagreements arise because of "misunderstandings" or a failure of internal Alliance structures, so ducking central political questions. Unless the organization is prepared to mobilize its two million members in an overt political struggle against government policy, it will continue to play second fiddle to business. Despite nationwide demonstrations, orchestrated by COSATU, in May and August 2000 and against privatization in August 2001, reflecting an increasingly restless rank and file, this action is seen as secondary to the desire to seek compromise and consolidate the Alliance.

The role of the SACP is central in this, as it maintains a disciplined line among its members and demobilizes them in the process of cementing the cracks in its political pact with the government. It seeks to be the natural political home for workers, while remaining a member of the Alliance to ensure that the ANC is not "hijacked by reactionary forces." With attacks on workers mounting, the SACP refuses to blame the ANC explicitly, instead choosing to blame a range of enemies of the "national democratic revolution." Take the announcement in May 2000 by the state-run train company, Spoornet, that it was sacking eighteen thousand workers as part of ANC government plans to "restructure" state assets.[56] In a typical piece of political obscuration, the SACP urged managers of public assets to "stop playing with workers' lives," accusing them of operating "outside of the political goals and supervision of the government and the tripartite alliance."[57] The implication is that public sector managers are to blame for sacking workers, not the ANC government or the minister of public enterprises and SACP national office holder, Jeff Radebe.

Shaping up for the future somewhere over the rainbow

The ANC government, as the new guardian of South African capitalism, faces perplexing dilemmas, and the question of how to resolve them goes to the heart of the political predicament facing the government and its Alliance partners. It is clear that the government intends to continue to put its faith in the free market. However, the structural problems that dog the economy will obviously be an important factor, as will the ANC's insistence on adhering to a neoliberal agenda through the strategy of GEAR. In Egypt, Zambia, Zimbabwe, and elsewhere, this recipe has been a disaster for the working class and peasants. But with a highly organized and politicized working class there is every reason to believe that serious political destabilization will happen if the ANC does not make demonstrable strides in addressing the apartheid legacy by creating jobs and delivering social services.

The snapshot of change presented in this chapter is still unfolding before our eyes. The national and international bourgeoisie (exemplified in the World Bank, IMF, MNCs, and domestic business) are doing what they can to see that change occurs in a conservative political environment. "Give us more time" is a plea of every government seeking to be reelected, but is it so audacious to have expected, as millions did, that much more would have been done since 1994? Discontent is simmering in labor and community circles among those who would like to contest the manner and direction of what is taking place. The shape of future developments in a fluid and fragile political environment cannot be determined in advance.

Yet despite everything that the ANC has done to woo big business and co-opt the labor movement, it still has not satisfied international capitalism. The pointlessness of this route is there for all to see. Just three days after the June 1999 election, Mark Mobins, president of one of the largest investors in South Africa's financial markets, said: "If the ANC gains the power to unilaterally amend the Constitution, we will adopt a very conservative cautious approach to further investment."[58]

Surely the time has come to acknowledge that the Alliance leadership are rapidly losing their political direction and that they have "squandered an opportunity of world-historic proportions."[59] The social fallout from broken dreams cannot be predicted, but we know that frustrations can turn to crime and apathy, borne of a feeling of power-lessness and alienation. Always penetrating the dark clouds of life under capitalism, however, are the rays of hope generated by resistance through strikes and social protests. The number of days lost to strike action is lower than in the mid-1980s, but 1999 saw the second highest number of days lost since the ANC was elected, 3.1 million. In April 2000 an incredible four million workers took part in a national one-day strike as part of COSATU protests against job losses and poverty.[60]

This structural power of the working class at the point of produc-tion, in the mines, on the farms, in the factories and shops, brought the apartheid regime down and is the key to unlocking the future. The growing separation of the ANC from those whom it aspires to repre-sent is a trend replicated globally. That professional politicians have moved closer to the neoliberal, pro-market policies of the parties of capital can clearly be seen with the social democratic parties in the UK, France, and Germany. While COSATU might continue to sup-port the ANC electorally, although this is subject to constant specula-tion, it may replicate another trend by shaping its own political agenda. In part this has happened in Europe amongst trade unions formerly associated with communist parties (France, Spain, and Italy) and for labor federations across Asia, Latin America, and Africa.[61] One of the most enduring bonds between the labor movement and a social democratic party can be found in the UK, but even today the trade unions are seriously debating whether to continue to pay a political levy to the Labour Party. An electoral alliance of left-wing groups, for-mer Labour Party activists, and community campaigners has been formed. With few resources and in a short time, the Socialist Alliance, according to an authority on electoral behavior, has achieved "easily the best record for the far left in postwar Britain."[62]

It is not hard to see this happening in South Africa. In fact, with ten-sions and differences persisting, together with continuing strikes and opposition to the privatization of public services among working-class community groups, it was no surprise to see former ANC supporters standing as independent candidates in the December 2000 local elections. With the emergence of new community groups, such as the Concerned Citizens' Group in Durban, the basis for sustained opposition to the ANC may already be taking shape in townships across the country. These are very welcome moves and underscore a central tenet of revolutionary socialism: that the real opposition in any society is to be found not in parliament, but in extra-parliamentary politics.

The development of a campaigning and electoral alliance incorporating the trade unions and working-class community groups to the left of the ANC would be a huge step forward. What is tentatively emerging is an alternative set of policies and ideas, ones that are taking up daily bread-and-butter issues and struggles. But what seems important is that they link these and the causes of the problems to the subordination of lives to capitalist social relations; social relations that the Alliance seeks only to fiddle with, but not fundamentally to transform. The intentions of the best governments, packed with "heroes and heroines" fresh from the struggle, are not the answer. Neither well-meaning policies nor sympathetic governments can fundamentally alter our lives unless they are part of a fundamental challenge to capital. That means making alternatives possible, and it requires a movement that seeks to change the political culture—the assumptions we bring to how society should work. It must also aim to bring more people collectively into everyday struggles, while deepening the understanding and skills of activists and developing an organized network of revolutionary socialist activists.

INTERVIEW WITH TREVOR NGWANE

Trevor Ngwane was elected as an ANC councillor in 1995 but was expelled in 1999 for "bringing the party into disrepute." His crime was to condemn the ANC's planned privatization of local government services in Johannesburg. Refusing to make a public apology, he continued to oppose the privatization of public services and helped to set up the Anti-Privatization Forum (Johannesburg, August 2001).

Can you tell us about yourself and your political background?

I am forty years old. I was born in Durban. I studied at Roman Catholic schools and spent four years at Fort Hare University. I could not complete my BA degree due to political disruptions at what was then a "bush college," a derogatory name given to Bantustan universities during those days. In 1989 I turned my full attention to the workers' literacy project we had founded and spent the next four years working there. In 1993 I joined the Transport and General Workers' Union, an affiliate of COSATU, as their national education officer. During this period in South Africa all the banned organizations were operating freely and a lot of work was being done by capital to woo the prospective new rulers to their capitalist agenda. With my comrades I wrote a paper called "Is holding hands with the bosses the way for new South Africa?," which was circulated widely and caused a lot of controversy, leading to my expulsion and subsequent reinstatement by workers into the union. But after this I could not last long and was eventually expelled in 1995.

All the time I was working in the township during my spare time, organizing residents into civics, i.e., local community bodies. I also joined the ANC in 1990 when it was unbanned and was elected into the first Jabavu Branch, Soweto, executive committee as a political education officer. In 1995 I stood for election as local government councillor on an ANC ticket. Winning was a walkover but the real challenge was trying to push progressive policies inside council. I worked well with the community, rose up inside the ranks of the ANC, but the debate and polemics were sharpening until in October 1999 I was suspended from all my ANC positions and my work as the chairperson of the town planning tribunal inside the council. The reason was that I had written a newspaper article denouncing the Igoli 2002, a plan by the Greater Johannesburg Council to privatize local government services. At this point I took notice of the anti-globalization movement and this made sense since Igoli 2002 was a World Bank brainchild. I helped form the Anti-Privatization Forum of which I am secretary. This is a coalition of organizations opposed to privatization, including the Soweto Electricity Crisis Committee and the working-class Community Coordinating Committee. I also attended the World Social Forum where I got a good idea of the anti-globalization movement, its dreams, hopes, and strategies. I believe that socialists must be at the forefront of such movements, ensuring that they address working-class issues and are under the leadership of workers.

What were your expectations of an ANC government when you voted in 1994?

I voted for the ANC because I believed that this party would roll back the legacy of apartheid or at least provide an avenue for the working class to push forward the socialist agenda. The ANC has been a great dis-appointment and that is despite my ongoing critique of the limitations of its nationalist politics long before it took power. As soon as it took power it threw away even the RDP, a reformist program which at least genuflected to redistributive economics. GEAR was adopted on advice from the World Bank, which actually helped write this neoliberal policy.

Privatization, deregulation, liberalization, retrenchments, currency crashes, etc., are the order of the day in South Africa.

What relationship does the ANC have with the working class? Does it still command a lot of loyalty?

Many workers are still loyal to the ANC. This is because of the prestige it carries, and makes sure no one forgets, as the party that delivered national liberation. At the same time this loyalty is steadily but surely diminishing. This is due to the absolute failure of the ANC to deliver significantly to the working class. In particular, the recent attacks on the working class have taken center stage in workers' minds despite their loyalist wish to trust the ANC. These workers tend to be either cynical, demoralized, or opt out of politics. But since these workers understand workers' power they need to see something powerful before they can move away from the ANC. On their own they will remain hostage to ANC politics.

What is life like in the townships for working-class people today?

Life in the townships is still the same if not worse. There are pockets of black middle classes, more freedom and dignity due to the absence of the apartheid police, more informal businesses due to the same reasons, more unemployment especially among youth. Recently the scourge of the townships has been the neoliberal cost-recovery policies, which led to massive water and electricity cutoffs due to nonpayment. The non-payment is attributed to a "culture" which started during the anti-apartheid boycotts. But in fact many working-class residents simply cannot afford to pay. Crime is also a great problem with many communities pushed to vigilantism. Child abuse has reached an all-time high. South Africa is the world's capital of rape and murder. On a Saturday afternoon you will see long queues of working-class people hoping to win the national lottery.

The life of workers improved a bit with the winning of worker rights in the workplace. But now these rights are under attack. Sunday work will no longer be paid double, various exemptions to circumvent minimum rights are granted using various excuses, flexible labor is talked about and practiced openly, outsourcing, retrenchments, and so on. This is how workers live today, always under attack. The government's privatization program is leading to untold misery for workers. The trade union bureaucracy sits like a dead weight on top of workers. The bosses have not been sleeping too. Union bashing is frequent. Expulsion of radical worker leaders and intimidation by management on the shop floor is on the rise again. Mamphele Ramphele, former vice-chancellor of the University of Cape Town and former close associate of Steve Biko, now a director of the World Bank, made a point of breaking the union NEHAWU's back before she moved on to greener pastures.

As you have said, the ANC are now openly pursuing a self-imposed World Bank neoliberal agenda through GEAR. How do you interpret what has happened?

The ANC introduced GEAR because it is carrying out the bosses' agenda in South Africa. This happened because of the age-old petty bourgeois politics of the ANC since the days it was formed by chiefs and western-educated African leaders. At the heart of this politics is nationalism and its method is class collaboration. Other factors also played a role in increasing the speed with which the ANC turned its back on working-class interests. This [one] is the collapse of the Soviet Union and as a result the total ideological disorientation which visited the SACP, the paramount partner, left flank watcher, and adviser of the ANC. This disorientation also visited many on the left in South Africa, especially the academic types.

Conspicuous consumption is the hallmark of the culture of the emergent black bourgeoisie in South Africa. There is an attitude of triumphalism, "we defeated the mighty apartheid state," and self-righteousness, "we liberated the people," and entitlement, "we worked and sacrificed a lot," among the new governing elite. The whiff of arrogance of the nouveaux riches is to be expected from this conundrum.

To what extent do workers exert control over the main union federation, COSATU, today?

I think things have gotten worse since I was in the unions and the situation was bad enough even then. Earlier in the year I was attending the local [shop stewards council] and found it weak and not really discussing building the struggle of the workers under workers' control. Important decisions were understood to be made by "higher" structures. It is impossible to resist the attacks against labor without fighting the ANC government. But this is exactly what COSATU leaders are loath to do. Many leftists call for the breaking of the Alliance between the union federation, the ANC, and the SACP. My point of view is that the ANC long ago broke the Alliance. The ANC does what it likes in government without consulting its Alliance partners at all and then, when opposition mounts, calls them to meetings which change nothing. The direct attacks on labor broke the Alliance.

Are there signs that this can change? Are there the stirrings of resistance?

Working-class people are talking about the hardness of life under the new South Africa. They talk about unemployment and crime, about the job losses, about casual jobs. About what is for supper tonight. They fantasize about winning the lottery and whether the national soccer team will win or not. However, there seem to be the beginnings of a change in mood with some sections of the working class more willing to fight back, as evidenced by the march against electricity cutoffs in Soweto, action against water cutoffs in Durban, a two-week strike by post office workers, the burning down of Pretoria station by angry commuters, etc. The fact that the ANC lost considerable voter support, through failure to vote by many workers in the last local government election, is a sign of things to come. There is the beginning of a new movement against neoliberalism—this is the same as a struggle against the ANC government given its undisguised neoliberal stance. However, the main obstacle is the freshness of national liberation and the ability of the new governing elite to raise symbols of national liberation to assure the people of their good intentions.

You are the secretary of the Anti-Privatization Forum (APF). Is the growth of this coalition a sign of the times?

In the Anti-Privatization Forum there is a dynamic which points to great things to come and indicates the potential which is ready to be plucked. Despite marginalization and demoralization, many ordinary workers, at least in Gauteng, know that there is some kind of opposition to what is going on. The community-based organizations such as the Kathorus Concerned Residents are truly grassroots-based and have been created out of dire need in defense of communities under attack from neoliberalism. The challenge now is to deepen the politics and educate wider and wider layers in the politics of anti-capitalism.

What have you learnt from your experiences as an activist?

A lesson from South Africa is to never allow the middle-class leadership or the bourgeoisie nationalists to take over the political leadership of working-class organizations. Another lesson is to be always wary of the ruling class. The only correct orientation I think is to hate the bosses and to always maintain the line that to get what it needs the working class must build a struggle against them. The left also needs to overcome its sectarianism and cooperate more and not allow differences to stand in the way of standing together in the face of the enemy.

Our struggle was able to achieve what it has achieved because the working class was active and at the forefront of the struggle despite the wrong politics. Another lesson is that no country is unique and independent from the inexorable laws of political and economic development whose engine is class struggle itself. There are no miracles in history and this has been decisively proven in South Africa, where the miracle is turning out to be nothing but the betrayal of workers by its self-appointed liberators.

You participated in the World Social Forum (WSF) in Porto Allegre, Brazil. How do you feel about the anti-capitalist movement and the possibility of socialist transformation in the twenty-first century?

What was great about the WSF is that almost everyone claimed and saw a continuity between the discussions and the various protest actions such as Seattle, Washington, and so on. There was so much hope and enthusiasm among delegates and such a marked aversion to neoliberal policies which destroy our planet that all were inspired to believe that this cannot and must not be allowed to go on any further. There was a lot of patience, tolerance, and understanding during discussions and an amazing warmth of feeling among delegates. It was like being at home for me, always the romantic revolutionary.

I also had the good fortune to spend three days with the Brazilian Workers' Party's Democratic Socialist current—three days of Marxist lectures and discussions, which really inspired me and introduced me to some of the most current debates taking place among Marxists. I learned about the need to revisit some basic Marxist propositions, which have been forgotten or distorted after decades of Stalinism and the struggle against it. I learned about how Marxism has to understand and incorporate in its armory the issues of environmentalism, racism, culture, and so on. I left convinced again that what we need in South Africa is a mass workers' party.

REVOLUTIONARIES, RESISTANCE, AND CRISIS IN ZIMBABWE

Munyaradzi Gwisai

In the last six years, the urban working masses of Zimbabwe have waged massive struggles that have shaken to the roots not only the postcolonial authoritarian state, but also the vicious neoliberal paradigm imposed by our rulers in Africa and across the world in the last two decades. But during this period, and in particular the last decade for Africa, the continuing and deepening attacks on the living conditions of workers, students, peasants, and the urban poor have provoked major bursts of resistance. These have been against both the fall in living conditions and also the undemocratic and authoritarian regimes that have implemented them. These struggles have swept aside entrenched regimes in places as far apart as Indonesia and Serbia and in southern Africa in Malawi and Zambia.

The struggles in Zimbabwe raise fundamental questions about the movement against capitalism and the possibilities of socialist revolutions led by the working class. The working-class resistance against the ZANU-PF government has gone further and deeper than most on the continent, giving rise to a political movement, the Movement for Democratic Change (MDC), that in the recent elections shook and nearly defeated one of the continent's most entrenched and violent ruling classes. Under mass pressure, the regime was forced to make a partial retreat from the neoliberal agenda, thereby inviting its current isolation and demonization by the global capitalist order. But the subsequent transformation of such a movement into right-wing neoliberalism also raises important questions for the working class.

How events will unfold in Zimbabwe remains unclear and will depend on a number of factors. Objectively, these include the extent to which the economic crisis continues to deepen in the light of an international recession, the resilience of the ruling party and the development of the emerging international anticapitalist struggle. Subjectively, an important factor will be whether the working-class movement will develop a sufficiently strong and independent ideological and organizational alternative to its current leadership, which is located in the organized labor movement (the Zimbabwe Congress of Trade Unions, ZCTU) and politically in the MDC. Another factor is the emergence of a new radical and anti-neoliberal movement in society, linked to the struggles against globalization.

Events in Zimbabwe assume further importance not only because it is an important capitalist state in Africa, but also by its connection to South Africa, the biggest and most important center of global capitalism on the continent. Zimbabwe is South Africa's biggest trading partner on the continent (and fifth globally) and shares similar colonial traditions. There are also an estimated one million migrant workers from Zimbabwe in South Africa, many of whom have taken a keen interest in the development of the MDC. South Africa has the continent's biggest and historically most militant working class. The possibility of the two movements in the two most important capitalist states in the region, linked to one another in struggle, shows the potential for socialist transformation in southern Africa. Revolts from below could radicalize the entire movement as part of the emerging anticapitalist struggle. This chapter looks at the critical role of the working class in this scenario, assessing the strength and weakness of the class from its historical development in the last fifty years.

Combined and uneven development:
the emergence of the industrial proletariat

The Zimbabwean working-class movement has grown on the basis of one of the more developed industrial economies in Africa.[1] This is probably one of the reasons why the response and resistance of the Zimbabwean working class has been much deeper than in many other African countries. It is the working class in Zimbabwe that has suffered most under the deindustrialization effects of globalization during the 1980s and 1990s.[2]

Unlike most African countries, where manufacturing is dominated by the production of consumer goods or the processing of primary goods, in Zimbabwe the manufacturing sector produces a wide range of consumer goods, intermediate products, and a small but significant range of capital goods in sub-sectors like engineering, chemicals, metals, and transport. Manufacturing is also the highest contributor to GDP, comprising about 24.8 percent in 1990 before the free market reforms were started, which is about two to three times that of an average African country. The manufacturing workforce constitute 16.5 percent of formal employment, second only to agriculture, while contributing 17–20 percent of total export revenue. The manufacturing sector is well connected to other sectors of the economy that also enjoy a high level of development, including one of the biggest large-scale capitalist agricultural sectors in Africa. A highly diversified range of products, such as tobacco, wheat, cotton, coffee, and beef, make agriculture the second biggest contributor to real GDP (at about 14 percent) and the highest contributor to formal employment and total exports at 25 percent and 34.5 percent respectively.[3] Similar developments are shown in the mining, service, and financial sectors.[4]

But this impressive base, which emerged out of an industrialization drive starting during the Second World War and extending to the late 1960s, was on an uneven, unequal, and racist platform that has only accentuated with time.[5] The economy has highly skewed ownership and control characteristics, such that today over 50 percent of manufactured output comes from Harare, the capital city, with another 25 percent coming from Bulawayo. Around 80 percent of products in the industrial sector are produced under monopolistic conditions. Nearly 60 percent of the urban population is concentrated in Harare and Bulawayo, while up to 60 percent of industrial activity is in foreign hands.[6] In the agriculture sector, a mere four thousand mainly white commercial farmers control almost 70 percent of the most productive land, thereby completely dominating the sector, while seven million or so peasants are squeezed in barren regions with little rain.[7] The top 5 percent of the population, including the traditional white upper classes and an increasing stratum of the post-independence black political and economic elites, enjoys about 70 percent of national income, while 76 percent of the population has been categorized as living below the official poverty line. Indeed, Zimbabwe has been ranked amongst the top five most unequal societies in the world in terms of income distribution.

The necessity to protect and sustain such an unequal and uneven economic base resulted in the emergence of one of the most authoritarian and undemocratic state structures in the British Empire, rivaled only by apartheid South Africa. Zimbabwe was established as a company "state" under Cecil John Rhodes's British South Africa Company in 1890, and was characterized by the imperatives of the maximum and quickest investment returns possible at the expense of the local population. Under growing pressure from below, this repressive structure continued to expand such that "the history of white rule in Zimbabwe is largely a history of a steady succession of shifts to the right."[8] It reached a climax under the white Rhodesia Front government of the 1960s and 1970s, leading one scholar to observe that "during the Rhodesia Front rule…the repressive instruments of the settler colonial state were perfected and ruthlessly implemented—it was an era of a racially founded police state."[9] This repressive structure remained substantially intact even after independence, clothed in "populism" (hence its characterization by some as "populist authoritarianism").[10] The post-colonial state took advantage of the inherited regime to consolidate its own political hegemony and contain rising working-class militancy. The state continued to be involved in waves of oppression, including the massacre of oppositionists in Matabeleland in the early 1980s.[11]

The development of the class struggle

After the decisive defeat of the anticolonial uprising or "Chimurenga" by British imperialism in 1896–98, the next forty years marked the development and consolidation of the new capitalist state, in which the natives were not only politically disenfranchised but also brutally dispossessed of independent means of production—mainly land and cattle—in order to turn them into low-paid wage slaves ("chibharo") in the new mines and farms, and to pay colonial taxes to fund the new developments.[12]

From the start, the new order faced resistance not only from the peasantry but also from the new proletarians, but such resistance was isolated and divided. Where it did occasionally break out into open class conflict, such as the strikes at Wankie Colliery in 1912 and Shamva Mine in 1922 and 1927, it was brutally and quickly suppressed by the state. The only serious attempt at building organized structures was the Industrial and Commercial Workers' Union (ICU), formed in 1927 mainly by migrant workers who had been inspired by a similar organization in South Africa. But the ICU floundered during the Great Depression in the 1930s, a victim not only of immense state harassment but also of the very nature of an economy based on unskilled, semi-migrant laborers who came to work only for intermittent periods and then returned to their rural homes in and outside Rhodesia.

The only section of the working class that could have provided leadership was the white working class, which being drawn from South Africa and Britain was already familiar with proletarian forms of organization and struggles, including the 1917 Russian Revolution. In 1916 railway workers formed the Rhodesia Railway Workers'

Union (RRWU), while the Rhodesia Mine and General Workers' Association (RMGWA) was formed in 1919, both of which, taking advantage of the shortage of skilled labor after the war, led some spectacularly successful strikes demanding pay increases and a forty-eight-hour week. There was even a Rhodesia Labour Party, modeled on the British one.

Following the end of Rhodes's company rule and the establishment of internal self-government in 1923, the political representatives of this government, the Reform Party, built on its legacy with a form of state capitalism based on strong state intervention in the economy, enabling the subsidy and protection of weak and peripheral petty bourgeois capital and labor. In Rhodesia, state capitalism became "socialism for whites,"[13] with white workers enjoying the exclusive right to form trade unions and to bargain collectively, but surrendering their rights to independence and to take strike action.

The white labor aristocracy became one of the strongest bulwarks for this racist state, a position that retarded the development of the working-class movement in Zimbabwe and was therefore particularly welcomed by both domestic and international capital. The new prime minister, Godfrey Huggins, stated:

> The European in this country can be likened to an island of white in a sea of black...with the artisan and the tradesman forming the shores and the professional classes the highlands in the centre. Is the native to be allowed to erode away the shores and gradually attack the highlands? To permit this would mean that the leaven of civilization would be removed from the country, and the black man would inevitably revert to a barbarism worse than before.[14]

However, there was a possibility of developing an independent socialist movement through the fledging Southern Rhodesia Communist Party, which had been formed from radical elements in the Rhodesia Labour Party, and those who had been associated with the South African Communist Party and the Communist Party of Great Britain. But at that time Russia was pushing "Popular Front" unity of all classes, which in Rhodesia meant unity with the white liberals. The price the party had to pay for this unity was to stop the work it had begun with the emerging black working class, as this was deemed antagonistic toward the increasingly racist, white labor force. This ultimately destroyed the party, as it divorced it from a real working-class base.

Parallel to this was the emergence of organizations representing the emerging black petty bourgeoisie, whose agenda was limited to putting pressure on the colonial state to grant more opportunities to certain black Rhodesians. One of the leading organizations was the Southern Rhodesian African National Congress (SRANC), formed in the 1930s, but until the emergence of the struggles of the black working class in the late 1940s it remained small and largely irrelevant, looking to white reformists for direction and leadership.[15]

The proletariat enters the stage

On the basis of state capitalist policies driven by war demand, an expanded European market and the federation with Zambia and Malawi, the Rhodesian economy underwent rapid industrialization between the late 1930s and the 1960s, leading to the emergence of a true industrial proletariat.[16] For instance, using an index of 100 for 1939, gross manufacturing output rose to 470 percent by 1953 with annual growth rates of 11.7 percent, and thereafter, for the next ten years of the federation, the country's GDP grew by 8.7 percent.[17] By 1950 the total black workforce had more than trebled to reach 469,000, of whom about half were industrial workers concentrated and overcrowded in the two centres of Bulawayo and Harare, working and living under very harsh conditions without the right to organize in trade unions or political organizations. Accommodation and health facilities were completely inadequate, failing to take into account the explosion of the black industrial population. Settler policy remained mired in an ideology that viewed black workers at best as a pre-industrial, semi-migrant force that would eventually retreat to its rural hinterland, and at worst as unwanted vagrants in the white man's growing cities.[18]

The most decisive class struggle of the pre-independence era was the April 1948 general strike, "the first strike which threatened the white man" and which laid the foundation of the anticolonial nationalist movement.[19] Starting on April 14 in Bulawayo, despite the pleas of the middle-class leaders of the union federations and the SRANC, tens of thousands of black workers downed tools to protest at poor wages and to demand a living national wage and adequate accommodation and health facilities. Within days the strike had spread nationally, supported by militant pickets and demonstrations and engulfing even the most backward sections of the working class, including farm workers, domestic workers, the urban unemployed, and housewives. The colonial state was only able to suppress the strike by a massive and unprecedented use of force, including soldiers, and as a result of the cowardly actions of the middle-class leaders of the movement. Nevertheless, the government was forced to grant significant concessions, including a national minimum wage and recognition of black trade unions.

Two months before the strike, meetings called by various organizations, which only a year earlier had attracted fewer than two hundred thousand people, were now attracting thousands of people in Bulawayo and Harare. These meetings united the various strata of the urban masses across national, ethnic, and gender lines. The final meeting preceding the Harare strike, at Stoddard Hall, was attended by workers, mothers, and the unemployed. Police spies were witness to the power of the movement, and reported:

> Several mass meetings were convened at Bulawayo by the Bulawayo Federation of African Workers' Union...and the African Workers' Voice Association between the 16th March and the 6th April at which signs were manifested that Bulawayo Africans were losing faith in their leaders' handling of affairs. The mood at these mass meetings was developing ugly characteristics and strike action was being called for.[20]

On April 13 a mass meeting in Bulawayo, attended by over forty thousand people, triggered the general strike. Despite the frantic efforts of the black and white middle-class leaders and advisers of the organizations that had called the meeting, "the mob…refused to listen to the leaders" and shouted: "We are not going to work. Chia! Chia! [Strike! Strike!] The leaders are cowards; they have taken our money; we must strike. We don't want leaders who are afraid. We are not going back to work. We want to strike."[21]

The strike that erupted the following morning was marked by intense militancy, with groups of pickets preventing workers from leaving the location, while others (including youth gangs and the unemployed) left for the towns and industrial regions to argue with workers to join the strike. The class dimension of the strike was shown by striking workers attacking not only the symbols of colonialism but also the properties of the black middle classes, seeing them as allies of the colonial ruling class.

However, there was an ideological immaturity in the strike that was initially exploited by radical members of the middle class, who by identifying with the strike were able to ride on its wave to political eminence. One of the most notable examples was Benjamin Burombo, a small shop owner who joined the strike and then rose to the leadership of the movement on the back of his radical, but opportunistic oratory. But far from being the heroic leader of the strike, recent research has now revealed that Burombo was actually a scab who tried to cash in on the strike, but whose "militant" transformation in support of the strike made him its mythical leader.[22]

Another example was Joshua Nkomo, the railway's first black graduate, who was employed to set up a social welfare department to prevent working-class action like the 1945 railway strike. Yet Nkomo's rise to become the most eminent nationalist in the entire country also reflected the very rich traditions of 1948; that Nkomo, a member of the Ndebele ethnic minority, could rise to such a position reflected the unifying power of the strike. Nkomo came to epitomize the new middle-class leaders, a graduate employed by the railways as a social officer.[23]

The 1948 revolt laid the basis for the development of the first viable working-class economic and political organizations, starting with the Southern Rhodesia Trade Union Congress (SRTUC), which was formed in 1954 and led by Nkomo. In 1957 the first real nationalist party, the African National Congress (ANC), was formed: a working-class-based mass movement that took most of its leaders from the labor movement, with Nkomo as president.

The "Zhii" strike movement of 1960–61 saw massive strikes in Harare and Bulawayo and combined economic and political demands. Its brutal suppression led to twenty-three deaths and the arrest of the leaders of the National Democratic Party (the successor to the banned ANC). At a time when most of Africa was achieving independence, the black middle-class leadership accepted the state's offer of black elections in fifteen out of sixty-five parliamentary seats. This was subsequently rejected by workers at an SRTUC congress in March 1961, who also demanded a national minimum wage and the immediate release of all political detainees.

The rising resistance of the black working class was only stopped by the transformation of the colonial state under Ian Smith's Rhodesia Front, which won power in 1962 and which in 1965 made a Unilateral Declaration of Independence (UDI). Thereafter the anticolonial movement could only move forward by mass open confrontation with the regime based on the militant working class. The leadership of this movement was unable to rise to the occasion, under Nkomo's leadership seeking but failing to achieve a decisive intervention on its behalf by the UK's Labour government. A section of the radical intelligentsia headed by Ndabaningi Sithole and Robert Mugabe broke with Nkomo in 1963 to form the Zimbabwe African National Union (ZANU). From the 1970s, the epicenter of the anticolonial movement shifted from the working class to radical middle-class intellectuals, whose ideology mixed radical nationalism with Maoist and Stalinist ideas. They led the peasant-based guerrilla war of liberation, which ultimately brought independence in 1980.

The seeds of this working-class failure were sown in 1948. While the general strike offered a major threat to the Rhodesian state, the absence of socialists to provide direction led the working class to look to the African middle class for leadership. A second key factor in the survival of racially based, state-led capitalism was the state's reorganization in the early 1950s when, under a banner of liberal enlightenment, it sought to foster this black reformist leadership for its own ends. In the words of Prime Minister Huggins:

> what we are witnessing here is nothing new, it has already happened in Europe. We are witnessing the emergence of a proletariat, and in this country it happens to be black.... We shall never be able to do much with these people until we have established a native middle class.[24]

The economy, which grew rapidly in the context of the postwar "long boom," made available relative increases in the previously ultra-low wages of black industrial workers, and minor breaches were made in the color bar that had generally prevented the training and advancement of skilled black workers. The centerpiece of this new liberal paradigm was the 1959 Industrial Conciliation Act, which created "multiracial" trade unions, although in reality, the union movement continued to be dominated by white labor and militant class action like strikes was prohibited.

Forced to recognize the existence of black labor by the sheer force of class struggle, colonial capital "gave in" in a way that was designed to protect its real class interests by granting a few crumbs to the emerging black "aristocracy," hoping that this group would become the immediate policemen of a rising black industrial population. This process was accelerated and aided after 1958 by international capital and right-wing union bodies, particularly the International Confederation of Free Trade Unions (ICFTU) and the African American Labour Centre, both right-wing bodies of American imperialism in the Cold War.

Some unions split and maintained links with the nationalist parties, such as the Southern Rhodesia African Trade Union Congress

(SRATUC), which was aligned to the Zimbabwe African People's Union (ZAPU). But one by one the subsequent federations succumbed to "economism"—by which trade union activity is limited only to "economic" issues—under a variety of pressures, including the repressive state machinery. This was especially true after the Unilateral Declaration of Independence in 1965. After 1965 more political unions were savagely repressed under such legislation as the Law and Order Maintenance Act and the Emergency Powers Act, whereby hundreds of trade unionists were jailed for going on illegal strikes or receiving or associating with "unlawful organizations," either nationalist parties or the Stalinist World Federation of Trade Unions (WFTU). The split in the nationalist movement between ZAPU and ZANU, which was increasingly "tribalist," also took its toll on the remnants of the political trade unions. Most trade unions were of secondary importance in the 1970s when the nationalist movement turned into a peasant-based guerrilla movement. In reality, they ceased to be real trade unions but instead became the labor wings of the guerrilla movement. The decline in working-class struggle is shown by the decrease in the number of strikes, from 138 in 1965 to only nineteen in 1971.[25]

In such a state and under the severe repression of the Smith regime, the working class had become emasculated and to all intents and purposes irrelevant to a struggle that it had itself initiated. The sorry state of the labor movement was shown in the estimation of its utility by its international paymasters, such as the ICFTU and the American Federation of Labor and the Congress of Industrial Organizations (AFL-CIO), who increasingly saw their role as ensuring that the labor movement would be pro-western in the event of the establishment of majority rule.

The 1980–81 explosions: pains of rebirth

In the two years after independence in 1980 there were an estimated two hundred strikes, in virtually every sector of the economy.[26]

The main demand was for higher wages in response to the attacks on workers under the Rhodesian state from the mid-1970s onwards. But there were also other issues, such as racism and the cumbersome and anti-working-class dispute settlement machinery. The strikes had a massive impact: "the effect of the April [1980] strikes was to wipe out the surplus for May, while exports went down by 10 percent," and they have been described as "one of the most severe industrial relations crises in the history of the country." But the massive militancy under-lying the strikes had greater impact, in so far as it pressurized the new state to introduce the most far-reaching welfare reforms since those of the 1930s.[27]

The main difference this time was that the new leadership sought to extend these reforms to the black majority, in the process consoli-dating its ideological hegemony by falsely proclaiming such reforms to be "socialism." The truth of the new regime was contained in Mu-gabe's Reconciliation Speech at independence, in which he assured white capital that its property would not be touched. The new black regime hoped to extend the use of welfarist programs to as large a por-tion of the black majority as possible: "Socialism for Blacks too." Thus in education the number of primary schools doubled, while second-ary school enrolment jumped from sixty-six thousand in 1979 to nearly one hundred fifty thousand by 1981. In the health sector an ex-tensive primary health care system was set up, which by 1990 had re-sulted in a reduction of infant mortality rates by 16 percent, while nearly eighteen thousand peasant families were resettled in the first three years.[28]

However, when the initial concessions to labor, coupled with early appeals to "patriotism," failed to quell workers' rising militancy, the new black government responded in a similar manner to the settler regimes. This response was a combination of repression, using the same laws and machinery that had been used by the colonial regime, and mea-sures aimed at fostering and co-opting a labour bureaucracy to weaken a rank-and-file workers' movement. Prime Minister Robert Mugabe at the end of 1981 denounced striking teachers and nurses as people with unrevolutionary minds, whom he claimed had never experienced the real hardships of the struggle for independence. Striking workers were soon being arrested, detained, or beaten by riot police under the Emergency Powers Act and the Law and Order Maintenance Act, the very cornerstone of colonial legislation that had been introduced in the 1960s to contain rising black working-class and nationalist militancy.

In 1981, the state succeeded in creating the Zimbabwe Congress of Trade Unions (ZCTU), whose national executive was completely dominated by staunch supporters of the ZANU-PF government, including its president, Alfred Makwarimba, and general secretary, Albert Mugabe, the brother of the prime minister. The driving aim of most of the leaders was to use the unions as a platform for ascendancy into the state machinery. Thus the ZCTU president denounced striking workers: "This country needs a disciplined workforce to encourage development—we are not going to achieve anything by going on strike, no matter how genuine our grievance."[29] By the end of 1984 there was widespread disillusionment with the existing group in charge of the Congress.[30]

"Social partnership" and the regime

The new "social partnership" was formalized in the Labour Relations Act. Under the act, registered unions were granted monopolistic rights to collective bargaining and representation, including a union dues check-off system, under the act's "one industry, one union" provisions, while the workers' committees were formally subordinated to the unions, thus addressing one of the main grievances of the labor bureaucracy. While strengthening the central ZCTU, the act firmly restricted independent rank-and-file activity. It effectively outlawed virtually all strikes, and continued the ban on the use of union funds for political purposes. The state reserved immense powers to interfere in internal union affairs, including supervision and regulation of elections, union dues, and the registration of unions.

This new bureaucracy proved unable to deliver even the state's aims of effective control of the working class. The immense disenchantment that this leadership created, alongside its ostentatious corruption, led to its removal in 1985 as the state made its peace with some of the marginalized old unions.[31] The leaders elected in 1985 and at the subsequent 1988 Congress, Jeffrey Mutandare and Morgan Tsvangirai, came from the ZCTU's largest affiliate, the Associated Mine Workers of Zimbabwe. Tsvangirai oversaw the creation of ZCTU regions and districts, which increasingly became an important organizing platform for militant lower-level unionists.

For a brief period between 1988 and 1992 there was a radical leftward shift in key sections of the labor bureaucracy, reflecting the tension created by the regime's adoption of free market policies from 1988, and the influence of Stalinist intellectuals at the University of Zimbabwe, whose sense of betrayal following ZANU's neoliberal shift was shared by some union leaders. The 1991 May Day celebrations were organized under the themes and banners, "Employers liberated, workers sacrificed" and "Are we going to make 1991 the Year of the World Bank Storm?"[32] The labour bureaucracy developed growing ties with radicalizing university students, hundreds of whom attended the May Day rallies. When the University of Zimbabwe was closed in October 1989 with the arrest of student leaders, the ZCTU general secretary, Tsvangirai, denounced the closure in very strong terms and was himself detained.[33]

In the 1990 elections, the growing autonomy of the ZCTU was demonstrated by its refusal to endorse ZANU-PF, while many workers tacitly supported a new breakaway party, Edgar Tekere's Zimbabwe Unity Movement (ZUM). Stalinism influenced a key section of the labor bureaucracy and demonstrated the fundamental importance of socialist intervention in the working class. However, this shift to the left lasted only until 1992. Thereafter, the labor bureaucracy assumed a more reformist position, calling for a "social contract" involving the state, capital, and labor in the implementation of the IMF-supported economic structural adjustment program (ESAP).[34] This new ideological position of the labor bureaucracy, aiming to offset the worst effects of structural adjustment rather than opposing it outright, was captured in the ZCTU's "Beyond ESAP" policy document. The term "comrade" was quietly replaced with "brother" and "sister."

The storm clouds gather—the failure of neoliberalism

But the long-term stability of the "social contract" or the reconciliation paradigm depended on the ability of the postcolonial state to guarantee improving working and living conditions for the black masses, as the colonial state had done for white workers. And in turn the state premised its ability to do so on a deepening of state capitalist policies. But therein lay the ultimate weakness, for the state of local and international capital had changed, and such policies were now being replaced at a global level by neoliberalism, aimed at resuscitating capitalism after the deep crisis of the 1970s. The ascendancy of political figures advocating this new ideology in the UK and United States accelerated this approach, arguing for privatization, tax cuts for businesses, the deregulation of the labor market, and an end to market-distorting state subsidies on health and education.

However, ESAP failed to address these problems. In fact, during ESAP economic performance actually worsened: whereas annual economic growth averaged 4.2 percent (5 percent in non-drought years) in the 1980s, in the 1990s it averaged less than 2 percent against a target of 5 percent. Export earnings declined by 10.7 percent in 1991, and the contribution of manufacturing to GDP declined by 14.2 percent.[35] Over fifty thousand jobs were lost, of which 56 percent were in manufacturing, while real wages declined as the consumer price index rose massively. According to the Consumer Council of Zimbabwe, a quasi-official body, "Prospects of getting the promised cake from ESAP are bleak as consumers continue to suffer severely from the so-called temporary shocks of the programme which appear to be permanent."[36]

But the strikes and demonstrations by an increasingly politicized middle and working class and university and college students pointed to the future. As long as these remained isolated struggles, the regime and the ruling classes remained relatively safe. But clearly this could not go on for long. The growing economic crisis and poverty were radicalizing ever-increasing numbers of the working masses. Things were bound to explode sooner or later. And explode they did, starting in 1996 and setting the working-class movement on an unprecedented path of development.

The government workers' general strike, 1996

For about three weeks starting in August 1996, tens of thousands of government workers went on a nationwide general strike in protest against low wages, denials of bonuses, poor working conditions, and corruption in government. For months, under pressure from below, the official public sector unions, such as the Public Service Association (PSA), the Zimbabwe Nurses' Association (ZINA), and the Zimbabwe Teachers' Association (ZIMTA) had been threatening to go on strike, but they had kept postponing the call for action. On the last payday in August, health sector workers from doctors to cleaners spontaneously walked out, holding a mass meeting at the central hospital in Harare. They elected a strike committee representing all the sectors of the ministry to lead and generalize the strike. Within a day the strike had spread to all sections of the civil service and nationwide to the smallest towns. For over two weeks the civil servants, under the leadership of an eleven-person strike committee called the United Civil Servants' Negotiation Committee, paralyzed government services, even when the official trade union leaders, who had by then joined the strike, tried to stop it a few days later. They failed, and the strike continued for twelve more days, forcing the government to grant a 26–29 percent increment and to reinstate seven thousand strikers.

After some tough talking by the union leaders, the strike ended with the striking workers receiving a significant pay increase, bonuses, and promises of a new Labour Act that would cover all workers and give recognition to the public sector unions. However, health sector workers, especially the nurses, were not happy with the compromise and resumed the strike in November, continuing until February 1997. Now isolated, they were ultimately defeated, but not before they had inspired masses of workers in the private sector generally.[37]

The government workers' strike was a watershed, shattering the social partnership of the 1990s, drawing on the militant traditions of 1980–81 and 1948 and developing new ones. The first significant element was its sheer size. For instance, while the two thousand striking workers in 1995 were the highest number since 1980–81, these were completely dwarfed by more than two hundred thirty-five thousand strikers in 1996, almost exclusively representing the general strike.[38] As in the 1948 general strike, the key driving force was the mass meetings of thousands of workers in Harare at Africa Unity Square and Harare Hospital and on a smaller scale in the other centers. It is at these mass meetings that the demands of the strikers became increasingly political, including cutting the size of the government, providing adequate resources in hospitals, and enacting a new harmonized labor law. The meetings were also forums through which leaders were made accountable and from where flying pickets were sent daily to government offices in Harare, to persuade those who had gone back to work to rejoin the strike.

But the 1996 general strike represented two major developments in the working-class movement. The first one was that, for the first time, a radical rank and file emerged to become the de facto leadership of the movement, drawing up a radical program uniting all workers. This was the eleven-person strike committee that was elected on the second day of the strike from militants among the strikers, including doctors and nurses. The government was forced to negotiate with the strike committee, while the traditional union leaders struck a compromise deal that eventually ended the strike. The result was the persecution of members of this committee who initially lost their jobs and careers, only to be reinstated after a long legal battle.[39]

The election of the strike committee and the militant conduct of the strike were closely tied to the second key development: namely, the intervention of a revolutionary socialist group in the strike. The International Socialist Organization (ISO) is a tiny Trotskyist organization based on the principles of workers' self-activity and opposed to a top-down approach centered on the party or union bureaucracy.[40] The role of the group has been consistently and deliberately ignored by most historians and political commentators, despite the fact that a cursory look at the newspapers and magazines of the period clearly shows its importance.[41]

On the second day of the strike, as workers started assembling at Africa Unity Square and Harare Hospital, small contingents of ISO members, mainly students from the Harare Polytechnic, joined the strikers and gave solidarity messages calling for the unity of the two groups. ISO issued a small leaflet calling for an indefinite strike, broader demands, and the election of a strike committee. These ideas were adopted by workers and ISO members became a key part of the strike in Harare and Bulawayo, conferring with the strike committee on the way forward. ISO members also traveled to other small centers, encouraging workers on strike.

Recognition of the key role of ISO in the strike came from two opposing sources. The government daily, the *Herald*, ran a comment on the strike calling on workers to dissociate themselves from "groups which were bent on transforming their legitimate strike into some Bolshevik revolution."[42] At the same time, ISO's slogan, "*Shinga Mushandi Shinga! Qina Msebenzi Qina!*" ("Worker, be resolute! Fight on!") became the official slogan of the striking workers. In the 1997 strikes, this slogan was to spread to the private sector workers and became the official slogan of the ZCTU.

The 1996 strike was decisive. The strike signaled the reemergence of the working class as the leading agent of political and democratic transformation in periphery capitalist societies, just as it showed the critical role of socialist intervention in class struggle. It was the great dress rehearsal for the struggles that exploded in the next few years.

The explosion of 1997

The year 1997 was to witness the largest number of strikes and demonstrations in the history of Zimbabwe. Workers, students, and even the previously marginalized war veterans and peasants came out in protest against the massive fall in their living standards that resulted from a continuing economic crisis, accelerated by the reforms of the 1990s. Every sector of the economy was hit as recalcitrant employers, used to years of docile workers and unions, initially refused to budge. There were militant strikes in the construction, clothing, and catering industries, and even in the agricultural sector, where the last strike had been in 1948. In 1997 there were fifty-five recorded strikes involving over 1,073,000 workers—almost the entire workforce in the private sector and higher than any year since independence in 1980.[43]

Similarly, for the first time since independence, landless peasants and war veterans invaded white commercial farms, and for some time resisted efforts by the police and senior government/ZANU-PF leaders to evict them. They even attended demonstrations in Harare. Significant too was the presence of former guerrillas who had fought the liberation war, but who had been discarded soon after independence, many of them now destitute, without job, pension, or land. Inspired by the mass struggles erupting around them, they started demonstrating against the government, demanding pensions. These demonstrations and the state reactions against them were key in delegitimizing the post-colonial ruling class.[44]

Reeling from massive pressure from below, in November 1997 Mugabe's government gave in to the war veterans' demands, awarding them a lump sum and pensions to be financed by ordinary people through a newly introduced 5 percent "War Veterans Levy" and a 2.5 percent increase in sales tax. A section of the ZCTU leadership, led by Tsvangirai, like Burombo before them, realized that the new radicalization in the working class meant that they needed to retreat from the ideas of "social partnership" and adopt a more militant outlook. They helped initiate mass meetings and labor forums in the major towns and cities, to consider the way forward. They called a two-day national strike, starting on December 9, which was to become

> the largest and most successful strike since independence—and probably since the national strikes of 1948. Almost all businesses and workplaces shut, involving more than one million workers, management, informal sector entrepreneurs and civil servants. In most cities, there were large demonstrations supported by a broad range of civic and professional organizations.[45]

When the police violently stopped workers from assembling at Africa Unity Square, now the traditional assembly point of striking workers, there were riots that left the city center a ghost town. Running scared, the ZCTU leaders, Morgan Tsvangirai and Gibson Sibanda, called off the strike, stating that the action would resume in January when workers returned to work from the annual Christmas holiday.

In early January 1998, given the continued delays by the ZCTU leaders in calling the action they had promised in December, housewives in one of Harare's poorest suburbs started demonstrating against increases in bread prices. Riots quickly spread to the unemployed and workers in Harare and a few other towns, despite the frantic efforts of the ZCTU leaders to disassociate themselves from the protests. The ISO leaflet entitled "Todya Marara Here?" ("Do They Want Us to Eat Dirt?") was quickly adopted by the rioting masses, leading to the arrest and harassment of leading ISO members in Harare and Bulawayo (including the author), as the organizers of the riots.[46]

The January riots were a powerful example of the direction that the struggles that had started in 1996 were now taking. What lay behind these explosions? The first was the increasing radicalization of sections of the working class. The strikes faced more resistance from the state, forcing even greater radicalization, which in 1996 was to explode in a generalized manner. The reemerged workers' committees became rallying points of resistance outside the unions. While the committees had been co-opted by the state and bosses in the 1980s, in the 1990s large workplaces became an increasing focal point of struggle, and began to include non-active groups of workers, the more educated and skilled white-collar workers. Such workers started participating in and leading workers' committees, especially at the larger workplaces such as the National Railways of Zimbabwe (NRZ). An underlying factor at play here was the change in the form of the working class.

By the 1990s a new type of worker, young, ambitious, and fairly well educated, had emerged partly as a result of the massive expansion of the education system in the 1980s. Many of these young workers had also grown up in urban areas (a factor caused by among other things the failure of the state to distribute land in the rural areas), in contrast to the rural background of their parents. Yet it is precisely these workers who were on the receiving end of the neoliberal reforms, particularly the casualization of labor, which meant that most were employed as contract or casual workers with very little if any job security. Workers' committees became much more flexible and open forums for expressing their discontent not just against the bosses, but increasingly also against their own unions.

The strikes of 1997–98 had a significant impact on the state. One of the most entrenched and violent ruling elites in Africa was forced to retreat before the power of the working-class-led revolts. Aware of the fate of earlier African regimes, Mugabe now conducted a partial economic and ideological retreat from neoliberalism, returning to a level of state intervention in the economy and a degree of radical rhetoric. Ideologically, Zanu-PF adopted an increasingly anti-imperialist and racist rhetoric centered on the land issue and, with the support of war vets leader Chenjerai Hunzvi, designated the largest-ever number of farms for acquisition (over eight hundred). It was in this context, attempting to breathe new life into a pseudo-radical "Third Worldism," that the regime sent Zimbabwean troops into the Democratic Republic of the Congo in 1998.

However, Mugabe faced resistance to this leftward lurch not from within ZANU-PF, but from local and international capital. The value of the Zimbabwean dollar crashed by 75 percent in November 1998, and subsequently in October 1999, with the suspension of IMF and World Bank loans, which in turn massively accelerated the economic crisis.[47] A campaign for Mugabe's international isolation was instituted. Although Mugabe came under increasing pressure to return to neoliberal policies, such was the impact of the revolt from below that he had no alternative but to make concessions to this movement.

From economics to politics: the formation of the Movement for Democratic Change

The discussions held in the ZCTU produced an increasing demand for it to lead the formation of a workers' party. Given its economist ancestry, this was initially opposed by the leadership, but by the end of 1998 pressure from below helped bring about a sharp U-turn. In February 1999, the ZCTU convened a National Working People's Convention. This established the Movement for Democratic Change, which on September 11 was officially launched as a political party, and which in June 2000 came close to defeating ZANU-PF in the parliamentary elections.

The period between March and September 1999, when party structures were being put in place, was a bustle of activity among the working class. MDC committees were built in the factories, usually around the most militant members of the workers' committees. Regular meetings were convened in the major towns by the ZCTU regions, which had been the engine of the stay-aways, and which now acted as the de facto MDC provincial structures. Of the eight or so provincial structures of the MDC, seven were dominated by organized labor; the party was routinely referred to as a "labor party."

Despite this, there had been signs from the first that the dominance of the MDC by the working class would be contested. The February 1999 convention that established the MDC was dominated by the liberal middle-class intelligentsia. In contrast, ISO was stopped from attending. Worker militants had called for a "labor party" to be formed, but the "movement" that was set up demonstrated a popular front ambiguity. As ISO warned, the declaration adopted was "a very dangerous document that will perpetuate the suffering of workers and the poor.... It is in fact a clever cover up for the drafters' intention of continuing with ESAP should they get into power."[48]

It was at the launch of the MDC in September 1999 that the party's class direction became clear. Without any consultation or involvement of its regional structures, the labor bureaucracy that dominated the MDC imposed an "interim" national executive that was drawn largely from the neoliberal middle classes, especially from the National Constituent Assembly (NCA, see below) and the Forum Party (which disbanded). The rank-and-file unionists who had built the movement were marginalized.

This was evident in the June 2000 elections, by which time the union bureaucracy had itself been marginalized. Trade unionists composed less than 20 percent of the parliamentary candidates, and most of these, including the party's president, Morgan Tsvangirai, were selected for unsafe rural constituencies, which they mostly lost. Nevertheless, following the referendum victory, the MDC won nearly half of the contested seats, sweeping the board in the urban centeres where the working class was strong. ZANU-PF achieved a narrow victory thanks to its violent and intimidatory rural campaign, but also due to Mugabe's opportunistic land policy, a position helped by the MDC's conservatism on the issue.[49] While the MDC had been propelled into near power by the working class, it was clear that the class character of the party was in opposition to the aspirations of the masses who had built it. How had this happened?

The relative ease with which a movement with so much potential was turned into a neoliberal popular front lay in the historical and continuing weakness of the working-class movement, and the lack of a significant socialist movement. While the 1997–98 mass actions had rocked Mugabe and generated the first significant challenge to his rule in twenty years, they had not developed into an independent rank-and-file movement that could challenge the stranglehold of a reformist labor bureaucracy. Under pressure from below, the bureaucracy had participated in and endorsed mass actions, gaining significant moral authority in the process. However, it remained prone to vacillation and fundamentally untransformed, as shown by its cancellation of the second day of the December 1997 strike. Threatened by the workers' growing radicalization, and vulnerable to state repression (such as the 1998 regulations outlawing strikes, and attempts to ban the ZCTU), the labor bureaucracy sought to rein in the workers. From March 1998, they shifted from strike-based demonstrations to "peaceful stay-aways" in which workers were told to stay at home. This reduced the militancy and impact of the action, individualized workers and made them vulnerable to intimidation; it also prevented the mass gatherings that had been the basis for pressure on the union bureaucracy, reducing its accountability. In late 1998 and early 1999, the ZCTU unilaterally canceled two major stay-away actions.

The ZCTU's sudden support for the formation of the MDC should be understood in this context. In late 1998, it argued that stay-aways were no longer useful; instead, what was needed was to build a political party and win the 2000 elections. Mass struggles were discouraged as falling into the enemy trap, which would give ZANU-PF an excuse to declare a state of emergency. These ideas appealed to many workers, and this partly accounts for the growth of reformist parliamentary illusions and the subsequent decline of more militant struggles.

Another key factor in the right-wing takeover of the rising working-class movement lay in the role of the middle-class intelligentsia. The neoliberal agenda had been imposed by an authoritarian system in Zimbabwe, as it had been in most of the periphery societies by one-party state regimes or military juntas. In such societies the distinction between economics and politics became infinitesimal. Thus the revolts that emerged against the worsening conditions of the masses, as a result of the deepening economic crisis, inevitably assumed a political form—democratic struggles against the authoritarian superstructure that had "imposed" the crisis in the first place. At that stage, the forces of global capitalism, aware of the revolutionary potential of the emerging struggles, were forced to abandon the old authoritarian forms of domination in the periphery, and instead to assume a more democratic face, so as to intercede and neutralize the rising movement.

The groups to whom their cynical appeals to bourgeois democratic values, such as "rule of law," "human rights," and "good governance," appealed the most were the middle-class intelligentsia, who were being radicalized under the impact of the crisis and who could be organized in NGOs and "civic society." In the absence of a rival ideological alternative, given the demise of "communism" and the accompanying bourgeois triumphalism of this period, many of these groups went to bed with neoliberalism, without interrogating the true nature of their partner. In any case, the thinly disguised bribes that global neoliberalism poured into the civic groups, academia, "independent media," and NGOs that mushroomed were too much for most to resist. And thus from Poland to Serbia, Zambia to Zimbabwe, such middle classes became the midwives who delivered the militant but ideologically immature working-class movement into the arms of neoliberalism.

In Zimbabwe the critical middle-class body that negotiated the neoliberal takeover of the rising workers' movement was the NCA. The NCA had been formed in 1997 as a vehicle for mobilizing the middle class around the demand for a new constitution, and was financed and mentored by German and Scandinavian social democratic foundations and unions. Its role in the MDC gave the new party respectability in the eyes of international financial organizations, which could now write off Mugabe, who had previously done their bidding, but who no longer had the authority to impose their reforms.

Just ahead of the 2000 elections, the IMF, World Bank, and western bank loans were suspended, accelerating the economic crisis.

Neoliberalism, the MDC, and the ISO experience

What was the role of the International Socialist Organization in this? One of its leading members was actually a member of parliament for the MDC. Was the ISO's participation an act of opportunism or would remaining outside be an act of "left-wing infantilism"? Many groups will be confronted by similar questions as the crisis of neoliberalism grows globally.

To remain outside and criticize a party that represented a rising working-class movement and had a massive following in the class risked the danger of being identified with a hated neoliberal regime and condemned to irrelevance. On the other hand, entryism risked "right-wing liquidation." After intense internal debate centred on the principles developed by Lenin, it was resolved to "enter" the MDC based on two interrelated principles. The first principle was Lenin's argument for entryism based on the nonnegotiable principle of absolute freedom of expression. The aim was to ruthlessly expose the bankruptcy of the ideas and leadership of the party, which the ISO did by opposing the party's neoliberal manifesto with its own anti-neoliberal "Action Programme," and by producing a monthly newspaper, *Socialist Worker*. The second principle was organizational autonomy based on Trotsky's united front, whereby the ISO resisted the MDC leadership's attempts to disband it, but instead sought constantly to use the party's platforms, including the parliamentary seat, to relate to and recruit rank-and-file militants.

The ISO did this with relative success first in the two biggest provinces of Harare and Bulawayo and, secondly, to build rank-and-file industrial committees in the industrial areas surrounding its constituency, which provided it with its first real roots in the working class. These groups subsequently played a critical role in defending the

ISO against the MDC, which sought to expel it as a result of its attacks on the increasingly right-wing nature of the party. The central idea was that, in time and with the benefit of experience, the masses would be able to identify with the ISO's communist propaganda, creating real opportunities for the growth of the revolutionary organization.

In December 2000, the MDC leadership unilaterally canceled a popular and long-awaited mass action to remove Mugabe, which was modeled on the Serbian revolts that had brought down Slobodan Milosevic. This was due to pressure from local and international capitalists, who feared the radicalizing effect of such action on the masses.[50] Disillusionment among ordinary members of the MDC, which had developed from the failure of its parliamentary representatives to raise their bread-and-butter concerns, crystallized around this decision. ISO concluded that this event marked the decisive break of the MDC leadership with its mass base. However, because of the importance of the 2002 presidential elections, which still fostered reformist illusions in workers, it was resolved that such a break would not be made by ISO. Instead, an accelerated ideological offensive was launched against the MDC leadership. In February 2001, I presented a document to an MDC leadership seminar, which laid the blame for the party's declining fortunes on the "hijacking of the party by the bourgeoisie, marginalization of workers, adoption of neoliberal positions and cowardly failure to physically confront the Mugabe regime and bosses."[51] This was followed, on May Day 2001, by ISO support for factory invasions by war veterans, but combined with a call on workers to take similar actions themselves, to stop retrenchments and win better conditions.

The ISO was unable to stop the final neoliberal takeover of the MDC fundamentally because it lacked the necessary size and penetration of the working class to offer a sufficient counterweight to the might of local and international neoliberal forces, vindicating Trotsky's imperative that the revolutionary party has to be built before the revolutionary explosions occur. The experience of the ISO operating in the MDC was nevertheless important: the limited influence it exerted, its survival and growth, doubling in size during this period, justified its tactics.

Despite the decision of the ISO not to campaign for Tsvangirai in the presidential elections in Highfield, the constituency that I represented, the MDC share increased from 73 percent to 82.1 percent, making it by far the best-performing constituency of the MDC. Of course, the entryism was not easy, as was shown in July 2001 when some of the older comrades in Harare, unwilling to break with the MDC, split to form what they called Left Wing. But overall the experience laid the basis for a sizeable socialist organization with sufficient roots in the working class to be in a much stronger position to play a leadership role in the future.

Conclusion

As I write, the results of the 2002 presidential elections have just been announced and Mugabe has been declared the winner after receiving 56.2 percent of the votes compared to Tsvangirai's 42 percent share. Thus for now one of the main aspirations of a movement that started around 1996 with so much promise has ended in a massive electoral defeat. What went wrong?

The MDC and its local and western allies have alleged electoral fraud and massive intimidation, and have refused to recognize the results, with the West imposing sanctions and calling for fresh elections. While violence was real in the elections, especially in the rural areas, such violence had been anticipated, with Brian Raftapoulos, a key liberal of civic society and a strong associate of the MDC, warning in mid-2000: "The MDC must face the prospect of a violent presidential election." However, the MDC dismally failed to do this, instead relying on the belief that change was "in the air."

It was the ideological and strategic crisis of the MDC that was crucial. It centred on the party's shift to right-wing neoliberalism, coinciding with Mugabe's partial retreat from structural adjustment to assume a nationalist and anti-imperialist stance, based on the land question. As the ISO warned: "That Mugabe's strategy has worked and could work around the presidential elections has in no small measure been helped by the wrong tactics and strategies adopted by the middle classes who now dominate our party. Their obvious pro-West, pro-commercial farmer, pro-IMF positions were a godsend to Mugabe. The MDC could only have dealt with Mugabe by outflanking on the left on bread and butter issues. . . ."

So in the end Mugabe's delivery on land and his radical rhetoric separated the urban poor from the rural poor, ensuring him victory. Mugabe's share of the vote increased by 7.9 percent from 2000, while the MDC's declined by 5.1 percent. His key gains were in rural areas, where voter turnout and his share of the vote increased significantly, including in the MDC Matebeleland strongholds; seven peri-rural MDC constituencies were lost.

On the other hand, the MDC moved to the right, to the alarm of most of its supporters. As the crisis deepened and the masses called for action, the MDC failed to deliver. Its leadership dithered and eventually rejected the Serbian route, opting for western pressure, the courts, and winning the elections. All militant action was frowned on as threatening an election that the MDC increasingly believed it would win. So the working classes were massively demobilized and disillusioned as they continued to suffer under a growing crisis. Not surprisingly, apathy in the urban areas in the elections ran at over 50 percent. This is a key reason why the revolts that had been predicted against a stolen election have dismally failed to materialize. The roar of the 1997 lion had by March 2002 been reduced to less than a kitten's meow, and the three-day stay-away called by the ZCTU to protest the results was a disastrous failure.

But neither Mugabe's victory nor the deceptive post-election calm means the end of the crisis in Zimbabwe. The depth of the economic crisis is extremely severe, including massive food shortages. The polarization of the Mugabe state from its bourgeois base is deep and growing; imperialism also regards Mugabe as a massive threat to a key centre of capitalism on the continent, South Africa.

It must be remembered that, while Mugabe is an intelligent and ruthless operator, capable of sophisticated tactical shifts, he and Zanu-PF are not immune from the tensions arising from the economic crisis. Zanu-PF remains a party dominated by the black national bourgeoisie who, in the context of the weak private capitalism prevalent in peripheral states like Zimbabwe, have sought to use the state, like their white colonial predecessors, as a channel for accumulation. This gives Zanu-PF a contradictory relationship with the free market that dominates the international economy: it resists the forced reduction of its capacity to develop economic polices that enable its own state-based accumulation, but at the same time greedily eyes the potential gains it can make from privatization. Opposed to the black national bourgeoisie are the lower structures of the party, especially those around the radicalized war veterans, whose underlying aspirations are clearly similar to those of the working class. As the economic and political crisis worsens, under Western pressure, these tensions can only grow.

These factors might force the regime to attempt to co-opt the MDC as a junior partner in a neoliberal government of national unity. There might be some constitutional reforms allowing for the eventual (and graceful) retirement of Mugabe and his replacement by a figure more acceptable to the West. It is the desire for such a result that is driving Washington and London to increase pressure on Mugabe, and he has already shown an inclination to drop his cynical anti-imperialist posture of the campaign period by stating in his victory speech that the neoliberal New Millennium Economic Recovery Program will be the basis of his economic policies.

Mugabe has no solution to the growing crisis, but nor does the MDC. Rapprochement with ZANU-PF, favored by most of its leadership, would amount to its "kiss of death," while its right-wing degeneration has gone too far for it to be anything other than a rapidly declining electoral force. The MDC's electoral defeat marks a disillusionment with the middle-class opportunists who hijacked the rising movement of 1997–98. The defeat of the neoliberal route in the context of a growing crisis means that the return of struggles or *jambanja* to finalize the unfinished business of 1997 is a distinct possibility.

Herein lies the most fundamental question confronting the Zimbabwean working class and socialist movement today: the issue of leadership. Under the pressure of the growing crisis, with socialist intervention, will rank-and-file union activists break through the suffocating air of the old union bureaucracy? Can the post-independence generation, which is educated, casualized, and extremely militant, create its own leadership and mobilize other sections of the oppressed, such as the war veterans, peasants, students, and unemployed, as it did in 1997–98? Can it join other struggles in the region, critically those of South Africa? The process has begun in some unions, but at a very slow and hesitant pace, stifled by the ZCTU leaders. Alternatively, the movement could be co-opted and neutralized by the new splinter unions being created by ZANU-PF through Joseph Chinotimba's war-veteran-dominated Zimbabwe Federation of Trade Unions.

As the history of Zimbabwe has shown, unless there is a substantial socialist intervention in the rising working-class movement, it remains vulnerable to co-option by its class enemies and may prove unable to fulfil its potential. Such intervention is critical in giving the movement appropriate organizational and ideological direction. It can help generalize the experience of the class, and act as its memory bank, sharing the lessons of 1948, 1980–81, and 1997–98. It can demonstrate the connection between the individual struggles of the different sections of the oppressed, and show that these are neither accidental nor confined to Zimbabwe, but are the inevitable consequence of an international system that is based on unplanned production for the maximization of profit. It can argue for the need to construct a working-class-led, antineoliberal united front to smash this system, and can demonstrate it in the concrete circumstances of struggle.

To play such a role, the experience of the ISO shows the need to construct a sizeable revolutionary organization with sufficient roots in the working class. To achieve this in the twenty-first century requires a radical reorientation to meet the new challenges we face. Socialists must turn outward to lead and to learn from the emerging movement, and from among the varied experiences of different socialist groups.[52] Socialists must leave behind the legacy of sectarian practices based on toy "internationals," personality cults, undemocratic structures and practices, and unprincipled splits and expulsions. Socialists must appreciate that a theoretical understanding of the nature of the period, and the strategies necessary to relate to it, is only the first step on a long journey. For without experience and the willingness to learn from it, even some of the best movements have failed the real test of their times. Given the demise of Stalinism and the great opportunities opened by the growing anti-globalization movement across the world, it would be a terrible crime to continue with old practices that divide and demobilize the international revolutionary movement, at a time when its potential has never been greater, nor its task more urgent.

INTERVIEW WITH TAFADZWA CHOTO

Before she became active in socialist politics, Tafadzwa Choto was involved in the women's movement in Zimbabwe. She is now the national organizer of the International Socialist Organization (ISO) in Zimbabwe. She has been involved in many strikes and demonstrations during the last five years. During the 2001 May Day celebrations in Harare, she was attacked and savagely beaten by Mugabe's thugs. Undeterred she remained active and continues to fight for socialist change in Zimbabwe (School of Oriental and African Studies, London, July 2001).

What events have shaped your political evolution?

To begin with the events that have really politicized me: the first one was when a woman at the University of Zimbabwe was stripped of her skirt. It was said to be a miniskirt and it was publicly ripped off her. I was disgusted. And this is at the highest institute of learning. I think that was in 1993. And then in 1995 in Harare, in the city center about three civilians were shot by the police, while the police were chasing after some thieves who had stolen a manual typewriter. Three civilians were shot dead and for what? There were riots in Harare. People reacted on the same day by burning cars and police property. By that time I was already in ISO; we organized a demonstration based on a united front with other organizations against police brutality. It was a huge success.

What were the events that drew you to the ISO? What did you know about the organization? How did you find out about it?

[Laughs] Actually it wasn't really an "event" as such. Because before I joined the ISO I used to be a member of a feminist group in Zimbabwe, a feminist organization. But by that time I wasn't really attending meetings because they were constantly attacking men, men, men. There was not much politics. I wasn't comfortable with it. At the same time I used to work at a certain company as a typesetter and the ISO meetings were held next door, so that is how I came to know of them. And one day I just said let me go and attend their meetings. Very simple really.

Can you say a few words about the organization? How is it responding to political events at the moment?

I have to look back to 1995 and the way it is right now and there is a big difference. Not only in terms of growth—it has really grown, unlike when I joined when there were less than twenty members. But also now most of the members are involved in the participations that are taking place on the ground. We are seeing the involvement of many, many workers. When ISO was formed in Zimbabwe it was basically a middle-class group but now it has really become a working-class group. On a day-to-day basis I am a national organizer for ISO. I am mainly involved in helping branches every now and then and in organizing the interventions and so forth. I also help in the typesetting of *Socialist Worker*.

And to bring us up to date, the events that everyone is talking about: the MDC and the rapid rise of the opposition in Zimbabwe. Can you talk about the working class and trade unions in the MDC and what way that is going to develop?

I can say that the role of trade unions in the MDC today is minimal. From independence to about 1987 the trade unions were very sympathetic to ZANU-PF. But what happened was a change of the top leadership, that's when we saw the original leadership being removed, replaced by Morgan Tsvangirai and others. And they created district structures and provincial structures and those are the ones that were very strong and those are the ones which formed the MDC. But now most of those who were part of the structures have drifted off, and some have been co-opted into the national executive of the MDC and some of them are now MPs and with the nature of the party right now they are also moving, together with the party, to the right. So I can't say that the working class or trade unions are playing a very important role in the MDC; the middle classes have a much stronger voice than the workers.

And that has been over the last year or so?

Yes, I think it really became apparent last year before the parliamentary elections. I think before that the bourgeoisie were not really convinced that the MDC would change the government. But when the MDC, ourselves and the NCA [National Constitutional Assembly] campaigned for a no vote at the referendum and the no vote won, that is when they became really convinced that the MDC is something and from then onward that is when we saw them hijacking the party and funding the parliamentary election campaigns. And afterward when the MDC got fifty-seven seats, you know gaining a strong voice, their influence has increased. Before the middle class were part of the structures making some decisions but now most of them are bourgeoisie. I met a middle-class activist before last year's elections, who really campaigned, and he was very frustrated about the results. So it is not only the workers who are frustrated!

In what way will the tensions resolve themselves? What do you think will happen?

Right now we have been working with the labor movement, saying that the labor movement should take an independent role. If you remember, last year [2000] Tsvangirai made statements that Mugabe was going to be removed—if he didn't resign, he was going to be removed by violence and there was going to be mass action. That never took place, and the reason: the MDC was given advice by European countries not to do so. So the mass action did not take place, and at that time the labor movement was not very organized to push for mass action on its own, so the only way to solve the tension and the

differences and for the working class to gain an upper hand is to organize independently under the ZCTU.

There have also been attacks on the ISO…

Yes, quite a lot, particularly over the issue of land. We agreed that land
should be given to peasants and also farmers shouldn't be compensated,
because in the first place they stole that land and after stealing the land
they oppressed the people working on it. So we saw no reasons why the
farmers should be compensated yet the MDC were saying that they
should be. Also the other issue was about workers themselves—workers
should use mass action to push for their demands and this thing of negotiating with the bosses through courts is nonsense. Negotiations
haven't worked and more and more workers can see that they can only
liberate themselves in the streets and not in parliament or the courts.

How in your opinion can the workers' voice be heard in Zimbabwe? There is some talk about an independent "labor" party.

For the workers to be heard I think they have to form an independent body and that requires rebuilding the structures of the ZCTU
and really making them strong so as to challenge both parties: the
MDC and ZANU-PF. And later on it can move to form its own party.
We were almost there, as the MDC was formed by workers, but it was
later hijacked. I just want to add that it doesn't only apply to workers
in Zimbabwe but also to South Africa—COSATU should become an
independent body out of the ANC and the SACP. So the challenge to
workers in Zimbabwe, Zambia, and South Africa is to now form independent parties to make the movement strong.

In what way has the anti-capitalist movement shown itself in Zim-babwe? Are there people talking about the mass demonstrations across the world against the IMF, WTO, etc.?

Yes, I can say people are beginning to talk about it after the disillusionment of the last year, with fifty-seven MDC MPs in parliament

doing nothing. Increasingly you meet students and the radicalized middle classes and some sections of the advanced workers who are talking about the movement. And we have to thank Mugabe [laughing] for taking the "anti-imperialist" stance because all of these demonstrations are being covered in Zimbabwe—if he wasn't "supporting" the demonstrations, we wouldn't see them. After Gothenburg there was a long article which was in one of the bourgeoisie papers saying that the anticapitalist and anti-globalization mood was led by the Trotskyites and anarchists—so the talk is now there in Zimbabwe.

What do you think are the prospects for socialism in Zimbabwe? What is the prospect for socialist transformation?

Well, after the fall of the Berlin Wall and the USSR ten years ago there was confusion about which way forward and I can say that in the early nineties the left weren't very radical and were disillusioned about the changes. But what is happening now is that the left are now gaining confidence and are beginning to talk about socialism and not the Stalinism that we had. So there is now a section of the left, from workers to students, who are talking about socialist transformation. Even Mugabe sometimes uses "socialism" at the time of the elections, but he has mostly abandoned that term since he decided to follow the IMF and the World Bank.

Can you reflect on your experiences as a socialist and as a woman fighting for socialism in Zimbabwe?

Well, I can say that it hasn't been that easy. But women have played a very important role in the strikes that have taken place, like the government workers' strike. Women were at the forefront of it because most of them are nurses, and nurses are the ones who started the strike. Even with the formation of the MDC there were quite a number of women who were at the forefront of it, and also the food riots of 1998 were actually kicked off by women. But the pity right now is that women often still think that they shouldn't push themselves forward and you see women saying, "You take the position." So those women who might want to challenge these assumptions are put in difficult positions.

Lastly, I would want to say one major disappointing thing is that because of the economic conditions, the worsening economic situation, women are being taken advantage of, even if they are outspoken. They are often forced through poverty to resort to desperate measures [female students at the University of Zimbabwe have been pushed into prostitution: see *Socialist Worker* (Harare), July–August 2001]. I am not happy about the position women are in right now in Zimbabwe; we hope that things will get better.

What lessons have you learned from your political activity as a revolutionary?

I want to quote Trotsky. I don't know if I'm quoting him correctly, but when he was older he said that he was much more convinced about the struggle and the need for socialism than ever before. I can say the same today: I am much more convinced of the need for a socialist society. Our world is very beautiful and it has so much to offer—so that is a challenge that I keep on fighting for. And I can say the experiences I have had in the past have really given me confidence and made me see the need to fight against our oppressive society, though in between the struggles you meet with challenges and at times you just think of stopping. After I was beaten on May Day, afterward I was really under . . .

Can you explain what happened?

OK, we went to attend May Day this year and we had produced a poster saying that the war veterans are not the answer to workers' problems because they were invading factories. And while we were putting up these posters the war veterans were around, so myself and another comrade, the coordinator for Highfield branch, we were attacked by ZANU-PF thugs. I think I was beaten by about six or so and sustained injuries to my eardrum and eye and the same with the other comrade. Afterwards my family played a very important role in assisting me, but

I was under pressure from some members of my family and some friends that it has become a serious danger for me to remain in politics. But I managed to overcome those pressures and I told them this is what I think is right to fight for and I stood by this. I don't expect the pressure to end right now—it will continue—but I think I have overcome the major challenges from them and gradually they will just accept it.

You are part of an international revolutionary tradition. How important is that for you?

It is very important because at times when you are back home in a Third World country you feel isolated and you wonder, "Will we ever achieve socialism here?" but when you come here [Marxism 2001—a yearly international socialist forum organized in London] you see organizations from all over the world and you know that you are not alone in the struggles that are taking place and you see that there is real hope for international socialism.

I want to thank you for helping to sustain that international tradition yourself.

We have been encouraged quite a lot, and also inspired by events taking place here as well. So I think it goes both ways.

CONCLUSION:
"SHINGA MUSHANDI SHINGA!
QINA MSEBENZI QINA!"[1]

Peter Dwyer and Leo Zeilig

The African continent has been tied to the international accumulation of capital since the first slave ships from Europe anchored off
the West African coast. Globalization, as such, is not new to Africa.
Long enmeshed in a complex web of uneven capitalist expansion that
enveloped the world, the continent was turned into a source of raw
materials for the North. The birth of global capitalism came "dripping
from head to foot, from every pore, with blood and dirt."[2] Africa was
savagely underdeveloped by its inclusion into an emerging capitalist
world. The great black intellectuals and liberation leaders of the twentieth century, Fanon, Cabral, and Walter Rodney, would be amused to
hear talk of globalization and the opportunities that we are told it offers to Africans. But there are two realities linked to what is now called
"globalization" that do offer real hope. First, globalization has buried
the myths of independent capitalist development, national autonomy, and "socialism in one country," and secondly, it has given birth to
resistance at each stage of this globalization.

Another global economic crisis in the early 1970s forced capitalists
to respond by taking up a renewed offensive (often referred to as "neoliberalism") against the exploited across the globe to restore profitability. In Africa this had the devastating effect of attacking the social

consumption of the poorest in an already devastated continent. As the previous chapters have shown, the result has been violent cuts in spending on health, education, food, and transport. In Zambia structural adjustment has meant that spending on social services was cut from 7.4 percent of GDP in 1991 to 0.4 percent in 1993.[3] Several African counties now spend more on servicing their debts to the West than they spend on education and health combined. In April 1995 an official of the World Bank expressed his satisfaction at the advancement of structural adjustment in Chad, where the economy had been completely destroyed, arguing that the country was now "ripe for the development of a free market economy."[4]

Yet while the neoliberal dogma is still peddled, two crucial problems persist. First, Africa has an extraordinary dependence upon a few export commodities that has always exposed it to international market forces. Secondly, the debt crisis has provided the leverage to enforce the economic and political diktat of international capitalism.[5] While millions suffered untold poverty and misery, much of the money raised by development loans was lavished on military expenditure and the import of luxury goods for the consumption of national ruling classes. The hypocrisy of the International Monetary Fund and the World Bank is unequaled; while today they hail "good governance," yesterday they granted loans to the likes of Mugabe, Mobutu, and the racists who ran the apartheid regime. Capitalism in Africa is built upon the enduring legacy of slavery, colonialism, and the continuation of the structural adjustment policies imposed by international financial institutions in the 1980s and 1990s.

The absurdity of the crisis of capitalism in Africa is today epitomized not least in the AIDS pandemic that is sweeping the continent. The problem (and potentially the solution) lies with the concentrated ownership of resources and lack of accountability of Glaxo SmithKline, Merck, Pfizer, and Eli Lilly, the big four pharmaceutical MNCs. These monopoly capitalists do not believe in the free market, whose virtues they so slavishly recite. Forget that in Africa millions are dying of diseases such as diarrhea, malaria, and AIDS that are preventable or treatable in the West. The retroviral drugs such as AZT and 3TC that could keep alive the thirty-two million or more men, women, and children infected by HIV in developing countries will not reach them because in capitalism profit comes before people. If there is no profit then what is the point in sending medicines to the people who need them but can't afford them? This fact is not lost on those of us around the world involved in the emerging specter that haunts the IMF, the World Bank, the MNCs, and national governments: anticapitalism. It is no coincidence that the most popular slogans of this new movement are "Our world is not for sale" and "People before profit."

African ruling classes are an intricate part of this disaster; not least through implementing IMF and World Bank programs and profiting, like their western counterparts, from capitalist "globalization." The result has been, to name a few examples, that Chiluba (Zambia), Mandela and Mbeki (South Africa), Mugabe (Zimbabwe), Nujoma (Namibia), and the previously self-proclaimed "socialist" governments in Mozambique and Angola have espoused and implemented free market economic policies, with only token reference to a socialist rhetoric that they used to champion. Even those opposition parties who claim to represent the poor are more often than not a form of recycled elites with no mass constituency, as in the case of Kenya and Nigeria. The kind of democracy and "good governance" being advanced by international and national ruling classes has been characterized as a form of democratic elitism, where the poor majority are disregarded as political actors and their needs play second fiddle to the profit of MNCs.[6]

This form of so-called liberal democracy does not require active participation but the "stability" and the political containment of social deprivation. Mass political passivity, commonly and patronizingly referred to as "apathy," is seen as an essential feature of stable democratic systems. Not only are the poor sidelined as active citizens, but their needs are excluded from discussion. More absurd is that the international and national ruling classes and many of their apologists in the universities and media pretend that capitalism has not failed Africa historically, exacerbating the problem further by insisting that more of the same medicine is applied.

However, to see these developments only from the point of view of the devastation of the continent is to miss the point of this book. At every stage in their development, popular movements in Africa, often led by the urban working class, have fought furiously and often successfully against this devastation. The last thirty years, as well as being a record of capitalist destruction across the continent, have also been an astonishing record of anticapitalist protest and revolt. To miss this is to revert to the often racist assumptions of the "hopeless" continent.[7] If these revolts and movements have not, in the final analysis, been able to solve the crisis of African capitalism, they should not be disregarded; we must learn lessons from them, analyze their weaknesses, draw on their strengths, and celebrate their victories. Only by doing this can we ensure that such revolts endure and are strengthened in the future.

So what are we to do? If we want a genuine globalization of democracy and an equitable redistribution of resources, not some imagined past of national autonomy, then the people this book has focused upon, the working class, hold the key to unlocking the chains that still enslave them. Moreover, they now have the potential to make a greater impact than ever before because of the global anticapitalist movement against the "dictatorship of the market."

This book has argued that across Africa there is a need for a radical socialist alternative. The way forward is to draw together a movement led by the working class in alliance with other oppressed and exploited groups. The argument for revolutionary politics is based not on predictions of instant insurrection, but on the understanding that it is through continued and organized mass struggle (campaigns, strikes, protests, land invasions, and workplace occupations) that the aspirations of the working class and poor can be realized.

Such a movement must link the struggles of those in employment with the unemployed and those in the informal economy. Workers in factories, shops, and mines must link up with those on the farms, in transport and construction, and with students and intellectuals who side with the poor against the privileged. But to do this there needs to be an organization of the working class that fights not for a renewal of the "nation" or for "real" independence, delinked from the capitalist world, but for revolutionary change rooted in an international struggle for socialist transformation. The role of such an organization is different from that of a trade union, civic organization, or NGO. It is a political organization that aims to strengthen and unite our disparate struggles. It should articulate the bond between the struggle for women's rights, work for all, decent affordable housing, and free health care. It must link the struggle to change the education system to one that serves society instead of the market, to expose corruption and defend ourselves against the violence that is the daily reality of capitalism.

But we must recall two points. First, the working class and poor can and do change the world, but never in circumstances they choose. Secondly, the liberation of the exploited must be undertaken by them, not simply because only they, collectively, have the power to do so, but because in the process of fighting for change, people themselves change. It is through struggle, grassroots politics, and political education in democratic organizations that people begin to create their own ideas of social transformation. This is not an abstract notion but the reality of every social movement in Africa since independence: from the struggle against apartheid to the ongoing struggles in Nigeria and Zimbabwe for democracy. Each of these struggles has allowed people to develop skills and talents they might otherwise not have had the chance to use. Central to these ideas is that politics must emphasize the ability of ordinary women, men, and youth, not great leaders, to act and change their world. Study any such process, ask anyone involved in social protest, and this theme emerges every time.

In struggling together we can begin to break down the artificial barriers that are purposely erected between us by the machinations of international capitalism: politicians, the media, academics, and "globalization." Each seeks to divert attention from the real causes of the crisis. During the struggle against apartheid in South Africa, the mistrust that existed between "African" and so-called "Coloured" people was vitally broken; Zimbabwe, constantly divided and redivided by Mugabe, was united on an unheard-of scale during the protests in 1996–98. This is not an accident. Unity against oppression encourages solidarity in a climate that extols, through political organization and education, a greater understanding of the real roots of the problems we face. We can say with certainty that only revolutionary action led by the working class can prevent the Balkanization of Africa.

Nor is the call for revolutionary organization a "western" one, residing in the heads of "European" Marxists. The need for revolutionary politics has been argued over for decades on the continent. It was the lack of a revolutionary socialist party that left organized labor and popular struggles without the political direction essential for carrying forward the movements described in this book. The need for revolutionary politics and activity was recognized repeatedly by activists and socialists in Africa. In Nigeria during the general strike of 1964—when the Joint Action Committee of labor leaders, supported by over five hundred thousand workers, brilliantly confronted the federal government—a strike leader made a telling point. He argued that, while the cause of the strike was based on economic demands, its development raised the potential of political action that, aided by a revolutionary socialist organization, could have led to a social revolution.[8]

In 1968 in Senegal, in a movement that started before the events in France, the country was effectively controled by the trade unions and radicalized students. While Senghor, the "great" leader of independence, sought protection with the French military, "power had become vacant...faced by the social explosion the ruling party could not act...ministers were consigned to government buildings. And leading figures in the ruling party hid in their houses. It was strange behaviour from a ruling party that said they were the majority in the country."⁹ But ultimately there was not the political direction that could push the movement forward.

The politics we argue for must be rooted in internationalism: a counterglobalization of solidarity that sees resistance across the world, North and South, as part of the same anticapitalist struggle, linked to worldwide socialist transformation. But to build this type of tradition it is imperative to grasp an immutable point: that only a movement headed by the working class, organized in its own revolutionary socialist party, holds the key to unlocking the creativity and power of millions of Africans to transform their lives.

Some will say this is utopian. But it has always been a question of where you look in society for inspiration, either to the top, to the bitter rivalry and murderous hypocrisy of the ruling class, or below, to the extraordinary capabilities and power of "ordinary" people. Hope of a better world comes from understanding the potential of this "power." We should not forget that a series of political mass strikes by national workers' movements have shaken the world in recent years, from Taiwan in 1994, France in 1995, and Greece, Italy, and Colombia in 1997, through to the incredible events in Indonesia in 1998–99 and in Argentina and South Africa as we write. Unsurprisingly, a report by the World Development Movement into the growing phenomenon of political resistance was called *States of Unrest*.¹⁰ This report lists a wave of struggles across the world in the ten months following the protests in Seattle in November 1999. This included strikes and protests in Kenya, Malawi, Nigeria, South Africa and Zambia.

Recent events in Madagascar show the great possibilities of revolutionary struggle, and the huge dangers. After disputed elections in December 2001, Madagascar was paralyzed by the country's fiercest general strike and daily mass demonstrations that seemed unfeasibly large. The "legitimate" government almost seemed to vanish from the scene, while the opposition was urged by the movement to "seize power" by force if necessary. The leadership prevaricated, sought negotiations, then rejected them and sought international respectability.

This vacillation gave the incumbent president, Didier Ratsiraka, and his supporters crucial breathing space. He retreated from the capital to his home province, where he launched an economic blockade on the capital. Still the opposition hesitated. Delegations from the former colonial power, France, and the Organization of African Unity, came and went.

In March 2002 the opposition leader, Marc Ravalomanana, insisted that his supporters return to work, ending the general strike that had galvanized the country. At the same time, Ratsiraka organized counterdemonstrations that led to the first casualties of the struggle. As the two leaders continued to outface each other, politicians started to bring ethnicity into play, in an attempt to divide the islanders.

Madagascar shows the possibility for mass action to oust an incumbent president and it reminds us of the passion and hope of revolutionary change, which was described by one striker as "like a holiday every day." But it also reminds us, crucially, of the crisis of leadership. There is no sizeable revolutionary current inside the Madagascan working class that can push the movement beyond the timidity and conservatism of the official opposition. This failure meant that Ravalomanana, himself a product of the strikes and demonstrations, eventually forced Madagascans to retreat from the general strike that had been at the heart of the mobilization.

Resistance like this, against the World Bank, the IMF, and privatization, took place in Africa long before the development of what is commonly called the anticapitalist movement, encapsulated by events in such places as Seattle and Genoa between 1999 and 2001.[11] But now it is part of a new movement, global in protest and aspiration, and the reason for it is simple: we live not in an era of peace and stability, but in one of incredible instability. While capitalism continues to exploit and oppress the vast majority of humanity, it constantly produces a class that has the potential of changing our world fundamentally. For capitalism continuously compels people to resist it, and even if resistance ebbs, the history of Africa tells us that it will rise again. As Femi Aborisade comments:

> There is enormous opportunity for radical social change. But unless socialists who aim at genuine democracy lead the broad forces for change, upheavals may come without real transformation. The absurdity of the American-led war against terrorism and the acute poverty in Africa have confirmed Marx's position that at every stage in the crisis of capitalism, it is either the victory of socialism or the re-entrenched rule of capitalism and the mutual ruin of contending classes. In a word: socialism or barbarism.[12]

FURTHER ACTION

Action is the most important ingredient for social change, but to act we have to understand and interpret the modern world. The two are inseparable for anyone who wants to change the world. This section is intended to help the reader access useful Web sites with information on Africa or to contact activists, campaigns, groups, and trade unions on the continent. It also suggests a number of books, recommended by the contributors, to help understand the political economy of the continent. It is, however, by no means a definitive list.

Web sites

Pambazuka News: weekly news for social justice in Africa

www.pambazuka.org/en

Marxists Internet Archive

www.marxists.org

Archive of Marxist texts in English and German

www.marxists.de/index.htm

Downloadable recordings of Left discussions and meetings

www.resistancemp3.lpi.org.uk

Contacts

Zimbabwe

International Socialist Organisation
Web: iso.zim.googlepages.com
Email: iso.zim@gmail.com

Keep Left

Web: socialismfrombelow.googlepages.com
Email: socialismfrombelow@gmail.com

Botswana

International Socialists Botswana
Email : isbots@yahoo.com

Ghana

International Socialist Organisation
Email: isogh@hotmail.com

Nigeria

Nigeria Socialist League
Email: nigeriasocialistleague@yahoo.com

Books

Franz Fanon, *The Wretched of the Earth* (London: Penguin, 2001).

John Walton and David Seddon, *Free Markets and Food Riots: the politics of global adjustment* (Oxford: Blackwell, 1994).

Leon Trotsky, *The Permanent Revolution: Results and prospects* (New York: Pathfinder, 1969).

Tony Cliff, *Marxism at the Millennium* (London: Bookmarks, 2000); *Deflected Permanent Revolution*, www.istendency.org/origins/pamphlet.html.

Alex Callinicos, *The Revolutionary Ideas of Karl Marx* (London: Bookmarks, 1996).

Basil Davidson, *Modern Africa: A social and political history* (London: Longman, 1994).

Walter Rodney, *How Europe Underdeveloped Africa* (London, Bogle l'Ouverture Publications, 1972).

David Renton, Leo Zeilig and David Seddon, *The Congo: plunder and resistance* (London: Zed Books, 2007).

Femi Aborisade, *Nigeria Labour Movement in Perspective* (Lagos: The Effective Company, 1992).

Miles Larmer, *Mine Workers in Zambia* (London: Tauris Academic Studies, 2006).

Patrick Bond and Masimba Manyanya, *Zimbabwe's Plunge* (London: Merlin, 2002).

Patrick Bond, *Looting Africa* (London: Zed Books, 2006).

Leo Zeilig, *Lumumba: Africa's lost leader* (London: Haus, 2008); *Revolt and Protest: student politics and activism in sub-Saharan Africa* (London: Tauris Academic Studies, 2007).

NOTES

Introduction
Resisting the Scramble for Africa

1. Quoted in 'Africa's strong growth,' 19 October 2007 http://www.economist. com/agenda/displaystory.cfm?story_id=10006712.
2. 'Oil boom fuels Dubai dreams in Angola's capital', Reuters News, 22 November 2006.
3. Lara Pawson, 'Peace is not enough for Angolans', 4 April 2007, http://news.bbc. co.uk/2/hi/africa/6522741.stm.
4. Lara Pawson, 'Angola: worlds in collision', 11 April 2007, http://www. opendemocracy.net/democracyafrica_democracy/angola_collision_4514.jsp.
5. 'Heady excitement dampened by doubt', *Financial Times*, 23 June 2008.
6. Watts, Michael, 'Africa: the next victim in our quest for cheap oil,' 14 July 2008, http://www.alternet.org/audits/89692.
7. 'The new middle classes: Market forces create a local infrastructure for aspiration', *Financial Times*, 23 June 2008.
8. See Prunier, Gerard and Gisselquist, Rachel 'The Sudan: A Successfully Failed State', in Rotberg, R (ed) *State Failure and State Weakness in a Time of Terror* Washington, DC: Brookings Institution, 2003.
9. Soares de Oliveira, *Journal of Modern African Studies*, 'Business success, Angola-Style: post-colonial politics and the rise and rise of Sonangol' (45, 2007), p. 614.
10. But these attacks are often undertaken by groups paid, manipulated, and driven by local politicians. In this respect the *Financial Times* report on the Niger Delta is probably correct: 'In Delta and Bayelsa States, security consultants say the governors are paying armed groups to act as semi-official protection forces for the waterways they would otherwise terrorise.' Legitimate demands and movements against years of repression and plunder by international oil companies have been subverted by regional politicians. 'The Niger Delta:

Fragile strageties for a complex conflict', *Financial Times*, 23 June 2008.

11. Watts, 'Africa: the next victim in our quest for cheap oil.'

12. Rice, Xan, 'The best thing that could happen to the country is if no oil is found' *The Guardian*, 14 June 2008.

13. The term seems to have been first used in the 1960s. See Clower, Robert W. *et al, Growth without Development: an economic survey of Liberia*, (Evanston, IL: Northwestern University Press), 1966.

14. Bond, Patrick and Ashwin Desai, 'Explaining Uneven and Combined Development in South Africa', in Bill Dunn and Hugo Radice (eds), *Permanent Revolution: Results and Prospects 100 Years On* (London: Pluto Press) p.239.

15. Rose, David, *A rich seam—who really benefits from the commodity price boom*, Christian Aid, January 2007, p. 21.

16. Ibid., p. 22.

17. 'Why China is trying to colonise Africa', *Daily Telegraph*, 31 August 2007.

18. Sautman, Barry and Hairong, Yan, 'Friends and Interests: China's Distinctive Links with Africa', *African Studies Review*, 50, no.3 (2007), pp. 75–114.

19. Soares de Oliveira, Ricardo, 'Business success, Angola-Style', p. 617.

20. Bond, Patrick and Kamidza, Richard 'How Europe underdevelops Africa', 13–15 June 2007, www.counterpunch.org/bond06132008.html.

21. UNSC, *Final Report of the Panel of Experts on the Illegal Exploitation of Natural Resources and Other Forms of Wealth of the Democratic Republic of the Congo* (New York: UNSC, October 2002).

22. See UNSC reports: *Report of the Panel of Experts on the Illegal Exploitation of Natural Resources and Other Forms of Wealth of the Democratic Republic of the Congo* (New York: UNSC, 2001); *Interim Report of the Panel of Experts on the Illegal Exploitation of Natural Resources and Other Forms of Wealth of the Democratic Republic of the Congo* (New York: UNSC, May 2002); *Final Report of the Panel of Experts on the Illegal Exploitation of Natural Resources and Other Forms of Wealth of the Democratic Republic of the Congo* (New York: UNSC, October 2002); *Report of the Panel of Experts on the Illegal Exploitation of Natural Resources and Other Forms of Wealth in the Democratic Republic of Congo* (New York: UNSC, October 2003). All these reports are available online: http://www.globalpolicy.org/security/issues/kingidx.htm.

23. See Volman, Daniel 'Africom: the new US military command for Africa,' 17 January 2008, http://concernedafricascholars.org/?p=82.

24. 'USS Fort McHenry Returns From Africa Partnership Station Maiden Deployment' 5 May 2008, http://mt-milcom.blogspot.com/2008/05/uss-fort-mchenry-returns-from-africa.html.

25. Davis, Mike, *Planet of Slums* (London: Verso, 2006) p.7.

26. Ibid., p. 8.

27. Ibid., p.10.

28. Ibid., p. 13.

29. Ibid., p. 14.

30. Ibid., p. 16.

31. Ibid., p. 201.
32. Ibid., p. 201.
33. The heterogeneity of classes has never been the reason for their political decay rather a factor of their real condition. As Lenin argued in 1920: 'Capitalism would not be capitalism if the proletariat pur sang were not surrounded by a large number of exceedingly motley types intermediate between the proletarian and the semi-proletarian (who earns his livelihood in part by the sale of his labour power), between the semi-proletarian and the small peasant (and petty artisan, handicraft worker, and small master in general), between the small peasant and the middle peasant, and so on, and if the proletariat itself were not divided...according to territorial origin, trade, sometimes according to religion, and so on.' *Left Wing Communisim: an Infantile Disorder* in *Selected Works*, (London: 1969 [1920]).
34. These arguments are dealt with in more detail in an article by Zeilig, Leo and Ceruti, Claire 'Slums, resistance and the African working class,' *International Socialism* 2, no. 17 (2007).
35. Davis, Mike, *Planet of Slums*, pp. 44–45.
36. Morris, Alan, *et al, Change and Continuity: A Survey of Soweto in the Late 1990's*. University of the Witwatersrand: Johannesburg, 1999.
37. Quoted by Ceruti, Claire, 'Divisions and Dependencies among Working and Workless', *South African Labour Bulletin*, 2, no. 31 (2007), p.22.
38. Ceruti, Claire, 'Divisions and Dependencies,' pp. 22–23.
39. Thompson, E. P., *The Making of the English Working Class*, (London: Penguin 1980), p. 8.
40. Ceruti, Claire, 'South Africa: Rebirth of a mass movement', *International Socialism*, 2, no. 16 (2007), p. 22.
41. Quoted in Aborisade, Femi 'Nationwide strikes in Nigeria,' 12 July, 2007 www.pambazuka.org/en/category/comment/42507.
42. Morelli, Carlo 'Behind the world food crisis', *International Socialism* 2, no. 119 (2008), p. 38.
43. 'Solution to food crisis must address inequalities—UN human rights chief,' 22 May 2008. http://www.un.org/apps/news/story.asp?NewsID=26762&Cr=food&Cr1=crisis.
44. 'Food price rises are "mass murder"—U.N. envoy,' 20 April 2008, http://in.reuters.com/article/worldNews/idINIndia-33134320080420.
45. See Rosa Luxemburg's classic, *The Mass Strike*, (London; Bookmarks, 1995).
46. Alexander, Anne 'Inside Egypt's mass strikes,' *International Socialism* 2, no. 118, (2008), pp.126–27.
47. Interview with Sameh Naguib, *International Socialism*, 2, no. 116, (2007).
48. See David Seddon's chapter in this collection.
49. The appeal for radical political alternatives has been stimulated by the development of the Social Forums—tied to the global anti-capitalist movement—on the continent. Even the problematic though important World Social Forum held in Kenya in 2007 was a significant development.

50. For a fuller analysis of the crisis in Zimbabwe, see Zeilig, Leo, 'Zimbabwe: imperialism, hypocrisy and fake nationalism,' *International Socialism*, 2, no. 119, (2008).

Chapter 1
Marxism, Class, and Resistance in Africa

1. Cited by Engels in a letter to Conrad Schmidt (5 August 1890). See Marx and Engels Internet Archive: http://www.marxists.org/archive/marx/letters/index.htm.
2. Isaac Deutscher describes classical Marxism as a body of thought developed by Marx and others, including Trotsky, Lenin, and Rosa Luxemburg. He contrasts it to Stalinism and European social democracy. Central to these ideas is the unity of theory and practice in working-class politics and the international scope of modern capitalism. See *Marxism in Our Time* (London: Jonathan Cape, 1972).
3. See S. Amin, *Delinking: Towards a Polycentric World* (London: Zed Books, 1990).
4. See K. Marx, *Revolution and Counter Revolution in Germany* (Peking: Foreign Language Press, 1977).
5. See V. I. Lenin, 'Critical remarks on the national question', in *Collected Works* (Moscow: Progress Publishers, 1964).
6. L. Trotsky, *The History of the Russian Revolution* (London: Pluto Press, 1977), p. 1235.
7. T. Cliff, *Deflected Permanent Revolution*, (London: Bookmarks, 1990).
8. See Amin, *Delinking*.
9. Ibid., p. 135.
10. Ibid., p. 158.
11. E. Guevara, *The African Dream* (London: the Harvill Press, 2000), p. 2.
12. See Babacar Diop Buuba, 'Trade unions, political parties and the state', in M. C. Diop (ed.), *Senegal: Essays in statecraft* (Dakar: CODESRIA, 1993).
13. T. Cliff, *Marxism at the Millennium* (London: Bookmarks, 2000), p. 46. See also Cliff, *Deflected Permanent Revolution*, (London: Bookmarks, 1990).
14. E. Hobsbawm, *Age of Extremes: The Short Twentieth Century, 1914–1991* (London: Abacus, 1995).
15. H. Adi, *The 1945 Pan-African Congress Revisited* (London: New Beacon Books, 1995).
16. See M. Sherwood, *Kwame Nkrumah: The Years Abroad, 1935–1947* (Accra: Freedom Publications, 1996).
17. See M. Kidron, *Western Capitalism Since the War* (London: Weidenfeld and Nicolson, 1968).
18. K. Nkrumah, *Africa Must Unite* (London: Panaf, 1963), p. 120.
19. T. Mboya, *Freedom and After* (London: André Deutsch, 1963), p. 167. Similar ideas are still fashionable today. George Alagiah writes, 'The search for togetherness finds expression in the uniquely African spirit', *Guardian*,

London, 8 September 2001.

20. General Paul Aussaresses caused a crisis in France when he admitted (what had been know for years) that the French government routinely executed and murdered suspects. See *Le Monde*, Paris, 3 May 2001. There was also call for a 'Truth Commission' into the Algerian war: R. Badinter, *Le Nouvel Observateur*, Paris, 24 May 2001.

21. See F. Furedi, *The Mau Mau War in Perspective* (London: James Currey, 1990).

22. F. Fanon, *The Wretched of the Earth* (New York: Grove Press, 1963), p. 67.

23. R. First, *The Barrel of a Gun: Political Power in Africa and the Coup d'État* (London: Penguin, 1970), pp. 57–8.

24. See L. De Witte, *The Assassination of Lumumba* (London: Verso, 2001).

25. See S. Kelly, *America's Tyrant: The CIA and Mobutu of Zaire* (Washington, DC: American University Press, 1993) and M. Schatzburg, *Mobutu or Chaos: The United States and Zaire, 1960–1990* (New York: University Press of America, 1991).

26. R. Biel, *The New Imperialism: Crisis and Contradictions in North–South Relations* (London: Zed Books, 2000), p. 91.

27. K. B. Hadjor, *Nkrumah and Ghana: The dilemma of post-colonial power* (London: Kegan Paul International, 1988), p. 23.

28. Hobsbawm, *Age of Extremes*, p. 405.

29. P. Marfleet, 'Globalisation and the Third World', *International Socialism Journal* 81 (1998), p. 104.

30. See B. Davidson, *Africa in Modern History: The Search for a New Society* (London: Penguin, 1978).

31. See Joao Emilio Costa's interview, 'Since Pidjiguiti we never looked back', in O. Gjerstad and C. Saarrazin (eds), *Sowing the First Harvest: National reconstruction in Guinea-Bissau* (Oakland: Liberation Support Movement, 1978), pp. 35–7.

32. Lefort cited in D. Donham, *Marxist Modern: An ethnographic history of the Ethiopian revolution* (Oxford: James Currey, 1999), p. 17.

33. Lefort cited in ibid., p. 213.

34. See J. Walton and D. Seddon, *Free Markets and Food Riots: The Politics of Global Adjustment* (Oxford: Blackwell, 1994).

35. Cited in R. Sandbrook, *The Politics of Africa's Economic Recovery* (Cambridge: Cambridge University Press, 1993), p. 2.

36. Seddon and Walton, *Free Markets and Food Riots*.

37. See ibid. for a description of this process across the developing world.

38. M. Mayakiso and P. Bond, *Township Politics: Civic Struggles for a New South Africa* (New York: Monthly Review Press, 1996), p. 52.

39. For example, John Ndebuyue of the Kwame Nkrumah Revolutionary Guard spent most of the late 1980s in prison.

40. P. Nugent, *Big Men, Small Boys and Politics in Ghana* (London: Pinter, 1995); see also D. Ray, *Ghana: Politics, Economics and Society* (London: Pinter, 1986), which was produced for a series on Marxist regimes.

41. See the Library of Congress: http://www.loc.gov.

42. C. Harman, 'Where is capitalism going?', *International Socialism Journal* 60 (1993), p. 79.

43. See N. Harris, *The End of the Third World: Newly industrializing countries and the Decline of an Ideology* (London: Tauris, 1986).

44. Biel, *The New Imperialism*, p. 194.

45. See Davidson for these ideas: *The Black Man's Burden: Africa and the Curse of the Nation-state* (London: James Currey, 1992), pp. 232–33.

46. Cited in J. Wiseman, *The New Struggle for Democracy in Africa* (Aldershot: Avebury, 1996), p. 70.

47. See C. Harman, 'The storm breaks', *International Socialism Journal* 46 (1989).

48. Cited in Harman, 'Where is capitalism going?', p. 79.

49. See IMF, *World Economic Outlook*, which is produced by IMF economists twice a year: http://www.imf.org/external/pubs/ft/weo/2001/01/index.htm.

50. M. Bratton, *Democratic Experiments in Africa: Regime Transitions in Comparative Perspective* (New York: Cambridge University Press, 1997), p. 5.

51. Ibid., p. 2.

52. J. Saul and C. Leys, 'Sub-Saharan Africa in global capitalism', *Monthly Review*, July–August 1999, p. 26.

53. Wiseman, *The New Struggle for Democracy in Africa*, p. 49.

54. R. Abrahamsen, *Disciplining Democracy: Development discourse and good governance in Africa* (London: Zed Books, 2000), p.125.

55. See *Africa Research Bulletin* 37, no. 9.

56. A. D. Smith, *The Independent* (London, 26 June 2001).

57. M. Curtis, 'Just another false dawn for the poor', *Guardian* (London, 26 June 2001).

58. See Paul Richards' critique of these ideas in his book about the war in Sierra Leone, *Fighting for the Rain Forest: War, Youth and Resources in Sierra Leone* (London: James Currey, 1996).

59. Jean-François Bayart, *The Criminalization of the State in Africa* (Oxford: James Currey, 1999), p. 19.

60. See J. Drysdale, *Stoics without Pillows: A Way Forward for the Somalilands* (London: HAAN, 2000).

61. See the reports in *New African* (June 2001).

62. T. Hodges, *Angola: From Afro-Stalinism to Petro-diamond Capitalism* (Oxford: James Currey, 2001).

63. See the report on 'Angolagate' in *African Business* (May 2001).

64. Cited in the brilliant report, *Oil Development in Nigeria: A Critical Investigation of Chevron Corporation's Performance in the Niger River Delta* by the California Global Corporate Accountability Project, http://www.nautilus.org/ cap.

65. The Elf scandal rocked France in 2001, bringing down Roland Dumas, who was imprisoned for six months in May 2001 for receiving illegal funds from the state-owned Elf Aquitaine oil company between 1989 and 1992, while he was foreign minister.

66. See F. X. Verschave, *Noir Silence: Qui arretra la Francafrique?* (Paris: Editions

des Arènes, 2000) and *La Francafrique: Le plus long scandale de la République* (Paris: Stock, 1998).

67. S. Peterson, *Me Against My Brother: At War in Somalia, Sudan and Rwanda* (London: Routledge, 2000).

68. See the excellent book by Linda Melvern, *A People Betrayed: The Role of the West in Rwanda's Genocide* (London: Zed Books, 2000).

69. Fanon, *The Wretched of the Earth*, p. 174.

70. K. Marx and F. Engels, 'Address of the Central Committee to the Communist League' (London: March 1850). Full text available on the Marx and Engels Internet Archive: http://www.marxists.org/archive/marx/index.htm.

Chapter 2
Popular Protest and Class Struggle in Africa:
An Historical Overview

1. There is a considerable literature on this process. For a theoretical analysis with respect to Africa, see C. Coquery-Vidrovitch, 'Research on an African mode of production', in D. Seddon (ed.), *Relations of Production: Marxist Approaches to Economic Anthropology* (London: Frank Cass, 1974).

2. *Review of African Political Economy (RoAPE)*, 'Editorial', 3 (May–October 1975), p. 5.

3. See Chapter 1 of this book (particularly the latter part of the chapter, which takes the discussion and analysis into the more recent 'post' post-colonial period). See also J. Walton and D. Seddon, *Free Markets and Food Riots: The Politics of Global Adjustment* (London: Blackwell, 1994), *passim* but especially chapter 5 by S. Riley and T. Parfitt on Africa.

4. R. Cohen, P. C. W. Gutkind and P. Brazier, *Peasants and Proletarians: The Struggles of Third World Workers* (London: Hutchinson University Press, 1979), p. 25.

5. K. Marx, *Capital*, vol. 1, cited in Mbeki, *Review of African Political Economy*, 11 (January–April 1978), p. 7.

6. See D. Seddon, 'Unfinished business: slavery in Saharan Africa', in H. Temperley (ed.), *After Slavery: Emancipation and its discontents* (London: Frank Cass, 2000).

7. Ibid.

8. Not only the insidious violence that undermined and destroyed indigenous social formations, subordinating them to the powerful demands of capital, but the open violence supporting that process, which led to death and destruction on a massive scale: cf. B. Bradby, 'The destruction of natural economy', *Economy and Society* 4, no. 2 (May 1975), pp. 127–61, p. 138.

9. M. Crowder, *West Africa under Colonial Rule* (London: Hutchinson, 1968).

10. On the notion of 'articulation of modes of production' generally, see A. Foster-

Carter, 'The modes of production controversy', *New Left Review* 107 (January–February 1978), pp. 47–77. For discussion of 'articulation' in specifically African contexts, see, for example, P. Ph. Rey, *Colonialisme, neo-colonialisme et transitions au capitalisme* (Paris, 1971) and *Les alliances de classes* (Paris, 1973).

11. E. Hobsbawm, *Primitive Rebels: Studies in Archaic Forms of Social Movement in the 19th and 20th Centuries* (Manchester: Manchester University Press, 1959).

12. See chapter 3 in this book.

13. Seddon, 'Unfinished business'.

14. M. Mamdani, 'Class struggles in Uganda', *Review of African Political Economy* 4 (November 1975), pp. 26-61, p. 31.

15. I. Davies, *African Trade Unions* (London: Penguin, 1966), p. 33.

16. Ibid.

17. In 1956, 'thousands of workers were being sentenced every year to prison with hard labour' according to Basil Davidson: B. Davidson, *The African Awakening* (London: Cape, 1956), p. 75.

18. From interviews with Mozambican peasant women, in H. Johnson and H. Bernstein, *Third World Lives of Struggle* (London: Open University, 1982), p. 32.

19. Cited in J. Woddis, *Africa: The Roots of Revolt* (London: Lawrence and Wishart, 1960), p. 50. Further details can be found in R. W. Thomas, 'Forced labour in British West Africa: the case of the northern territories of the Gold Coast, 1906–27', *Journal of African History* 14, no. 1 (1973), pp. 79–103.

20. P. Mosley, *The Settler Economies: Studies in the Economic History of Kenya and Southern Rhodesia, 1900–1963* (Cambridge: Cambridge University Press, 1983), p. 134.

21. In 1907, Winston Churchill, as undersecretary at the Colonial Office, condemned the treatment of native labor in Natal; later that year, visiting British East Africa, he was apparently outraged by the official policy of labor conscription for settlers and in 1908 was able to change the policy to one of 'encouragement' of labor: cf. J. Sender and S. Smith, *The Development of Capitalism in Africa*. (London and New York: Methuen, 1986), p. 48.

22. Davies, *African Trade Unions*, p. 35.

23. Tom Brass asks 'when has running away not been, in a very general sense, an act of resistance?': T. Brass, 'At their perfect command? The struggle of/over post-emancipation rural labor', *Journal of Peasant Studies* 28, no. 3 (April 2001), p. 168, footnote 16. Labor conscripted from the northern territories of the Gold Coast to work in the gold mines regularly deserted in large numbers: in 1922–23, 483 men out of 2,524 so 'recruited' had absconded before reaching the south, according to J. Crisp, *The Story of an African Working Class* (London: Zed Press, 1984), p. 48.

24. See R. Cohen, 'Resistance and hidden forms of consciousness among African workers', in Johnson and Bernstein (eds), *Third World Lives of Struggle*, pp. 244–58; J. Scott, *Weapons of the Weak: Everyday forms of peasant resistance* (New Haven, CT, and London: Yale University Press, 1985).

25. L. Vail, 'The state and the creation of colonial Malawi's agricultural economy', in R. Rothberg (ed.), *Imperialism, Colonialism and Hunger: East and Central Africa* (Lexington, MA, and Toronto: D. C. Heath, 1983), pp. 49–50.

26. T. Mbeki, 'Domestic and foreign policies of a new South Africa', *Review of African Political Economy* 11 (1978), p. 12.

27. Saul *et al.*, cf. E. P. Thompson, *The Making of the English Working Class* (London: Penguin, 1968).

28. N. Poulantzas, 'On social classes', *New Left Review* 78 (March–April 1973), pp. 27–54.

29. Davies, *African Trade Unions*, p. 75.

30. Aleksandr Lozovsky, *Marx and the Trade Unions* (London: Martin Lawrence, 1935).

31. For further details, see chapter 3 in this book.

32. 'We shall probably have a strike when a general reduction of labour is brought about; that will not last long—an African worships his stomach and will be back again to work before many days': cited in A. G. Hopkins, 'The Lagos strike of 1897: an exploration in Nigerian labor history', in Cohen, Gutkind and Brazier (eds), *Peasants and Proletarians*, p. 89.

33. Hopkins, 'The Lagos strike of 1897', p. 91.

34. R. Cohen and A. Hughes, *Towards the Emergence of a Nigerian Working Class: The Social Identity of the Lagos Labour Force, 1897–1939*, Occasional Paper Series, Birmingham: University of Birmingham, 1971. Hopkins, 'The Lagos strike of 1897', p. 105.

35. Davies, *African Trade Unions*, p. 56.

36. C. von Onselen, *Chibaro: African Mine Labour in Southern Rhodesia, 1900–1933* (London: Pluto Press, 1976); also 'Worker consciousness in black miners: Southern Rhodesia, 1900–1920', in Cohen, Gutkind and Brazier (eds), *Peasants and Proletarians*, pp. 107–27.

37. Davies, *African Trade Unions*, p. 56.

38. Ibid., p. 57.

39. Ibid., pp. 57–8.

40. For further discussion, see chapter 3 in this book.

41. Davies, *African Trade Unions*, p. 75; see also chapter 5 in this book.

42. Davies, *African Trade Unions*, p. 76.

43. R. Jeffries, *Class, Power and Ideology in Ghana: The Railwaymen of Sekondi* (Cambridge: Cambridge University Press, 1978).

44. J. Iliffe notes, in *A Modern History of Tanganyika* (Cambridge: Cambridge University Press, 1979), that 'railway workers were relatively skilled and numerous, and their occupation provided a natural framework of organization and communications', p. 396.

45. Davies, *African Trade Unions*, p. 75. The Labour governments of 1924 and 1929 paid some attention to colonial labor conditions in the British territories, but it was not until 1930 that the Labour government appointed a Colonial Labour Office Committee and Secretary of State Sydney Webb approved proposals to accord African trade unions formal legal rights.

46. Cited in Davies, *African Trade Unions*, p. 39.

47. Cited in ibid., p. 41.

48. S. Stichter, 'The formation of a working class in Kenya', in R. Sandbrook and R. Cohen (eds), *The Development of an African Working Class* (London: Longman, 1975); S. Stichter, *Migrant Labour in Kenya: Capitalism and African Response, 1895–1975* (London: Longman, 1982), pp. 119, 170.

49. Iliffe, *A Modern History of Tanganyika*, pp. 402–3.

50. Davies, *African Trade Unions*, p. 79.

51. Ibid., pp. 81–4.

52. R. Cohen, *Labour and Politics in Nigeria* (London: Heinemann, 1974), pp. 71 *et seq.*; P. Waterman, *Wage Labour Relations in Nigeria: State, Capitalists, Unions and Workers in the Lagos Cargo-handling Industry* (The Hague: Institute of Social Studies, 1982), pp. 92–3; see also Chapter 4 in this book.

53. Davies, *African Trade Unions*, p. 43; see also R. Montagne, *Naissance du Proletariat Marocain* (Paris, 1954).

54. See C. H. Allen, 'Union–party relationships in francophone West Africa', in Sandbrook and Cohen (eds), *The Development of an African Working Class*; S. Ousmane, *God's Bits of Wood* (London: Heinemann, 1970).

55. Davies, *African Trade Unions*, pp. 44–5.

56. M. Harbi, *Le FLN: mirage et realité* (Paris: Editions JA, 1980), pp. 140–2.

57. Cited in Davies, *African Trade Unions*, p. 46.

58. Ibid.

59. Ibid., pp. 47–9.

60. W. Elkan, *Migrants and Proletarians* (Oxford: Oxford University Press, 1961).

61. C. Allen, 'Understanding African politics', *Review of African Political Economy* 65 (September 1995), p. 303.

62. Davies, *African Trade Unions*, pp. 95–112. In some territories—notably in Egypt, Morocco, Tunisia, French Equatorial Africa, Nigeria, and Sierra Leone—the elite parties survived to form the first independent governments.

63. There is an issue of how best to characterize these regimes. While they were often self-defined as 'socialist', this is misleading. See Chapter 1 of this book.

64. In Libya, in 1969, Colonel Qaddhafi and other young officers overthrew the corrupt regime of King Idris; in the same year, a new military government in Sudan adopted a radical and strongly anti-imperialist rhetoric and Soviet-educated Siad Barre became Somalia's leader, nationalized foreign enterprises, and moved closer to the Soviet Union. Congo-Brazzaville became a 'people's republic' in 1970 and adopted Marxism-Leninism as its official ideology.

65. H. Alavi, 'The state in post-colonial societies: Pakistan and Bangladesh', *New Left Review* 74 (July–August 1972) began this debate; John Saul and Colin Leys arguably began the African debate: J. Saul, 'The state in post-colonial societies: Tanzania', *The Socialist Register*, 1974; C. Leys, *Underdevelopment in Kenya: The political economy of neo-colonialism, 1964–1971* (London: Heinemann, 1975) and C. Leys, 'The "overdeveloped" post-colonial state: a re-evaluation', *Review of African Political Economy* 5 (January–April 1976). Saul's article

criticized an important work by Issa Shivji on *Class Struggles in Tanzania* (Dar es Salaam, 1975).

66. See Leys' acknowledgement of previous discussions that had influenced his work: Leys, *Underdevelopment in Kenya*, p. 8.

67. M. Ougaard, 'The origins of the Second Cold War', *New Left Review* 147 (September–October 1984), pp. 66–7.

68. A. Cabral, *Revolution in Guinea: An African People's Struggle*, revised edn (London: Stage 1, 1969).

69. M. von Freyhold, 'The post-colonial state and its Tanzanian version', *Review of African Political Economy* 8 (January–April 1977), pp. 86–8.

70. Tom Mboya of Kenya, cited in Davies, *African Trade Unions*, p. 101.

71. As Shivji argued for Tanzania specifically, and Africa more generally. See I. Shivji, 'Peasants and class alliances', *Review of African Political Economy* 3 (May–October 1975), pp. 11–18, and I. Shivji, *Class Struggles in Tanzania*.

72. Leys, *Underdevelopment in Kenya*, p. 207.

73. Sender and Smith, *The Development of Capitalism in Africa*, p. 130.

74. J. Saul and G. Arrighi, 'Nationalism and revolution in sub-Saharan Africa', in *The Socialist Register* (London: Merlin Press, 1969).

75. Ibid., p. 149. A major influence here was the revolutionary writer Frantz Fanon, who had identified the explosive revolutionary potential of the lumpen proletariat and the peasantry, cf. Davies, *African Trade Unions*, p. 11. Others have been more skeptical: cf. R. Cohen and D. Michael, 'The revolutionary potential of an African lumpen proletariat: a skeptical view', *Bulletin of the Institute of Development Studies*, 5, 2–3 (1973), pp. 31–41.

76. Davies, *African Trade Unions*, pp. 10–11.

77. Ibid.

78. Ibid., p. 10.

79. R. Jeffries, 'The Sekondi-Takoradi general strike, 1961', in Johnson and Bernstein, *Third World Lives of Struggle*.

80. Ibid., p. 131.

81. Davies, *African Trade Unions*, p. 146, and more generally pp. 143–7.

82. E. Wolf, *Peasant Wars of the Twentieth Century* (London: Faber and Faber, 1973).

83. H. Bernstein, 'Notes on capital and peasantry', *Review of African Political Economy* 10 (September–December 1977), p. 73.

Chapter 3
Globalization, Imperialism, and Popular Resistance in Egypt, 1880–2000

1. See for instance, T. Mkandawire, and C. C. Soludo, *Our Continent, Our Future: African Perspectives on Structural Adjustment* (Asmara: Africa World Press, 1999).

2. Since the massive protests against the World Trade Organization in Seattle in 1999, a growing wave of 'anticapitalist' and 'anti-globalization' demonstrations have targeted the world's financial and political leaders. This diverse movement has brought a number of writers and thinkers to prominence including Susan George, Pierre Bourdieu, Naomi Klein, Noam Chomsky, Walden Bello, and George Monbiot. Susan George was already a well-known critic of the neoliberal system: see, for instance, George's writings on Third World debt, *How the Other Half Dies* (London: Penguin, 1976) and *A Fate Worse than Debt* (London: Pelican, 1988).

3. I. Wallerstein, 'Africa and the world system: how much change since independence?', in G. M. Carter and P. O'Meara (eds), *African Independence: The First Twenty-five Years* (London: Hutchinson, 1985), pp. 330–38.

4. M. Eltahawy, 'To Mubarak only the number of votes matters', *Guardian*, 27 September 1999.

5. M. Davies, *Late Victorian Holocausts* (London: Verso, 2001), p. 103.

6. A. Hourani, *A History of the Arab Peoples* (London: Faber and Faber, 1991), pp. 273–75.

7. R. Luxemburg, *The Accumulation of Capital* (New York: Monthly Review Press, 1968), pp. 425–38.

8. 'Suez Canal', *Encyclopaedia Britannica*, http://www.britannica.com.

9. Luxemburg, *The Accumulation of Capital*, p. 438.

10. Ibid., p. 437.

11. Davies, *Late Victorian Holocausts*, p. 105.

12. A. Schölch, *Egypt for the Egyptians!* (Oxford: Middle East Centre for St Antony's College, 1981).

13. J. Marlowe, *Cromer in Egypt* (London: Elek Books, 1970), p. 58.

14. J. Cole, *Colonialism and Revolution in the Middle East: Social and Cultural origins of Egypt's 'Urabi movement* (Princeton, NJ: Princeton University Press, 1993), pp. 87–8.

15. J. Beinin and Z. Lockman, *Workers on the Nile* (Princeton, NJ: Princeton University Press, 1987), p. 23.

16. *The Economist*, 17 June 1882, p. 735.

17. P. J. Vatikiotis, *The History of Modern Egypt* (London: Weidenfeld and Nicolson, 1991), p. 178.

18. *The Times*, 19 June 1882.

19. R. Owen, *Cotton and the Egyptian Economy 1820–1914* (Oxford: Oxford University Press, 1969), pp. 221–22.

20. S. Musa, quoted in E. Davies, *Challenging Colonialism: Bank Misr and Egyptian industrialization, 1920–1941* (Princeton, NJ: Princeton University Press, 1983), p. 45.

21. The British plutocrats are discussed in S. Haxey, *Tory MP* (London: Gollancz, 1939), pp. 43, 56; and A. Campbell, *Empire in Africa* (London: Gollancz, 1944), p. 54.

22. *The Economist*, 23 January 1947.

23. J. and S. Lacouture, *Egypt in Transition* (London: Methuen, 1958), p. 97; J. Damien, 'Social and political conditions in Egypt today', *Fourth International* 7, no. 7, (July 1946).

24. 'Egypte: Un Manifeste Programmatique des Trotskystes Égyptiens', *Quatrième Internationale* (July–August 1947).

25. *Saut al-Umma*, 7 September 1947, 8 September 1947. Copies of this paper can be accessed in the national library, Dar al-Kutub, in Cairo.

26. A. Alexander, 'National liberation or social revolution? The Communists and the nationalist movement in Egypt, 1945–1953', unpublished MA dissertation, Oxford University, 1997; Beinin and Lockman, *Workers on the Nile*, pp. 348, 356–7.

27. For Egyptian Trotskyism, see D. Renton, 'Soldats britanniques et trotskysme égyptien: Pain et Liberté', *Cahiers Léon Trotsky*, 68 (2000), pp. 95–120. Also R. J. Alexander, *International Trotskyism, 1929–85: A documentary analysis of the movement* (Durham and London: Durham University Press, 1991), p. 249; and S. Botman, *The Rise of Egyptian Communism, 1939–70* (New York: New York University Press, 1988), pp. 12–16.

28. 'Note on Communist policy for Egypt', undated document (c.1951), in the Communist Party of Great Britain archive (CP) in the National Museum of Labour History in Manchester: CP/CENT/INT/56/03.

29. Alexander, 'National liberation or social revolution?'

30. R. P. Mitchell, *The Society of the Muslim Brothers* (London: Middle East Monographs, 1969), p. 328.

31. T. Cliff, *Deflected Permanent Revolution* (London: Bookmarks, 1990), p. 22.

32. Hourani, *History*, p. 406.

33. One feddan is 1.038 acres.

34. National Bank of Egypt, 'Special studies: the Egyptian economy, 1959/60–1969/70', *Economic Bulletin*, 25, 4 (Cairo: National Bank of Egypt, 1972), p. 257.

35. See M. Kidron, *Western Capitalism since the War* (London: Pelican, 1968), pp. 48–64.

36. W. Bello, *Dark Victory: The United States and Global Poverty* (London: Pluto Press, 1994), pp. 42–5.

37. 'Infitah' comes from the Arabic root 'Fataha' meaning 'to open' and describes a process of 'opening up', in this context translated as 'economic liberalization'.

38. H. Abd al-Razzaq, *Misr fi 18*, 19 Yanayar (Cairo: Dar Shady, 1985), p. 27.

39. D. Hopwood, *Egypt: Politics and Society, 1945–1990* (London: Harper-Collins Academic, 1991), pp. 112–13.

40. See N. Klein, *No Logo* (London: Flamingo, 2000), pp. 195–229, for a full discussion of the impact of Export Processing Zones on employment conditions.

41. R. W. Baker, *Egypt's Uncertain Revolution under Nasser and Sadat* (Cambridge, Mass: Harvard University Press, 1978), p. 145.

42. G. Shoukri, *Egypt: Portrait of a President—Sadat's Road to Jerusalem* (London: Zed Books, 1981), p. 26.

43. Baker, *Egypt's Uncertain Revolution*, p. 144.

44. M. H. Haykal, *Autumn of Fury: The Assassination of Sadat* (New York: Random House, 1983), p. 183.

45. A. Richards and J. Waterbury, *A Political Economy of the Middle East* (Boulder: Westview Press, 1990), p. 242.

46. 'Masr wa sunduq al-naqd al-dawly', *Nashra iqtisadia l'l-bank al-ahly al-masry 1991 (4)* (Cairo: National Bank of Egypt, 1991), p. 309.

47. *Akbar al-Yawm*, 8 January 1977.

48. *Akhbar al-Yawm*, 15 January 1977.

49. *Al-Ahram*, 18 January 1977.

50. *Al-Ahram*, 20 January 1977.

51. *Al-Ahram*, 20 January 1977.

52. Shoukri, *Egypt*, p. 323.

53. *Al-Ahram*, 21 January 1977.

54. *Al-Ahram*, 21 January 1977.

55. C. Harman, 'The Prophet and the proletariat', *International Socialism* 64 (1994), pp. 3–64, 27.

56. P. Marshall, 'The Middle East after Sadat', *Socialist Review* (October 1981), pp. 12–15; 'State of terror', *Socialist Review* (February 1993), p. 12; Harman, 'The Prophet and the proletariat', pp. 25–30.

57. Hourani, *History*, pp. 457–8; H. Shukrallah, 'Political crisis in post-1967 Egypt', in C. Tripp and R. Owen (eds), *Egypt under Mubarak* (London: Routledge, 1989), pp. 53–103, 95–6.

58. H. El-Laithy, 'Structural adjustment and poverty', in A. El-Mahdi (ed.), *Aspects of Structural Adjustment in Africa and Egypt* (Cairo: Center for the Study of Developing Countries, 1997), p. 185.

59. N. C. Pratt, 'The legacy of the corporatist state: explaining workers' responses to economic liberalisation in Egypt', *Durham Middle East Papers*, November 1998 (Durham: Centre for Middle Eastern and Islamic Studies, 1998), p. 22.

60. T. Mitchell, 'Dreamland: the neoliberalism of your desires', *Middle East Report*, 210, available at http://www.merip.org.

61. M. H. Abdel Aal, 'Structural adjustment and farmers' voluntary associations', in A. El-Mahdi (ed.), *Aspects of Structural Adjustment in Africa and Egypt* (Cairo: Center for the Study of Developing Countries, 1997), pp. 295–96.

62. *Al-Ahram Weekly*, 25 March 1999.

63. 'Country report on Egypt', *Financial Times*, 2000, http://www.ft.com.

64. USAID report on agricultural projects in Egypt, http://www.usaid.gov/eg/proj-agr.htm.

65. El-Laithy, 'Structural adjustment', p. 162.

66. Ibid., p. 159.

67. Pratt, 'The legacy of the corporatist state', p. 29.

68. El-Laithy, 'Structural adjustment', p. 140.

69. Pratt, 'The legacy of the corporatist state', p. 24.

70. El-Laithy, 'Structural adjustment', pp. 154–62.

71. A. El-Mahdi, 'The economic reform programme in Egypt after 4 years of

implementation', in El-Mahdi, *Aspects of Structural Adjustment*, p. 28.

72. Mitchell, 'Dreamland'.

73. Ibid.

74. J. Stork, 'Egypt's factory privatization campaign turns deadly', *Middle East Report* (January–February 1995), available at http://www.merip.org.

75. F. Farag, 'Strike season hits the factories', *Al-Ahram Weekly*, 30 July—5 August 1998.

76. See M. Pripstein Posusney, *Labor and the State in Egypt: Workers, unions and economic restructuring* (Columbia: Columbia University Press, 1997) for a detailed discussion of the trade union movement in post-Nasserist Egypt.

77. Pratt, 'The legacy of the corporatist state', pp. 38–42.

78. O. El-Shafei, 'Rural development, organized labor and democracy in Africa: an overview', in El-Mahdi, *Aspects of Structural Adjustment*, p. 266.

79. *Al-Ahram*, 27 February 1986.

80. Markaz al-dirassat al-ishtirakiyya, *Filasteen, Ruyia Thawriyya* (Cairo, 2001).

81. *Al-Ahali*, 23 September 1998.

82. Associated Press, 24 October 2000, http://www.cnn.com.

83. Human Rights Watch, *Country Report on Egypt*, 1999, http:// www.hrw.org.

84. H. Shukrullah, 'Political crisis and political conflict in post-1967 Egypt', in C. Tripp and R. Owen (eds), *Egypt under Mubarak* (London: Routledge, 1989), p. 53.

85. P. Marshall, 'The children of Stalinism', *International Socialism* 68 (1995), p. 119.

86. K. Marx and F. Engels, *The Communist Manifesto* (various editions); also see D. Renton, *Marx on Globalisation* (London: Lawrence and Wishart, 2001), passim.

87. Quoted in D. Plavsic, 'Wars without end', *Socialist Review* (April 2001), p. 18.

Chapter 4
"There Shall Be No Property":
Trade Unions, Class, and Politics in Nigeria

I have referenced Colonial Office papers held in the Public Records Office as "PRO CO" followed by their relevant catalog number as well as title or date etc., where available.

1. Cited in T. Falola and J. Ihonvbere, *The Rise and Fall of Nigeria's Second Republic 1979–84* (London: Zed Books, 1983), p. 155.

2. See R. Cohen, *Labour and Politics in Nigeria* (London: Heinemann, 1974); U. Damachi, H. Siebel and L. Trachtman, *Industrial Relations in Africa* (London: Macmillan, 1979).

3. G. Andrae and B. Beckman, *Union Power in the Nigerian Textile Industry: Labour regime and adjustment* (Uppsala: Nordiska Afrikainstitutet, 1998); J. Ihonvbere and T. Shaw, 'Petroleum proletariat: Nigerian oil workers in contextual and comparative perspective', in R. Southall (ed.), *Labour and Unions in Asia and Africa* (London: Macmillan, 1988).

4. B. Freund, *The African Worker* (Cambridge: Cambridge University Press, 1988); P. Lloyd, *A Third World Proletariat?* (London: Allen and Unwin, 1984).

5. For example, see Andrae and Beckman, *Union Power in the Nigerian Textile Industry*; A. Peace, *Choice, Class and Conflict* (Brighton: Harvester, 1979); P. Waterman, *Division and Unity amongst Nigerian Workers* (The Hague: ISS, 1982).

6. Cited in A. Hughes and R. Cohen, 'An emerging Nigerian working class', in P. Gutkind, R. Cohen and J. Copans (eds), *African Labour History* (Beverley Hills, CA: Sage, 1978), p. 33.

7. J. H. Morrison, 'Early tin production and Nigerian labour on the Jos Plateau, 1906–1921', *Canadian Journal of African Studies* 11, no. 2 (1977), pp. 212–14.

8. See E. O. Akpan and V. I. Ekpo, *The Women's War of 1929* (Calabar: Government Printer, 1988) on the 1929 massacre of twenty-six women on Eguanga beach.

9. R. Cohen, *Contested Domains* (London: Zed Books, 1991), p. 76; T. Fashoyin, *Industrial Relations and the Political Process in Nigeria* (Geneva: ILO, 1981), p. 2.

10. O. Ojiyi, *The British Political Shooting of Nigerian Coalminers on November 18 1949* (Enugu Colliery Workers Union, n.d.), p. 12.

11. A. Phillips, *The Enigma of Colonialism* (Indiana: James Currey, 1989), pp. 48–9. See also P. Lovejoy and J. Hogendorn, *Slow Death for Slavery: The Course of Abolition in Northern Nigeria, 1897–1936* (Cambridge and New York: Cambridge University Press, 1993).

12. W. Ananaba, *The Trade Union Movement in Nigeria* (London: Hurst, 1969), p. 108.

13. M. Crowder, *The Story of Nigeria* (London: Faber and Faber, 2nd ed., 1966), p. 280; PRO CO 537/5785 'Coal Situation At Enugu Colliery'.

14. For example, see PRO CO 537/4727 (1949) *Political Intelligence Reports West Africa*, Document 'Nigerian Political Summary', January–March 1949, no. 29, p. 5.

15. Cited in Hughes and Cohen, 'An emerging Nigerian working class', p. 46.

16. Ibid., p. 53.

17. Crowder, *The Story of Nigeria* (2nd ed.), p. 233.

18. See G. Darah, 'Imoudu and the labour movement', *Journal of African Marxists* 9 (1986), p. 92.

19. M. Crowder, *The Story of Nigeria* (London: Faber and Faber, 4th ed., 1978), ch. 16, passim.

20. E. Isichei, *A History of Nigeria* (London: Longman, 1983), p. 432.

21. See G. Olusanya, *The Second World War and Nigerian Politics* (Ibadan: Evans Bros, 1973), p. 103.

22. Cohen, *Labour and Politics in Nigeria*, p. 158; J. S. Coleman, *Nigeria: Background to Nationalism* (Berkeley, CA: University of California Press, 1971), p. 256.

23. PRO CO 583 275/30625 (1945) Nigeria Trades Union Congress Doc. 9, telegram 4 June 1945.

24. Phillips, *The Enigma of Colonialism*, p. 147.

25. R. Sklar, *Nigerian Political Parties* (Princeton, NJ: Princeton University Press, 1963), p. 72.

26. Olusanya, *The Second World War and Nigerian Politics*, pp. 58, 126.

27. *West African Pilot*, cited in Olusanya, *The Second World War and Nigerian Politics*, p. 117.

28. See, for example, PRO CO 537/2638 *Fortnightly Review of Communism in the Colonies*, eighth report, dated 24 September 1948, p. 2.

29. Olusanya, *The Second World War and Nigerian Politics*, p. 121; Phillips, *The Enigma of Colonialism*, p. 141.

30. PRO CO 537/5807 *The Zikist Movement*, Doc. 22-2, February–March 1950.

31. See Olusanya, *The Second World War and Nigerian Politics*.

32. See PRO CO 537/5807 *The Zikist Movement*, Doc. 1.

33. Darah, 'Imoudu and the labour movement', p. 93.

34. Ibid. and PRO CO 859/764 *Trade Unions in Nigeria*, 1954–56, 'ANTUF Constitution' as appendix D.

35. R. Melson, 'Nigerian politics and the general strike of 1964', in R. I. Rotberg and A. A. Mazrui (eds), *Protest and Power in Black Africa* (New York: Oxford University Press, 1970).

36. Ibid., p. 780.

37. Cited in ibid., p. 776.

38. Membership rocketed from 353,000 to 518,000 from 1963 to 1964: see Cohen, *Labour and Politics in Nigeria*, p. 129.

39. Melson, 'Nigerian politics and the general strike of 1964', p. 771.

40. Cohen, *Labour and Politics in Nigeria*, p. 166.

41. Ibid., p. 167.

42. Crowder, *The Story of Nigeria* (2nd ed.), ch. 16.

43. A. Boahen, *Ghana: Evolution and change in the nineteenth and twentieth centuries* (London: Longman, 1975), pp. 206–08.

44. See E. Madunagu, *Nigeria: The Economy and People* (London: New Beacon Books, 1983).

45. *Daily Times*, cited in Melson, 'Nigerian politics and the general strike of 1964', p. 785.

46. Ibid., p. 787.

47. Ibid., p. 775.

48. Cohen, *Labour and Politics in Nigeria*, p. 93; R. Melson, 'Political dilemmas of Nigerian labour', in U. Damachi and H. Seibel (eds), *Social Change and Economic Change in Nigeria* (New York: Praeger, 1973), p. 132.

49. Crowder, *The Story of Nigeria* (4th ed.), p. 276.

50. L. Greene, 'Migration urbanisation and national development in Nigeria', in S. Amin, *Modern Migrations in Western Africa* (London: Oxford University Press, 1974), p. 293.

51. See Cohen et al., 'Introduction', in R. Cohen, P. Gutkind and P. Brazier, *Peasants and Proletarians* (London: Hutchinson University Library, 1979); P. Lubeck, 'Early industrialisation', dissertation, Northwestern University, Evanston, IL, 1975).

52. V. P. Diejomaoh, 'Industrial relations in a development context: the case of

Nigeria', in U. Damachi, H. Siebel and L. Trachtman, *Industrial Relations in Africa* (London: Macmillan 1979), pp. 187–8.

53. Ibid., passim.

54. Ibid., p. 184.

55. T. Turner, 'Nigeria: imperialism, oil technology and the comprador state', in P. Nore and T. Turner, *Oil and Class Struggle* (London: Zed Books, 1980).

56. T. Fashoyin, 'Trade unions, the state of labour mobility in ECOWAS', in R. Southall (ed.), *Labour and Unions in Asia and Africa* (London: Macmillan, 1988), p. 54.

57. Ihonvbere and Shaw, 'Petroleum proletariat', p. 84.

58. D. Otobo, 'The Nigerian general strike of 1981', *Review of African Political Economy* 39 (1981), p. 66.

59. Cited in Falola and Ihonvbere, *The Rise and Fall of Nigeria's Second Republic*, p. 163.

60. Ihonvbere and Shaw, 'Petroleum proletariat', p. 94.

61. Quoted in Fashoyin, *Industrial Relations and the Political Process in Nigeria*, p. 17.

62. Falola and Ihonvbere, *The Rise and Fall of Nigeria's Second Republic*, pp. 156–7.

63. Cited ibid., p. 157. See F. Aborisade, *May-Day: Genesis and Significance* (Ibadan: Centre for Labour Studies, 2000), which was originally presented at a workers' conference organized for the Nigerian Union of Railwaymen (NUR) in the early 1980s.

64. Otobo, 'The Nigerian general strike of 1981'.

65. Falola and Ihonvbere, *The Rise and Fall of Nigeria's Second Republic*, pp. 161–62.

66. *West Africa*, 25 July 1983.

67. *West Africa*, 9 January 1984, p. 53.

68. *West Africa*, 16 January 1984.

69. Fashoyin, 'Trade unions, the state of labour mobility in ECOWAS', p. 67.

70. Falola and Ihonvbere, *The Rise and Fall of Nigeria's Second Republic*, pp. 150–1.

71. Ibid., pp. 151–3.

72. Otobo, 'The Nigerian general strike of 1981', p. 81.

73. C. Kolande, Cadbury PLC, quoted in *African Guardian* (Lagos), 23 August 1993, p. 13.

74. Ibid.

75. Nigeria Survey, *Financial Times*, 16 March 1992.

76. *African Guardian*, 19 July 1993, p. 10.

77. Quoted in *Financial Times*, 9 August 1993.

78. *African Guardian*, 23 August 1993, p. 15.

79. Government press releases denying northern participation were carelessly copied out as news in some western papers. See London *Independent*, 24 August 1993, p. 8.

80. Quoted in *African Guardian*, 9 August 1993, p. 36.

81. *African Guardian*, 30 August 1993, p. 13.

82. *Newswatch*, 6 September 1993, p. 17.

83. Quoted in London *Economist*, 18 June 1994, p. 80.
84. Quoted in Manchester *Guardian*, 12 June 1994; *African Guardian*, 25 July 1994, p. 12.
85. *African Guardian*, 25 July 1994, p. 12.
86. *Newswatch*, 8 August 1994, pp. 15–17.
87. For example, see the report on Frank Kokori's arrest in Manchester *Guardian*, 12 August 1994.
88. Quoted in *Newswatch*, 29 August 1994, p. 9.
89. London *Economist*, 23 July 1994, p. 55.
90. London *Economist*, survey, 21 August 1993.
91. See *Newswatch*, 8 August 1994, pp.15–17.
92. *African Guardian*, 25 July 1994, p. 14.
93. *Tell*, 22 August 1994, p. 22.
94. *African Guardian*, 25 July 1994, p. 15.
95. *The NEWS*, 29 June 1998, p. 14.
96. *Newswatch*, 27 December 1999.
97. *Newswatch*, 1 January 2001.
98. Crowder, *The Story of Nigeria* (4th ed.), ch. 16, passim.
99. See R. Luxemburg, *The Mass Strike* (London: Bookmarks, 1986).
100. R. Cohen *et al.*, 'Introduction', p. 26.
101. K. Marx, *The German Ideology* (London: Lawrence and Wishart, 1970), p. 123.

Chapter 5
Resisting the State: The Trade Union Movement and Working-Class Politics in Zambia, 1964–91

1. For example, R. H. Bates, *Markets and States in Tropical Africa* (Berkeley, CA: University of California Press, 1981) and 'Party–union relations in the Copperbelt of Zambia', Massachusetts Institute of Technology Paper (Cambridge, MA, 1969); A. Martin, *Minding Their Own Business: Zambia's Struggle Against Foreign Capital* (London: Hutchinson, 1972); R. E. Baldwin, *Economic Development and Export Growth* (Berkeley and Los Angeles, CA: University of California Press, 1966); J. L. Parpart and T. M. Shaw, 'Contradiction and coalition: class fractions in Zambia, 1964–1984', *Africa Today* 30, no. 3, (Denver, 1983).
2. I. Henderson, 'Labour and politics in Northern Rhodesia, 1900–1953', PhD thesis, University of Edinburgh, 1972.
3. Quoted in J. L. Parpart, *Labour and Capital on the African Copperbelt* (Philadephia: Temple University Press, 1983), p. 47.
4. Quoted in C. Perrings, *Black Mineworkers in Central Africa* (London: Heinemann Educational, 1974), p. 224.
5. Bates, 'Party–union relations in the Copperbelt of Zambia', p. 6.

6. Quoted in Berger, *Labour, Race and Colonial Rule* (Oxford: Clarendon Press, 1974), p. 138.

7. A. L. Epstein, *Politics in an Urban African Community* (Manchester, 1958), p. 121.

8. J. L. Parpart in *Working-class Wives and Collective Labour Action on the Northern Rhodesian Copperbelt, 1926–1964* (Boston: African Studies Center, Boston University, 1982), argues that women were crucial in mobilizing support in strikes and to stop scabbing by unemployed men. In this and other respects, Copper Belt disputes were played out in the wider community as well as in the mines themselves.

9. This policy is described by UNIP leaders in D. C. Mulford, *Zambia: The Politics of Independence, 1957–1964* (Oxford: Oxford University Press, 1967).

10. For example, International Marxist Group, 'Zambia: humanist rhetoric, capitalist reality', *Africa in Struggle* (Occasional Papers), No. 2 (London, 1975).

11. Quoted in Bates, 'Party–union relations in the Copperbelt of Zambia', p. 29.

12. Ibid., p. 32.

13. R. Fincham and G. Zulu, 'Labour and participation in Zambia', in B. Turok (ed.), *Development in Zambia: A Reader* (London: Zed Books, 1979).

14. E. O. Akwety, *Trade Unions and Democratisation: A Comparative Study of Zambia and Ghana* (Stockholm: University of Stockholm, Department of Political Science, 1994), p. 48.

15. Zambia Department of Labour, *Annual Report*, 1968 (Lusaka, 1970), p. 7.

16. Ibid.

17. Quoted in R. H. Bates, *Unions, Parties, and Political Development: A Study of Mineworkers in Zambia* (New Haven, CT, and London: Yale University Press, 1971).

18. H. A. Turner, 'Wage trends, wage policies and collective bargaining: the problems for underdeveloped countries', University of Cambridge Department of Applied Economics Occasional Papers, No. 6 (Cambridge, 1965).

19. ILO, *Report on Workers' Education in Zambia* (Geneva, 1970), p. 6.

20. Turner, 'Wage trends, wage policies and collective bargaining', p. 23.

21. Ibid., p. 75.

22. ILO/UNDP/TAS, p. 22.

23. Ibid., p. 25.

24. Quoted in F. O. E. Okafor, 'The mining multinationals and the Zambian economy', *The African Review*, 17, 1 and 2 (Dar es Salaam, 1990).

25. 'Towards complete independence', speech by H. E., The President D. K. Kaunda to the UNIP National Council held at Matero Hall, Lusaka, 11 August 1969 (Lusaka: Zambia Information Services).

26. Ibid., p. 47.

27. Ibid., pp. 44–5.

28. A. Gupta, 'Trade unionism and politics on the Copperbelt', in W. Tordoff (ed.), *Politics in Zambia* (Manchester: Manchester University Press, 1974), p. 305.

29. M. Burawoy, *The Colour of Class on the Copperbelt* (Lusaka, 1972), p. 74.

30. Ibid., p. 80.

31. Ibid., p. 79.
32. Ibid., p. 80.
33. Ibid.
34. M. Burawoy, *The Politics of Production* (London: Verso, 1985), cited in E. H. O. Akwetey, *Trade Unions and Democratisation: A Comparative Study of Zambia and Ghana* (Stockholm: University of Stockholm, Department of Political Science, 1994).
35. C. Gertzel, 'Industrial relations in Zambia', in U. G. Damachi, H. D. Seibel and L. Trachtman (eds), *Industrial Relations in Africa* (New York: St Martin's Press, 1979), p. 332.
36. Quoted in M. Burawoy, 'Another look at the mineworker', *Constraint and Manipulation in Industrial Conflict: A Comparison of Strikes Among Zambian Workers in a Clothing Factory and the Mining Industry* (Lusaka: Institute of African Studies), p. 252.
37. C. Gertzel, C. Baylies and M. Szeftel (eds), *The Dynamics of the One-party State in Zambia* (Manchester: Manchester University Press, 1984).
38. M. Hamalengwa, *Class Struggles in Zambia* (Lanham, MD, and London: University Press of America, 1992).
39. Fincham and Zulu, 'Labour and participation in Zambia'.
40. *Africa Contemporary Record*, (London, 1970).
41. *Workers' Voice* (Kitwe, September 1980).
42. Gertzel, 'Industrial relations in Zambia', p. 348.
43. Economic Development Institute of the World Bank/R. Gulhati, 'Impasse in Zambia: The economics and politics of reform', Development Policy Case Series, No. 2 (Washington, 1989), p. 27.
44. *Africa Confidential*, 29, 19 (London, 23 September 1988).
45. Quoted in Hamalengwa, *Class Struggles in Zambia*, p. 115.
46. E.g., Gertzel et al., *The Dynamics of the One-party State in Zambia*.
47. World Bank Country Economics Department/C. Colclough, *The Labour Market and Economic Stabilisation in Zambia* (Washington, 1989), p. 1.
48. Ibid.
49. M. Martin, 'Neither Phoenix nor Icarus: negotiating economic reform in Ghana and Zambia, 1983–92', in T. Callaghy and J. Ravenhill (eds), *Hemmed In: Responses to Africa's Economic Decline* (New York: Columbia University Press, 1993).
50. P. Nordlund, *Organising the Political Agora: Domination and democratization in Zambia and Zimbabwe* (Uppsala: Uppsala University, 1996), p. 93.
51. Akwetey, *Trade Unions and Democratisation*, p. 102.
52. Nordlund, *Organising the Political Agora*, p. 115.
53. L. Rakner, *Trades Unions in Processes of Democratisation* (Bergen: Chr. Michelsen Institute, Department of Social Science and Development, 1992), p. 7.
54. Ibid.
55. Nordlund, *Organising the Political Agora*, p. 59.
56. K. Gostner, 'Playing politics: labour's role in Zambia', *South African Labour*

Bulletin 21, no. 3, (June 1997).

57. S. Buhkungu and L. van der Walt, 'Interviews with NCZ workers, *South African Labour Bulletin* 21, no. 3, (June 1997), p. 65.

58. *Workers' Voice* (Kitwe, July 2000).

59. Ibid.

Chapter 6
South Africa Under the ANC:
Still Bound to the Chains of Exploitation

Thanks to Dale McKinley, Trevor Ngwane, Weizmann Hamilton, Ken Cole, Alf Nilsen, and all the contributors to the DEBATE discussion list. To add your email address to the DEBATE mailing list, email: majordomo@sunsite.wits.ac.za.

1. Important differences aside, these offer a relatively common explanation of capitalist laws of motion and Marxist theory of crisis: C. Harman, *Explaining the Crisis* (London: Bookmarks, 1988); R. Brenner, 'The economics of global turbulence: a special report on the world economy, 1950–1998', *New Left Review* 229 (1998); R. Brenner, *World Economic Turbulence* (London: Verso, 1998).

2. For more on the global crisis of the 1970s and 1980s, see S. Clarke, *Keynesianism, Monetarism and the Crisis of the State* (Aldershot: Edward Elgar, 1988), pp. 279–360; D. Harvey, *The Condition of Postmodernity* (Oxford: Blackwell, 1989), pp. 180–97; P. Armstrong, A. Glyn and J. Harrison, *Capitalism since 1945* (Oxford: Blackwell, 1991), pp.169–260.

3. See C. Harman, 'Globalisation: a critique of a new orthodoxy', *International Socialism Journal* 73 (Winter 1996).

4. M. Castells, *The Information Age* (Oxford: Blackwell, 1998), Vol. III; M. Castells, *End of Millennium* (Oxford: Blackwell, 2000).

5. J. Baskin, *Striking Back: A History of COSATU* (London: Verso, 1991), p. 450.

6. For more on this early history, see J. Maree, *The Independent Trade Unions, 1974–1984* (Johannesburg: Raven Press, 1987).

7. The origins and operation of FOSATU can be found in D. McShane, M. Plaut and D. Ward, *Power, Black Workers, Their Unions and the Struggle for Freedom in South Africa* (Nottingham: Spokesman, 1984); S. Friedman, *Building Tomorrow Today* (Johannesburg: Raven Press, 1984).

8. *South African Labour Bulletin*, August 1984.

9. J. Lewis and E. Randall, 'The state of the unions', *South African Labour Bulletin* 11 (October 1985), pp. 74–6.

10. See M. Murray, *The Revolution Deferred* (London: Verso, 1994), p. 142; G. Kraak, *Breaking the Chains: Labour in South Africa in the 1970s and 1980s* (London: Pluto Press, 1993), p. 246.

11. Ibid., p. 502.

12. A similar process may already be happening. See B. Rostron, 'South Africa

glosses over its own history', *New Statesman*, 6 December 1999.

13. Personal interview, Cape Town, April 1998.
14. Personal correspondence, May 2000.
15. *Financial Times*, 7 May 1994.
16. *The Star*, 30 October 1994.
17. *Sowetan*, 5 March 1990.
18. *Financial Times*, 7 May 1994.
19. World Bank, *Global Economic Prospects and the Developing Countries* (Washington, DC: World Bank, 1996), p. 4.
20. C. Stals, 'The South African Economy: An Evaluation', in A. Handley and G. Mills (eds), *From Isolation to Integration: The South African economy in the 1990s* (Braamfontein: South African Institute of International Affairs, 1994), p. 16.
21. G. Mills, 'Introduction and acknowledgements', in Handley and Mills (eds), *From Isolation to Integration*, p. 2.
22. *Business Day*, 2 August 1996.
23. *Sunday Times*, 16 June 1996.
24. *The Citizen*, 27 July 1996.
25. Report by the labour relations group Andrew Levy and Associates, quoted in the *Business Report*, 14 February 2000.
26. P. Bond, *Elite Transition: From Apartheid to Neoliberalism in South Africa* (London: Pluto Press, 2000), pp. 193–94.
27. *Business Report*, 9 September 1999.
28. J. Herbst, 'Africa and the international economy', in Handley and Mills (eds), *From Isolation to Integration*, p. 75.
29. *New Nation*, 28 February 1997.
30. At an ANC Women's League meeting I attended in Gugulethu township, Cape Town, May 1999.
31. Personal interview, June 1999.
32. *Business Day*, 22 September 1999.
33. Fitzgerald has hardly been a good luck charm for those who work for Unilever. On top of the twenty-five thousand sackings announced in early 2001, another eight thousand were to be sacked. *Independent*, 28 April 2001.
34. See interview after this chapter.
35. *Mail and Guardian*, 21 October 1998.
36. 'April 1994–1997: what has changed?', *Mail and Guardian*, 1 January 2000; see also http://www.mg.co.za/mg/news/2000jan2/31jan-elite.html.
37. See the excellent article by Patrick Bond, 'The political economy of South African AIDS', *ZNet Commentary*, 17 July 2000 (www.zmag.org).
38. Personal interview, Cape Town, May 1998.
39. *The Star*, 17 February 2000.
40. Report conducted by South Africa's largest water NGO, Mvula Trust, and the Australian Development Aid, *African Eye News Service*, 9 May 1999.
41. See the SAMWU website, www.cosatu.org.za/samwu, for details on this and the campaigns against privatization programs such as Igoli 2002.

42. See the exclusive work done by J. Rudin, *Challenging Apartheid's Foreign Debt* (Cape Town: Alternative Information and Development Centre, 1997). Check out their website, http//:www.aidc.org.za, for the latest on that and the international debt cancellation campaign.

43. See their website at: http//:www.cosatu.org.za/samwu/apf.htm.

44. For a more detailed discussion of the theory of Colonialism of a Special Type, see A. Callinicos, *South Africa Between Reform and Revolution* (London: Bookmarks, 1988), pp. 65–72; R. Fine and D. Davis, *Beyond Apartheid: Labour and liberation in South Africa* (London: Pluto Press, 1991), ch. 11.

45. For example, No Sizwe (a pseudonym for Neville Alexander), *One Azania, One Nation* (London: Zed Press, 1979); Callinicos, *South Africa Between Reform and Revolution*; Fine and Davis, *Beyond Apartheid*.

46. See D. McKinley, *The ANC and the Liberation Struggle: A Critical Political Biography* (London: Pluto Press, 1997), ch. 3. While a very important critique of the ANC, this book does not capture the complicity of the SACP in this political process. A book on that has yet to be written.

47. *Business Day*, 1 October 1999, emphasis added.

48. Friedman, *Building Tomorrow Today*, p. 413.

49. Callinicos, *South Africa Between Reform and Revolution*, chapter 4, gives a detailed, yet not uncritical, account of this period and the organizations on the left in South Africa at the time. See also C. Jacquin, *The Trade-union Left and the Birth of a New South Africa* (Amsterdam: International Institute for Research and Education, 1999).

50. See also Jacquin, *The Trade-union Left*.

51. D. T. McKinley, *The ANC and the Liberation Struggle* (London: Pluto Press, 1997), p. 1.

52. For a discussion of the development of civics (working-class, township-based organizations) and the exciting debates they generated for the democratic possibilities in post-apartheid South Africa, see M Mayekiso, *Township Politics: Civic Struggles for a New South Africa* (New York: Monthly Review Press, 1996).

53. Quoted in H. Marais, *South Africa: Limits to Change—The Political Economy of Transition* (London, Zed Books, 1999), p. 94.

54. *Mail and Guardian*, 20 August 1999.

55. Personal interview, Cape Town, April 1998.

56. *Business Day*, 29 May 2000. See http://www.bday.co.za/bday/content/direct/0,3523,626143-6078-0,00.html.

57. Press release from Mazibuko K. Jara, Department of Media, Information and Publicity, South African Communist Party, 29 May 2000.

58. *Business Day*, 6 June 1999.

59. J. Saul, 'Cry the beloved country', *Monthly Review Press*, 52, no. 8 (January 2001). Just how disappointing the ANC has been in government is captured well in the very personal and tortuous way Saul recounts his return to South Africa. Although a welcome, if belated, contribution to the growing realization of just how little things have changed under the ANC by an

erstwhile key international, intellectual supporter, it says virtually nothing of the role of the SACP in this process.

60. *Daily Despatch*, 11 May 2000.
61. See K. Moody, *Workers in a Lean World* (London: Verso, 1997).
62. *Independent*, 23 December 2000. For more on this, see: www.socialistalliance.net

Chapter 7
Revolutionaries, Resistance, and Crisis in Zimbabwe

Thanks to a former student of mine who once remarked 'Munyaradzi has all sorts of good ideas but is too lazy to write and will die unknown', and to the editor, Leo Zeilig, whose untiring emails, calls, and brilliant editing ensured that at least this piece was done. This chapter is dedicated to the late ISO comrades Edwin Kabias Murambiwa and L. Briggs Chopa Zano and to a generation of other ISO and IS Tendency comrades, too many to mention, present and departed, who have soldiered on, and in recognition of the red-hot debates and experiences we have shared, and which in fact form the foundations of the ideas in this chapter.

1. See P. Bond, *Uneven Zimbabwe: A Study of Finance, Development, and Underdevelopment* (Trenton, NJ: Africa World Press, 1998).
2. See generally J. T. Chipika, S. Chibanda and P. G. Kadenge, *The Effects of Structural Adjustment in Southern Africa: The Case of Zimbabwe's Manufacturing Sector During Phase 1 of ESAP: 1991–1993* (Harare: SAPES Trust, 2000), pp. 51–5.
3. Ibid.
4. Ibid., pp. 15–19.
5. Bond, *Uneven Zimbabwe*; I. Phimister and I. Mandaza (eds), *Zimbabwe: A Political Economy of Transition 1980–86* (Dakar: CODESRIA, 1986).
6. Chipika, Chibanda and Kadenge, *The Effects of Structural Adjustment*, pp. 15–17.
7. J. Herbst, *State Politics in Zimbabwe* (Harare: University of Zimbabwe, 1990), p. 37.
8. L. W. Bowman, *Politics in Rhodesia* (Cambridge, MA: Harvard University Press, 1973), p. 11.
9. N. Tengende, 'Workers, students and the struggles for democracy: state–civil society relations in Zimbabwe', PhD dissertation, Roskilde University, 1994, p. 60.
10. Ibid.
11. See Amnesty International's report on state violence in Zimbabwe: http://www.amnesty.org.uk/news/briefings/zimbabwe0600.shtml.
12. See generally B. Raftopoulos and I. Phimister (eds), *Keep on Knocking: A History of the Labour Movement in Zimbabwe, 1990–1997* (Harare: Baobab Books/ZCTU/Friedrich Ebert Stiftung), pp. 1–41; Charles van Onselen, *Chibharo: African Mine Labour in Southern Rhodesia 1900–1933* (London: Pluto Press, 1976).

13. Term used by J. Herbst, *State Politics in Zimbabwe* (Berkeley, CA, and Oxford: University of California Press, 1990).

14. Raftopoulos and Phimister, *Keep on Knocking*, pp. 33–45.

15. B. Raftopoulos, 'The labour movement in Zimbabwe, 1945–1965', in ibid., p. 65.

16. See generally I. Phimister, *An Economic and Social History of Zimbabwe, 1890–1948: Capital Accumulation and Class Struggle* (London: Longman, 1988); Bond, *Uneven Zimbabwe*.

17. Chipika, Chibanda and Kadenge, *The Effects of Structural Adjustment*, pp. 6–9.

18. Ibid.; I. Phimister, *Wangi Kolia: Coal, Capital and Labour in Colonial Zimbabwe, 1894–1954* (Harare: Baobab Books, 1994).

19. Raftopoulos, 'The labour movement in Zimbabwe', p. 68.

20. Ibid., p. 64.

21. Quoted in A. Astrow, *Zimbabwe: A Revolution that Lost its Way?* (London: Zed Books, 1983), p. 21.

22. Raftopolous, 'The labour movement in Zimbabwe', pp. 69–70.

23. J. Nkomo, *The Story of My Life* (Harare: SAPES Trust, 2001).

24. Government of Zimbabwe, Ministry of Labour Manpower Planning and Social Welfare, *Labour and Economy: Report of the National Trade Unions Survey* (Zimbabwe, 1984), Vol. 1, p. 16.

25. Ibid., p. 19.

26. For details of these strikes and the response of the state, see Astrow, *Zimbabwe*, pp. 175–9; L. Sachikonya, 'State, capital and trade unions', in I. Mandaza (ed.), *Zimbabwe: The Political Economy of Transition, 1980–1986* (Dakar: CODESRIA, 1986), p. 268.

27. Sachikonye, 'State, capital and trade unions', p. 254.

28. R. Saunders, *Never the Same Again: Zimbabwe's Growth Towards Democracy, 1980–2000* (Harare: Richard Saunders, 2000), p. 18; Herbst, *State Politics in Zimbabwe*, p. 45. A very useful book on the post-1980 development of the labour movement and the emergence of the MDC, but which appeared after completion of this chapter, is B. Raftopoulos and L. Sachikonye, *Striking Back: The Labour Movement and the Post-colonial State in Zimbabwe, 1980–2000* (Harare: Weaver Press, 2001). Of particular importance is the chapter by P. Bond, 'Radical rhetoric and the working class during Zimbabwe nationalism's dying days'.

29. *The Herald*, 31 October 1981, quoted in E. Chikweche, 'History of the Zimbabwe labour movement, 1980–1990', LLBS Hons dissertation, University of Zimbabwe, 1991, p. 14.

30. *The Herald*, 31 October 1984; Chikweche, 'History of the Zimbabwe labour movement', p. 15.

31. Chikweche, 'History of the Zimbabwe labour movement', p. 15.

32. Tengende, 'Workers, students and the struggles for democracy', p. 426, citing 'The long march to a labour movement', *Social Change and Development*, 26 (1992), p. 5.

33. M. Gwisai, 'The legacy of Kempton Makamure', *Socialist Worker* (Harare),

October 2000, gives a participant's analysis of the contribution of the Stalinist left to the evolving movement of the late 1980s.

34. Zimbabwe Congress of Trade Unions, *Beyond ESAP* (Harare: ZCTU, 1996). ISO issued a severe critique of this neoliberal position of the ZCTU leadership in Lovemore B. Zano, 'What we think beyond ESAP', *Socialist Worker*, September 1996, republished in *Socialist Worker*, September–October 1999, p. 3.

35. Chipika, Chibanda and Kadenge, *The Effects of Structural Adjustment*, pp. 50–2.

36. Ibid., pp. 59–61.

37. For a participant perspective on the strike, see *Socialist Worker*, September 1996; November 1996; March 1998. For general accounts, see Raftopoulos and Sachikonye (eds), *Striking Back*, pp. 118–27.

38. Saunders, *Never Again*, p. 68.

39. For their seminal legal battles, whose challenge went to the core of the authoritarian legal structure of the 1960s, see cases like *Jiah and Others* v. *Chairperson, Public Service Commission*.

40. For a general treatment of the emergence and principles of the International Socialist Tendency, see T. Cliff, *A World to Win: Life of a Revolutionary* (London: Bookmarks, 2000).

41. Reports of ISO's role in key struggles like the 1995 police brutality demonstration include *Parade*, January 1996, *The Herald*, December 1996, and *The Herald*, January 1998. On the other hand, examples of glaring omissions not only of the role but even of the name of ISO include R. Saunders, *Never the Same Again*; Raftopoulos and Phimister, *Keep on Knocking*; Bond, *Uneven Zimbabwe*.

42. *The Herald*, August 1996.

43. Saunders, *Never the Same Again*, p. 68.

44. Ibid., pp. 85–9.

45. Ibid., p. 88; *Socialist Worker*, February 1998.

46. For an account of the riots, refer to *Socialist Worker*, February 1998; *The Herald*, January 1998; *Parade*, February 1998.

47. Saunders, *Never Again*, p. 86.

48. *Socialist Worker*, May–June 1999.

49. Saunders, *Never Again*, pp. 106–13.

50. As was publicly disclosed by one of the party's leading ideologues in an article on the party's website. David Coltart stated that one of the reasons why the mass action had been called off was that 'the international community pleaded with us to hold off on the use of mass action, promising at the same time that if we backed off, they would do all they could to increase pressure on Mugabe', D. Coltart, 'Some words of encouragement', Opinion, 16 December 2000, MDC Web site: http://www.mdczimbabwe.com.

51. For a full copy of the document 'MDC: revamp the party—go back to the working people', see *The Herald*, 13 February 2001, p. 8.

52. Besides our own International Socialist Tendency, some of the best advice and critiques that we have received have been from other socialist traditions. See,

for instance, the series of articles in the Communist Party of Great Britain's *Weekly Worker* on Zimbabwe in 2000–01, http://www.cpgb.org.uk; *Black History and the Class Struggle*, no. 1 (New York: International Communist League); B. Slaughter and C. Marsden, 'Zimbabwe: promotion of the MDC by middle class radicals politically disarms the working class', World Socialist Web Site, http://www.wsws.org, 7 October 2000.

Chapter 8
Conclusion: "Shinga Mushandi Shinga! Qina Msebenzi Qina!"

1. 'Worker, be resolute! Fight on!' Slogan used by Zimbabwean workers in the 1990s (see chapter 7).
2. K. Marx, *Capital*, Vol. 1 (London: Lawrence and Wishart, 1954), p. 712. See particularly all of ch. 31, 'Genesis of the industrial capitalist'.
3. R. Abrahamsen, *Disciplining Democracy: Development Discourse and Good Governance in Africa* (London: Zed Books, 2001), p. 123.
4. Cited in Jean-François Bayart *et al.*, *The Criminalization of the State in Africa* (Oxford: James Currey, 1999), p. 20.
5. For an excellent overview of the relationship between capitalist crisis, debt, structural adjustment, and the popular protests they gave rise to in the 1980s and 1990s, see ch. 1 in J. Walton and D. Seddon, *Free Markets and Food Riots: The Politics of Global Adjustment* (Oxford: Blackwell, 1994).
6. Abrahamsen, *Disciplining Democracy*.
7. It also leads to the common assumption that the problem of Africa is 'leadership', not in the sense used in this book, but referring to those in government and in positions of political power. The solution according to this formula is simply the search for honest, courageous people to lead Africa out of the contemporary impasse.
8. See a recent collection on some of these questions: C. Barker, A. Johnson and M. Lavalette (eds), *Leadership and Social Movements* (Manchester: Manchester University Press, 2001).
9. Abdoulaye Bathily, *Mai 68 a Dakar—ou la revolte universitaire et la democratie* (Paris: Editions Chaka, 1992), p. 80.
10. *States of Unrest: Resistance to IMF Policies in Poor Countries* (World Development Movement, 2000), http://www.globalexchange.org/ wbimf/statesofunrest.html.
11. See E. Bircham and J. Charlton (eds), *Anti-Capitalism: A Guide to the Movement* (London: Bookmarks, 2001). The best-selling anti-capitalist book in the UK (*Guardian*, 4 August 2001).
12. Personal communication, November 2001.

INDEX

ABOUT HAYMARKET BOOKS

Haymarket Books is a nonprofit, progressive book distributor and publisher, a project of the Center for Economic Research and Social Change. We believe that activists need to take ideas, history, and politics into the many struggles for social justice today. Learning the lessons of past victories, as well as defeats, can arm a new generation of fighters for a better world. As Karl Marx said, "The philosophers have merely interpreted the world; the point, however, is to change it."

We take inspiration and courage from our namesakes, the Haymarket Martyrs, who gave their lives fighting for a better world. Their 1886 struggle for the eight-hour day, which gave us May Day, the international workers' holiday, reminds workers around the world that ordinary people can organize and struggle for their own liberation. These struggles continue today across the globe—struggles against oppression, exploitation, hunger, and poverty.

It was August Spies, one of the Martyrs who was targeted for being an immigrant and an anarchist, who predicted the battles being fought to this day. "If you think that by hanging us you can stamp out the labor movement," Spies told the judge, "then hang us. Here you will tread upon a spark, but here, and there, and behind you, and in front of you, and everywhere, the flames will blaze up. It is a subterranean fire. You cannot put it out. The ground upon which you stand is on fire."

We could not succeed in our publishing efforts without the generous financial support of our readers. Many people contribute to our project through the Haymarket Sustainers program, where donors receive free books in return for their monetary support. If you would like to be a part of this program, please contact us at info@haymarketbooks.org.

ALSO FROM HAYMARKET BOOKS

Poetry and Protest: A Dennis Brutus Reader

Edited by Aisha Karim and Lee Sustar • A vital original collection of the interviews, poetry, and essays of the much-loved anti-apartheid leader. ISBN: 978-1-931859-22-6.

Sin Patrón: Stories from Argentia's Occupied Factories

Edited by the lavaca collective, with a foreword by Naomi Klein and Avi Lewis • The inside story of Argentina's remarkable movement to create factories run democratically by workers themselves. ISBN: 978-1-931859-43-1.

Subterranean Fire:
A History of Working-Class Radicalism in the United States

Sharon Smith • Workers in the United States have a rich tradition of fighting back and achieving gains that previously seemed unthinkable, but that history remains largely hidden. In *Subterranean Fire*, Sharon Smith brings that history to light and reveals its lessons for today. ISBN: 978-1-931859-23-3.

In Praise of Barbarians: Essays Against Empire

Mike Davis • No writer in the United States today brings together analysis and history as comprehensively and elegantly as Mike Davis. In these contemporary, interventionist essays, Davis goes beyond critique to offer real solutions and concrete possibilities for change. ISBN: 978-1-931859-42-4.

War Without End: The Iraq War in Context

Michael Schwartz • Schwartz argues that U.S. policy in Iraq is circumscribed by an interest in long-term regional hegemony, leading the U.S. to systematically dismantle, rather than rebuild, the Iraqi state and economy. He also debunks leading myths surrounding Iraq's Kurdish population, and traces U.S. involvement in provoking ethnic cleansing between Shia and Sunni Iraqis. ISBN: 978-1-931859-54-7.

No One Is Illegal:
Fighting Racism and State Violence on the U.S.-Mexico Border

Justin Akers Chacón and Mike Davis • A history of anti-immigrant vigilante violence in the U.S.—and the tradition of resistance in the factories and the fields. Now also available in Spanish! ISBN (Eng): 978-1-931859-35-3. ISBN (Esp): 978-1-931859-63-9.

Between the Lines:
Readings on Israel, the Palestinians, and the U.S. "War on Terror"

Tikva Honig-Parnass and Toufic Haddad • This compilation of essays—edited by a Palestinian and an Israeli—constitutes a challenge to critically rethink the Israeli-Palestinian conflict. ISBN: 978-1-931859-44-8.

The Communist Manifesto:
A Road Map to History's Most Important Political Document
Karl Marx and Frederick Engels, edited by Phil Gasper • This beautifully organized and presented edition of *The Communist Manifesto* is fully annotated, with clear historical references and explication, additional related texts, and a thorough glossary that together help bring the text to life. ISBN: 978-1-931859-25-7.

The Essential Rosa Luxemburg:
Reform or Revolution and *The Mass Strike*
Edited by Helen Scott • This stellar new introduction to Rosa Luxemburg's two most important works presents the full text of *Reform or Revolution* and *The Mass Strike* with explanatory notes, appendices, and useful historical contextualization. ISBN: 978-1-931859-36-3.

Myths of Male Dominance:
Collected Articles on Women Cross-Culturally
Eleanor Burke Leacock • Drawing on extensive ethnographic research, Leacock demonstrates that claims of inherent male dominance and female subordination are based on carefully constructed myths with no historical or factual basis. She also documents numerous examples of egalitarian gender relations. ISBN: 978-1-931859-57-8.

The Democrats: A Critical History
Lance Selfa • Offering a broad historical perspective, Selfa shows how the Democratic Party has time and again betrayed the aspirations of ordinary people while pursuing an agenda favorable to Wall Street and U.S. imperial ambitions. ISBN: 978-1-931859-55-4.

History of the Russian Revolution
Leon Trotsky • This detailed history, written by one of the revolution's central participants, still offers the most vivid and inspiring account of the upheavals of 1917, which overthrew the tyranny of the tsar in February and by October established the most radically democratic society in world history. ISBN: 978-1-931859-45-5.

The Revolution and the Civil War in Spain
Pierre Broué and Emile Témine • Broué and Témine's outstanding history shows how a promising workers' movement ended in a fascist victory, detailing the internal political dynamics that led the Popular Front to hold the fight back. ISBN: 978-1-931859-51-5.

The Comintern
Duncan Hallas • Ranging from its beginnings in 1919 as the center of world revolution through its degeneration at the hands of Stalinist bureaucracy, Hallas present the authoritative history of the Communist (Third) International. ISBN: 978-1-931859-52-3.

Order these titles and more online at www.haymarketbooks.org or call 773-583-7884.

ABOUT THE EDITOR

Leo Zeilig is a research associate at the Center for Sociological Research in Johannesburg and a senior lecturer in the department of sociology at the University of the Witwatersrand. His books include *Revolt and Protest: Student Politics and Activism in Sub-Saharan Africa* (London: I. B. Tauris, 2008) and *Africa's Lost Leader: Patrice Lumumba* (London: Haus, 2008).

Zeilig has worked as an independent journalist and coordinated the Independent Media Centre in Zimbabwe during the presidential elections in 2002. He has worked as a lecturer at Université Cheikh Anta Diop in Dakar, Senegal, and as a lecturer and researcher at Brunel University, London. Zeilig has written extensively on the struggle for democratic change, social movements, and activism in sub-Saharan Africa.